CAPISTRANO TRAILS:
RIDE FOR THE BRAND

An Oral History

San Juan Capistrano's Story
As Horse Capital of Orange County

DONNA L. FRIESS, PH.D.

2018

Library of Congress-in-Publication Data
All Rights Reserved
Copyright 2018 by Donna L. Friess

Friess, Donna L.
Capistrano Trails: Ride for the Brand
Donna L. Friess
1. History
Hurt Into Happiness Publishing, 31899 Del Obispo St. Suite 135, San Juan Capistrano, CA 92675

First Edition
        978-0-9815767-5-6
        0-9815767-5-3

This book is an oral history San Juan Capistrano's Story As Horse Capital of Orange County

Publisher's Cataloguing-in-Publication

Friess, Donna L., 1943-

        Capistrano Trails: Ride for the Brand. Donna Friess. -- San Juan Capistrano: Hurt into Happiness Publishing, [2014]

        Library of Congress
                Includes bibliography.

    Summary: This work is a collection of historical accountings and oral histories based upon the memories of those contributors described in the bibliography section. It is the horse story of San Juan Capistrano, California.

        Historian Donna Friess, Ph.D. brings San Juan Capistrano, California's vibrant horse story to life in this personally written narrative based upon interviews, written statements, field trips, as well as historical accountings. The history begins with the Ice Age when Equus Occidentalis walked the Western Coast of California, and includes the Mission and Rancho Periods of History, through contemporary times, illustrating that San Juan Capistrano is in fact the "Horse Capital of Orange County, California."

    To Order books visit Amazon.com or digitally through the Kindle app.

    Cover: This is a 2007 watercolor painting by Donna Friess from a photo taken in the 1970's of Donna racing Jimmy Jackson along the berm on the north side of San Juan Creek. Cover design by Diana Starr.

Books by Donna Friess

*Women Leaders of the Movement to Stop Child Sexual Abuse
A Doctoral Dissertation.* An Oral History 1992

Cry the Darkness: One Woman's Triumph over the Tragedy of Incest, 1993
2nd Edition, 2013

Whispering Waters: Historic Weesha and the Settling of Southern California (Oral History)
With Janet Tonkovich, 1998

A Chronicle of Historic Weesha and the Upper Santa Ana River Valley
with Janet Tonkovich, 2000.

Circle of Love: A Guide to Successful Relationships, 3rd Edition, 2008

One Hundred Years of Weesha: Centennial 2010. An Oral History, 2010

Cherish the Light: One Woman's Journey from Darkness to Light, 2013

Just Between Us: Guide to Healing (1995, out of print)

The Unraveling of Shelby Forrest 2014 – a Novel

True Animal Short Stories for Children:

Oh What a Big Surprise!

Three Little Kittens Lost in the Woodpile

Zoe's First Birthday

There's Something Scary in the Shed

Starving in the Woods

Winning the Horse Race

Jessica the Seal

About *Cry the Darkness*

Winner Indie Excellence Book Awards – Women's Issues 2014
Honorable Mention – Paris International Book Festival 2014
Honorable Mention – New York Book Festival 2014
Honorable Mention – Southern California Book Festival 2014
Honorable Mention – London International Books Awards 2014
Honorable Mention – New England Festival of Books 2014

"A real contribution to women everywhere." *Changes Magazine.*

Re-released by Bastei Lubbe Publishing. Germany, 2018

"It is a wonderful book!" Marilyn Van Derbur, Former Miss America, incest survivor.

"I couldn't put it down. It is inspirational!" *Alpha Gamma Delta International Quarterly*

"It is a gripping story…it keeps the reader moving." U.S. International University *Envoy.*

"A must read for everyone. One of the most important books available. It gives hope. Donna's life story is a beacon of hope and happiness for adult survivors of sexual abuse." Claire Reeves, Founder, Mothers Against Sexual Abuse.

Cry the Darkness is my most valued possession." Gina, Incest survivor and AIDS patient.

"It changed my life and gave me hope." Sonja, Incest survivor.

"*Tarer I Morket.*" Best selling non-fiction book in the history of Egmont (Virkelightedens Verden) publishing, Norway, 1990's. Egmont Bogklub.

"An inspiration for those working for victims of childhood trauma." *Changes Magazine.*

"Outstanding Donna! A good reminder that we DO have a choice in how we respond." Judy P., Reader.

About *The Unraveling of Shelby Forrest*

Winner Indie Excellence Book Awards – Best New Novel 2015
Honorable Mention- Pacific Rim International Book Awards 2015
Independent Author Network, IAN- Finalist Book of the Year Awards- Romance 2015
Honorable Mention -- Paris International Book Festival 2015
Honorable Mention – New York Book Festival 2015
Honorable Mention – Southern California Book Festival 2016
Honorable Mention – London International Festival of Books 2016
Honorable Mention – Los Angeles Book Festival 2016
Honorable Mention- Hollywood Book Festival 2016

About *Whispering Waters: Historic Weesha and the Settling of Southern California*

Finalist: International Book Excellence Awards. Non-Fiction. 2017

California Historian John W. Robinson's 1998 review of *Whispering Waters:* "Congratulations on your splendid book Whispering Waters. It's amazing the amount of research you and Janet Tonkovich have done to produce this comprehensive history not only of Weesha but all of the San Bernardino Mountains and Southern California! My previous knowledge of Weesha was quite rudimentary, but thanks to you two, I now have access to the full story. This book will quickly become a collector's item, I am sure. I will treasure my copy."

*For those who are working to protect
The cherished traditions and equestrian legacy
of San Juan Capistrano*

ACKNOWLEDGMENTS

This collection of memories and historical accounts would not have been possible without the cooperation and willingness to share on the part of all of my contributors. I appreciate their candid and personal stories. I am particularly indebted to Tony Moiso, Gilbert Aguirre, Emmy-Lou Jolly-Vann, Kathy Holman, Dana Butler-Moburg, Laura Freese, Richard Hill-Adams, Sam Allevato, Colonel Jim Williams, Steve Nordeck, Cherylin Von Aldenbruck, John Clifton, Sherry Clifton, Jim Verbeerst, Tom Baker, Joan Irvine Smith, Fred Love, Hilary Powell, Janet Harris Tonkovich and Renee Ritchie, who were generous in sharing materials with me.

I have relied heavily upon the photographic evidence of life in Southern California at the turn of the 20th Century to support this project. I am the grateful recipient of both of my grandmothers' meticulously documented personal histories. My maternal grandmother, Gertrude Haas Borwick, was born in 1888 in Ithaca, Nebraska. She took great pains to preserve photos of their lives: from hay harvests on her family farm, to trips to the market with her horse, Babe, pulling the wagon, to the family's 1920 move to California; and their proud acquisitions of early automobiles. My paternal grandmother, Vera-May Cooper Lewis, born in Los Angeles in 1901, also kept bulging albums of carefully labeled photographs.

This book would not have come together without my husband, Ken's, encouragement about memorializing the precious stories of our local horse-enthusiasts. Being at the forefront of the 1970's battle to preserve San Juan's character, coupled with his knowledge and extensive library of public City documents, Ken has been an invaluable resource for this project. In addition, he is a fine editor and owns a sensible head for bouncing off my ideas, but more than that, Ken is the one who supports me when the going gets tough. He has always been the wind beneath my wings and the great love of my life and I appreciate him very much. Thank you to my sister, Diana Starr, for all of her technical support and her love. Photographer, Mario Jeglinski's technical skill made it possible to use some of the antique photos. His contribution is very much appreciated. I appreciate Juanita Firestone's proof reading.

I deeply appreciate my sons, Rick and Dan Friess, and my daughters-in-law Jenny and Natalie, and my daughter, Julina, and my son-in-law Justin Bert, who inspire me to be the best I can be. I have written this history as a reminder to cherish the past for my eleven grandchildren: Jake, Jillian, Megan, Jaycelin, Emily, James, Elizabeth, Ella, Ashley, Katie, and Caroline. I find a deep purpose for living through all of you. Thank you for your faith in me.

PART I

I Smile When I Catch God Watching

Me Through the Eyes of My Horse

TABLE OF CONTENTS

The Code of the West:

1. Live Each Day with Courage
2. Take Pride in Your Work
3. Always Finish What You Start
4. Do What Has to Be Done
5. Be Tough, But Fair
6. When you Make a Promise, Keep it
7. Ride for the Brand
8. Talk Less and Say More
9. Remember: Some Things Aren't For Sale
10. Know Where to Draw the Line

(Owens and Stoecklein, *Cowboy Ethics: What Wall Street Can Learn from the Code of the West. 2004).*

At the Trail Head

CAPISTRANO TRAILS: RIDE FOR THE BRAND

"If we are not supposed to dance, why all this music?" (Gregory Orr)

Perhaps this story has been long in the making. I think it may have begun in the late 1940's when I was a little girl growing up on the beach in the area of Venice, California, which is now the Marina Peninsula in Marina Del Rey. When I was a child the land that is now the beautiful Marina was nothing more than a swampy area with weeds that included a local dumpsite. However, in one corner away from the weeds and refuse, was a magical area called Hoppyland where Hopalong Cassidy, a famous movie and television cowboy [William Boyd], would often appear. One day when I was about eight years-old I was visiting Hoppyland, when I got to meet him and he actually kissed me on the cheek. I was delirious with joy! Until then the even more famous cowboy, Roy Rogers, had been my favorite, but after that kiss, Hoppy had stolen my heart! Six years later my girl friend, Leanne, and I were visiting her parents' friends for the week in Palos Verdes, California, when I met a boy, and again, lost my heart. He was a special boy, and I became so enthralled by his shy ways that I was unable to eat nor sleep for the several days remaining of the visit. My emotions were further unhinged by the fact that our friends' mother came for an afternoon visit and seeing my 14 year-old state, began to sing, "the love bug's bitten and you can't sit still." I was horrified that my feelings were so transparent to her, and relieved when the week ended, and we went home some sixty miles away.

Hopalong Cassidy 1951 Hoppy Land

During the following school year, that quiet boy sent me a special delivery letter every single week. Plagued by shyness, and hampered by the cost of long distance, we did not even try to talk on the telephone, but feelings were running high. The next year my friend Leanne and I again visited the same friends. This time that boy came for us with his friend Jerry. They had invited us girls for a day's outing. You can imagine our surprise when they arrived on horseback!!

As I was writing this, I shared that 60 year-old memory with Leanne. Laughing she replied, "Do you remember how freaked out we were because we either had to wrap our arms around those boys or fall off! Apparently you were NOT holding on because when the horse you were on started up the hill you slid right off its back! After that we all just walked the horses up the hill! Do you remember?" We laughed. No, I had not remembered that part.

1

Heaven help me! I had fallen for a cowboy. Before too many years we graduated from college and I married him, his name was Ken Friess. Soon three children arrived. All the while, that boy, now a man, loved to reminisce about his horseback adventures in the hills of Southern California. In 1972 we purchase a weekend cabin with acreage in the San Bernardino Mountains. Soon, Ken arranged for horses to be stabled at the cabin so that we could enjoy them during time off. All the while we were aware that our lifestyle of dogs, cats, and kids did not seem compatible with the tract home environment which we were trying to live in Huntington Beach. Ken was attempting to grow a crop of corn in our three-foot-wide side yard while our big Weimaraner dog entertained himself by intimidating the mail man. One day, in an attempt to make good on his threats, that dog lumbered right through our cinder block fence, knocking it down. He didn't get the mail man, but delivery was stopped for all the residents on our street! We knew it was time to move, and the rural cabin had taught us that we needed more space.

Our home search brought us to a little town of about 4000 people named San Juan Capistrano. We found a two story house on two acres in an area at the end of a dirt and gravel road which was adjacent to the Lacouague Citrus Ranch. We liked the rural atmosphere and the children were ecstatic over the two Shetland ponies which came with the house. We opened an escrow. Our Huntington Beach escrow had to close two months before the San Juan home so we went to stay at our place in the mountains. With the new property's horse corrals in mind, Ken bought an unbroken Welch Pony from a camp near our cabin, so that I could learn to ride. Ken's thinking was that as I trained the mare to allow me on her back, that I would magically learn to ride! Thus my horse adventures began in earnest as that mare bucked me off time and again for weeks! I finally tamed her enough so that she allowed me to ride her, but it was not easy! Four and a half decades later our family is still engaged in many horsey adventures. Horses at all times are corralled in our San Juan back yard.

Mounted soldiers, cowboys, vaqueros, cattle, and horses are integral elements of the history of San Juan Capistrano. Recently, my husband, Ken, was lamenting the fact that some of the old-timer cowboys were moving out of town, or with time, would pass away. He pointed out that their stories could be lost if someone did not record them. That conversation became a seed that took root in my mind. This book reflects the result of our discussion that day. It consists of oral histories, anecdotes, old written accounts, memories, philosophies, my perceptions and thoughts, and a few, perhaps tall tales. More than a year into my research, and many personal interviews later, I realized that this work is a broad stroke capturing a part of the equestrian story of San Juan. During my conversations, I came to understand that entire books could be written about each of the many cowboys and

c. 1948 Ken Friess Inspired by TV Cowboys

cowgirls who have played a major role in the equine life of the City. There are some incredible tales to be recounted. Perhaps this is a challenge that others will take up. In the meantime, I hope you enjoy this ride while you take a personal look at the San Juan Capistrano horse story.

c. 1950 Ken Friess Inspired by Hopalong Cassidy

Hoppyland Ad

Chapter One

San Juan Capistrano

"The wind of heaven is that which blows through a horse's ears."

I recently began a new chapter of my life by becoming a certified docent at the beautiful Mission San Juan Capistrano. During my studies I read Father Saint John O'Sullivan's book, *Capistrano Nights*, published in 1930. It is an inviting collection of stories of pueblo life reaching back to the early years in San Juan. According to *Capistrano Nights,* in 1880 there were 376 people living in the pueblo. The book charmed me. I especially enjoyed reading about the old families whose many descendants are still in town.

Some are living on Los Rios Street and are counted among our friends. I was so taken with the simple stories in that book that I began to brainstorm on how I could add to the body of history of our town without repeating what others had already written. I was serious about it, wondering how I could contribute.

I was thinking hard the day I went to buy some sacks of grain for my horses from Fred Love at Ortega Tack and Feed. I had discovered that he was closing down in two weeks and moving away. I felt an urgency sweeping over me as I thought about Fred leaving. His presence in town has been something of an institution. Most everyone in the equestrian world in South Orange County knows Fred. He's been in the area since 1955, working as a horse trainer, trader, and farrier.

On the mile trip back toward my home, an idea began to take hold. My sensitivity to horses seemed to intensify as I passed the Horse Crossing signs at the La Novia Bridge, I then continued by Tar Farms where several beautiful sorrel

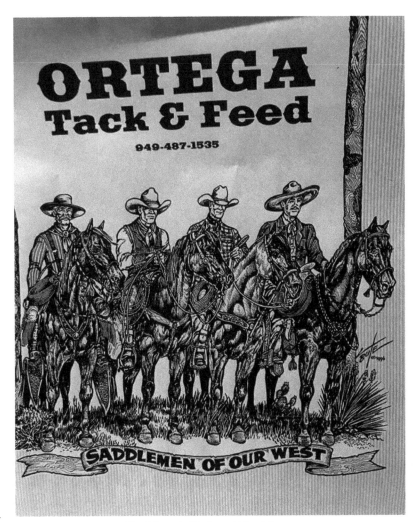

Fred Love's Tack and Feed Store

mares were grazing in the front pasture. I stopped the car as two riders entered the cross walk in front of me. I studied them. *Horses.* My thoughts scanned quickly to the bigger-than-life pair of brass lawn statues whose riders seem to greet any of us coming into town on Del Obispo Street from Dana Point. *Horses.*

In that moment I decided that, at the very least, I would interview Fred Love and preserve his story.

The Amazing Race

Later that day, sitting on my patio enjoying watching my three horses as they grazed on our lawn, I studied our thirty-one-year old thoroughbred which had once been a race horse. His name had been "Short Timer." In retirement we called him Mr. T as a nickname. Thinking about race horses and races, my memory took me back to two of the most significant events of my life.

Friess Horses at Friess Home 2017

It was 1975 and 1976. It centered on the Swallows Day Parade in San Juan Capistrano. Over the years, the parade had become a major event, drawing huge crowds to enjoy the biggest non-motorized parade in the West. It is over a two hour show of horses, carriages, school bands, Native American dancers, and so much more. It is an exciting annual community ritual marking the return of the swallows known as the Fiesta de Las Golondrinas. In 1975 our friends and neighbors decided on the spur of the moment that it would be fun to have a cross-country horse race after the parade. I had never really raced and only had three years of riding experience, but with my usual enthusiasm, I agreed to join the group and put up my entry money. There was to be a generous purse for the winner. I really had no idea what to expect and without any real preparation, I jumped in at the last minute, riding our adopted Appaloosa, Paiute. Caught up in the drama of the day, my husband and I took off with all the other crazy people in what was a barely organized chaos. Fortunately, we all survived without incident and afterward the participants agreed that the next year would stage a proper event.

During the weeks approaching the big day, for the second race, I took our Arabian/Quarter Horse, Windy, out for practice runs each afternoon when I returned home from teaching. We ran the course and got in shape. On the day of the event, I was surprised to see dozens of horse trailers parked throughout our rural valley. Word of this race had spread and riders had trailered in their horses from as far as 60 miles away.

The two-mile course was marked, and men were stationed with walkie-talkies along its rock-strewn route. It was far more organized than I had imagined. Spectators were gathering along the path and at the finish line. I felt nervous, and so did Windy.

What a mixed bag we riders were; middle-class businessmen turned weekend cowboys,

Donna Riding Piaute Racing Jimmie Jackson c. 1970's

construction workers who fancied themselves "real cowboys," working cow hands from nearby ranches, local blacksmiths, stable owners, horse enthusiasts, and me, a schoolteacher who only rode bare-back. I had not yet mastered the saddle and hadn't really wanted to since I had learned to ride without one. I felt most comfortable bareback because I felt in control with my thighs pressed against the horse.

I could tell that our blacksmith, Joe, thought my entry in the race was the funniest thing of all. That schoolteacher? What a hilarious joke! He delighted in teasing me about it. I could just hear him laughing good naturedly, "Donna?" he would say in an amazed tone, and break into laughter. I didn't care. It would be fun.

As race time approached, all of us lined up at the starting line, perhaps twenty or more riders. My heart was pounding, Windy was shivering beneath me. I heard the starting gun and we were off!

Pressing my legs tightly against Windy, we glided smoothly around the pack of riders as we headed into the riverbed. I knew that this was not unusual for Windy. She did not like to lose a race, not to anyone. She hated being in another horse's dust. We were racing like the wind, through rock and sand, past bamboo and bushes, up onto the dike that ran along San Juan Creek. Windy and I passed every one of the riders and were comfortably out in front when we approached the first look-out with his walkie-talkie carefully in hand. It was Joe. Later he said that he screamed into his walkie-talkie, "Jesus Christ, it's Donna!!!" He was almost shocked speechless. He repeated that line many times that night at the post-race party. He could not believe his eyes.

Windy, pacing herself now, kept the lead as we continued across the course. Along the top of the dike, I leaned low against her neck. Finally a sharp turn back into the riverbed, where the trail was uneven with rocks and stones. A horse could easily stumble and throw its rider off to be trampled by the pack of wild racers. The trail was much too narrow to avoid a catastrophe if someone fell. I was conscious of the danger, but I just kept crooning, "We can do it girl. Good girl. Bring us in Windy."

As we came into the final turn, I gave Windy one last kick and leaned down on her neck. As she turned the final corner the pad slipped and I fell halfway down her back.

"No! Not now!" I yelled aloud. "We're so close." And then to myself, "*You're almost in, Donna, hang on!!*"

I pulled hard, grasping Windy's mane and managed to right myself. My friends were applauding and yelling. I crossed the finish line and the crowd roared.

I had won the race! I was the champion! No one could believe it. The schoolteacher! The beach kid; a person opposite of the *real* cowboys and girls, the one wearing tennis shoes. I was elated, but in my heart I always thought I might have a chance to surprise everyone. I had practiced ahead and focused on what I was doing. And I knew that deep inside I had a streak of daring. I had experienced that before. I knew what my horse could do, and I knew my own determination.

My friends were thrilled, but some of the macho cowboys were not. One man, Hoss, (name changed for privacy), was so disgusted with his horse for not winning that he tied her up without walking her down. Maybe she needed to cool off more, or maybe the race was just too much for her, but she died a few hours later.

I knew this was a tough crowd, but that dead horse showed a callousness I wasn't used to. Some of the cowboys were missing teeth and others chewed chaws of tobacco and spit their smelly wads onto the dusty ground. Perhaps that was partly why it was so intriguing. I got to go up against real cowboys and win. That outstanding day with Windy came to be, in some ways, a symbol for my life. It gave me courage, to know that I could win in life against all kinds of odds.

San Juan Capistrano as Horse Capital

Sitting on my patio, that memory led to my idea. San Juan Capistrano is touted as the horse capital of Orange County; some even claim it to be the "Horse Capital of the West Coast." I have been told that the City's website described San Juan as the "Horse Capital of the West Coast" for many years. How is it possible that it has emerged to enjoy such an elegant distinction? Why are we residents so fortunate as to drive through our little city and see horses out among us, reminders of the past? Why indeed?

I have been living in town for nearly half a century. It's a frequent memory, as I leave home and drive on San Juan Creek Road, to pass Del Goodwin's old bunk house, now the home of Marguerite Kennedy, which sits across the street from the entrance to Tar Farms Stables, next to Ambuehl School. I often smile as the mental picture of Del bubbles up. My memory sees Del rounding up his cattle and driving them to the cow loading chute which was next to the bunk house. He corralled his cattle on the flat just above the bunk house. Today a beautiful custom-built Hidden Mountain home sits on that corral site. For decades, Del roamed the hills of San Juan, often with his Jeep. He ran some two

Del Goodwin Long Time Cowboy Ran Horses and Cattle in Hills

hundred head of cattle where San Juan Hills High School stands today and the land between our house and the bluff above the ocean near the flag pole.

During my interview with Fred Love, long time cowboy, I learned that he and Del had been good pals. As a farrier, Fred shod Del's horses every six weeks. It was a routine thing for Del to say, "So Fred, when you get through, how about we brand some calves today?" Fred says he'd shake his head, and conceal a grin. He was used to being pressed into helping Del. Life in San Juan in those days was like that. People helped each other. The sub-title of this book is "Ride for the Brand." It suggests 'all for one and one for all.' Fred and Del exemplified this spirit of loyalty, cooperation, and pitching in to help your neighbor.

Sometimes on Sunday afternoons our family would saddle up and ride around the hills. A favorite place was in the orange grove that was to be the site for the future Los Corrales homes. The grove had been abandoned, and thus created a fun place to ride. As Ken showed off his horsey tricks, swinging from the saddle to the ground, and back up again as the horse loped along, the kids would ride backwards in the saddle and show off tricks of their own. Del and his big horse might be riding by on the other side of the barbed wire fence witnessing our family's antics. Often I would catch his eye, and he would nod a greeting from under his wide cowboy hat. Other times, his serious expression broke into a smile and he would wave to the kids.

Ken joined me on the patio and I mentioned that I was thinking about Del.

Laughing Ken asked, "Do you remember when some of his calves got loose and they scrambled under the fence, dashed through Jean Lacouague's orange grove and were grazing on our back lawn?"

Grinning, I replied, "No, I don't …"

"Yes, and pretty soon, here comes Del on his horse, ready to herd the miscreants back into the pasture."

Later I was asking our son Dan about it. He recalled, "when I was four-years-old I remember being out on our back lawn when out of the corner of my eye I saw something big. It was alive! It moved. I just remember how scared I was and quickly went running into the house for help. I thought it was a coyote just standing on the lawn eating pears from the tree. Turned out it was a calf, but it scared me!"

Del Goodwin's Bunk House, Across From Tar Farms c. 1980.

Capturing the Horse Stories

As I pondered the project that was beginning to roll around in my brain, and thought of Ken's lament about old stories being lost, I realized that I had lived through a good part of San Juan's more recent equestrian story. It seemed like if I hurried I could capture the tales and experiences of the local equestrian set before they moved away or passed on, and their stories were lost. Certainly buildings and structures were disappearing. I had always planned to do a painting of the 113 year-old Cook Barn on Del Obispo Street, but when it went up in flames in 2011, I knew I had missed my opportunity. I didn't want to miss my chance to talk to others and gather the old stories and learn more.

I decided to interview those who had been in a position to shape San Juan's destiny when the heavy pressures to develop came to bear on the little valley in South Orange County. I decided to find as many people as possible who had been involved with horses, and shaping the City, and who would talk with me. I audio taped many of the interviews and transcribed them. The method of inquiry I relied upon is called Symbolic Interactionism, which rests upon studying the social interactions taking place between the individual contributor and his or her social environment (Blumer, 1962). It is a methodology that helps one to understand the reality of a particular contributor within the specific situation.

An oral history is all the richer for the "voices" of the individual story tellers. I have used a different *font* to distinguish between my narrative and that of others. The goal of this work is to shed some light on San Juan's emergence as an equestrian center while sharing some of the vibrant stories that have created our city's proud tradition. I have attempted to "mirror" the world through the ancient tradition of oral narrative.

San Juan Capistrano Remained a Village for Many Decades

I began digging through my many history books, searching for picturesque glimpses of the past way of life as it related to horses. I was reminded that before the railroad came through town in 1887, all transportation, except for one's feet, involved horses or mules. Horses were essential, the backbone of commerce and community life. As I read, my imagination grabbed hold of the image of the frequent and heavily wagered horse races that were a big attraction in the early days. They were held across the area, on the Ranchos [I was to learn that Rancho Mission Viejo at one time had a full race track where the Tree of Life Nursery stands today, on the north side of Ortega Highway], and some were held in the streets of downtown San Juan. I found testimony that races were also held on the "old road," El Camino Real below Mission Hill before any homes were ever built there. I could imagine the streets lined with spectators as horses galloped madly past the Mission and down Camino Capistrano! I found an 1859 newspaper ad which read:

Advertisement: $5000! $5000! Challenge to the backers of the Coyote. $5000 (or $6000) plus 50 horses & mares offered by Desiderio Burnel of Santa Ana and his associates on Azulejo v. Coyote for 1,000 yards. Fernando Sepulveda backer of Coyote." (*Southern Vineyard*, March 25, 1859) [Cleland.]

I knew I wanted to discover more about those races. The one advertised was just over a half a mile in distance. The Kentucky Derby, for example, is a distance of one and a quarter miles. I could just imagine the speed of those horses in such a short race. I was intrigued to research more fully

Rancho Mission Viejo Race Track 1976 - Racing a Favorite Pastime Across History. Courtesy RMV

Gretchen Stroscher Thompson Story
"The Fastest Horse in Orange County!"

One day in July of 2017, I was invited to a luncheon at El Adobe for the Board of Trustees and Directors of the San Juan Capistrano Historical Society. I was seated next to a descendent of an old San Juan family. She is Gretchen Stroscher Thompson, granddaughter of San Juan ranching pioneers, William and Fredericka Stroschein (the family name was later changed). These pioneers purchased a ranch in downtown San Juan next to the Mission and what is now Del Obispo Street where they grew English walnuts and citrus. As our luncheon talk continued, I explained about my writing project and that I had been busy gathering up people's memories involving horses. She smiled and replied, "I have two horse stories." Immediately my ears perked up and I turned on my recorder. This is her first story:

"I never knew my grandfather; he had died in 1915, but I knew that before he emigrated to America, he had been the head groom on a large estate in Germany and he loved horses and knew his horse flesh. Later in life, when he finally had enough money, he bought himself a 'fabulous' horse. He used it in two ways, pulling a carriage and for racing."

She continued, "My father grew up in San Juan, however, once he was trained as a dentist there was not enough population to support a practice, so he moved to Santa Ana, where I was raised and went to school. In the 1950's my father was running for school board and it was my job as a teenager to help him pass out his campaign literature. I was going from house-to-house one day when I knocked on a door and an old man answered. He looked at me with my red hair and asked, "Are you a Stroschein?"

I was a bit taken aback by that observation as I had not stated my name. "Yes I am." I answered suspiciously.

In a sudden burst he exclaimed, "I knew your grandfather!" He grinned at me and continued, 'I had a leather shop in Santa Ana and he would come up, bringing me sticks in the length of his children's feet. He'd say, 'this is a girl, this is a boy' and have me make shoes for them! Why he loved horses and prided himself on having the most beautiful animal around. He enjoyed racing his horses down in San Juan and was known for having the fastest race horse in all Orange County!'"

That story felt like a treasure to me. I appreciated that Gretchen shared it, and it whetted my appetite for more such accounts. It was only by chance that Gretchen had heard it in the first place. She had not known about the racing horses at all until she had encountered that gentleman at the door who had once known her grandfather. I felt lucky that she remembered it all these decades later.

As I continued my researching, I learned more. There had been bull fights in the great plaza in front of the Mission, and strutting caballeros. I learned that the town had to form a vigilance committee and that its members had to be ready at a moment's notice to ride out to capture horse and cattle rustlers. There were dangerous gun battles and masked robbers who made quick get-aways on their mounts. There were hangings and ambushes. My head began to spin with the tales from the old days. It reinforced for me how important it is to collect some of these old memories.

San Juan Capistrano – A City Unique in Celebrating Its Heritage

As the months of interviews and research continued, I came to realize that it is not so much that San Juan has "risen up" as the equestrian center of Orange County, or the West Coast, but rather that other cities have simply let that aspect of their rich heritage take a back seat to the sprawling progress of steel, glass, and concrete as high-rise office buildings, tracts of homes and apartment buildings cover the once serene landscape. I also came to understand that an implicit cooperation exists between the Rancho

Signs of a Vibrant Equestrian Life 2018

Mission Viejo, the entity of the City, and the townspeople, which has resulted in San Juan's unique celebration of the Western way of life. In fact, while interviewing Tony Moiso, of the great Rancho Mission Viejo, he recalled that during one of the Portolá Ride kick-offs, San Juan's native son and former Mayor, Larry Buchheim, once told the crowd of Riders, that, "from the very beginning the City, the Ranch and the Mission have been one."

As my studies continued, I came to realize how profoundly the Ranch has helped the City and the Mission. San Juan is fortunate in many ways because not only does Rancho Mission Viejo considers it its town, but so did the great Rancho Santa Margarita y Las Flores which is now Camp Pendleton. Many towns in early Orange County such as Forster City founded in 1876, on the north coast of Rancho Santa Margarita, failed, while San Juan maintained.

An Equestrian Kaleidoscope

In the galleria in the hallway of my home, every day I walk past some of the framed election flyers of my husband's bids for election and re-election to the City Council. In four consecutive elections he campaigned on the same platform, *"The quality of life in San Juan Capistrano is unique. We must preserve it,"* and he triumphed in each. He was first elected as part of a movement to contain excessive development in the City. In 1972 a new City leadership organized committees of citizens who worked long and hard on shaping a General Plan that would reflect the town's desire to preserve what it had. After two years of intensive effort on the part of many, the General Plan was revised and adopted in 1974.

The new plan reduced the ultimate city growth down from the 85,000 to a maximum build-out of only 40,000, with the preservation of the hillside and open space. At this writing, San Juan's population is less than 40,000. So this is the story I want to share with you: that San Juan Capistrano is unique, perhaps across America, that its citizens dared to dream of fighting to retain the City's rural charm.

Let's pause for some moments in the long-ago past, and then the more recent past, while enjoying an "equestrian kaleidoscope" of all that goes on which has allowed its distinctive character to be recognized.

There are many ways to approach a subject like this. I am by training an oral historian, it is natural for me to collect memories and piece together a narrative. However, memories like perceptions, vary with the individual and change across time. This history does not claim to be infallible. It is merely a gathering of stories, reminiscences, and historical accounts. As the year of gathering tales stretched forward, I came to realize that this project could almost be endless. I offer this portion up, hoping the next curious historian will pick up the baton, and continue the collection.

Ken Friess on Paiute 1980

As I share this with you, I would like you to join me in your imagination and see us sipping a cup of coffee on my patio and talking about what horses have meant to us in our little corner of the planet. I'm hoping you'll smile, perhaps even shed a tear, as you feel the spirit of San Juan Capistrano tugging at you as you step into the past and enjoy these often heartfelt tales.

Lacouague Citrus Ranch c. 1970's

Chapter Two

Prehistoric Equus

"When God wanted to create the horse, he said to the South Wind, 'I want to make a creature of you. Condense.' And the Wind Condensed." (Odeoncafedc.com)

Before long, word got out about my writing project. A flurry of excitement seemed to erupt around me when the topic of horses and local history arose. Acquaintances began sharing their horse experiences with me at lunch. During my weekly trail rides, I would frequently strike up conversations with others on their horses. They often provided me with an anecdote. I soon learned that some simply wanted to tell an amazing moment that had little to do with horses. When you live in a community with a common sense of history and purpose, sharing is something of a cultural norm. At Ralph's Market, for example, the twenty-five-pound bag of carrots in my shopping cart was all it took to open the conversational gates. This bag of carrots to horse people was clear evidence that I was a kindred spirit and we had a mutual love of horses. They eagerly shared their stories with me.

Metro Meteor

On one particular day, as I hefted my carrots into the cart, a lovely woman dressed as an equestrienne paused in the aisle and asked after my horses. As we exchanged words, I, of course, asked if she had a horse story for me. "Ah," she smiled. "I have a painting by the famous race horse Metro hanging in my home. I'm Holly. Here's my number, call me and I'll tell you more."

The minute I got home, I Googled "Metro." I learned that his story had recently been aired on morning television. It seems that a crippling knee injury sidelined Metro Meteor from his racing career at Belmont and Saratoga. In retirement he was to be a pleasure horse. His new owner, artist, Ron Krajewski, noticed that Metro liked to bob his head around for attention. Ron thought he might enjoy painting. With brush in his teeth, Metro began to paint bold, colorful abstracts.

Before long it became obvious that Metro's knee condition was worsening. Concerned, the Krajewskis took him to a veterinarian. The prognosis was bad. He had, perhaps, two years to live. In the meantime, the sales of his paintings were soaring. He became the best selling artist in Gallery 30 in Gettysburg. Using a portion of the money from the paintings, Ron and his wife, Wendy, found a young veterinarian who was willing to try an experimental treatment. It reversed Metro's condition. His knees are still a problem, but he can walk the trails. With his limitations he has more time than ever to devote to his paintings. Recently the Krajewskis donated $45,000 from Metro Meteor's paintings to the New

Vocations Racehorse Adoption Program. These funds help retired thoroughbreds find homes and new careers. Perhaps some will be inspired by Metro and try their "teeth" at painting as well.

Equus: San Juan's Prehistoric Horse Fossil

Equine stories were coming to me faster than I could get them down. There was an energy surrounding my project. I could feel it. It woke me up at night. As I continued with my daily routine, my thoughts would randomly slip back to horses and how important they have been across time. I also noticed that many of the people I encountered in town had some kind of a connection to the topic. One afternoon my friend, Rhonda DeHaan, a member of the San Juan Capistrano Friends of the Library Board of Directors, invited me to a lecture by professional paleontologist Eric Scott of the Cogstone Resource Management Center which specializes in authentications in paleontology, archaeology and history. Among his many credentials, I discovered that he had served as Chief Excavator at the La Brea Tar Pits. I attended his lecture on a warm June day in 2017 to learn about "The Story of Human Civilization which is the Story of the Horse," the title of his talk.

What I heard took my breath away. Eric Scott held the eager audience filling San Juan's library meeting room in thrall with his remarkable facts. He reported that contrary to what many of us have been taught, that the Spaniards brought horses to North America in the 15th Century, in fact, they simply

Donna Friess and Wendy Cast and Nephews La Brea Tar Pits August 2017

returned our horses to us! Equus, (horse) was native to North America and had flourished in past ages, evolving over some 50 million years from a small animal the size of a dog to the stunningly large animal we know today. Scientists believe that the relatives of today's horse evolved during the Pliocene epoch in North America and emigrated north across the Bering Land Bridge during the Ice Age to Eurasia. Sometime later the "horse" disappeared from the West. Anthropologists believe that humans lived for some 15,000 years on the Bering Land Bridge between Asia and North America. Reliable science suggests the land bridge was 600 miles wide and that humans remained there until the last Ice Age ended.

This information was new to me and got me so excited that during a family trip to Avalon on Catalina Island the next month, with my eleven grandchildren around me, one of my favorite topics was to quiz them about what they knew of the Bering Sea Land Bridge. I took guesses and made it suspenseful. Now I realize I could have taken bets on what scientists think versus what most of us know about it. Too late! Anyway, that Bering Land Bridge was my pet idea all summer, plus I found it amazing that scientists have an ancient horse fossil from San Juan Capistrano with a jaw and teeth! I won't bore you with all that. I love details, but you may not. I was sharing all these facts with my twenty-two year-old law school student, granddaughter, Jillian, over lunch one day. Thinking out loud about the fossils, amused, I admitted, "ah..It's possible I'm getting carried away with this!" Creating her own pun, she replied, "Mimi, you might want to *rein* it in some!" We both laughed as she knows me well! So if this topic of ancient equines is not for you, please just trot ahead!

I made a date with my niece and her dinosaur-loving boys and headed 60 miles north to Los

Fossil of Equus 13000 Years Old, La Brea Tar Pits

Angeles. We were going to get to the bottom of this prehistoric horse business. As a child, I frequently visited the Tar Pits with my grandparents who lived near them. In those days there was no museum, just messy pits sprawled across a park. It wasn't much back then, but I had done my homework and knew that it was unique in the world, yielding the most Ice Age fossils in existence anywhere, and has been continually excavated since 1906.

Horse Fossils at La Brea Tar Pits
The Spaniards Return Horses to North America

Upon arriving at the La Brea Tar Pits, we began our adventure in the Page Museum. As we ambled by the giant animated mammoth, of course we had to stop and take our picture with it. The boys were spellbound by its immensity, but I was eager to move on and find the ancient horse bones.

Finally, there they were! My heart skipped a few beats as I examined the roughly 13,000 year-old Western horse remains; Equus Occidentalis (Western horse). Its head and jaw were displayed with the teeth, as well as a leg. It was exactly what Eric Scott had described regarding the much older fossil of the same Western horse found in San Juan Capistrano. I was in heaven. The boys weren't so impressed and went on to examine a huge saber-toothed cat's skull.

I was still considering the ancient horse, learning that at one time there were something like twenty-seven genera of them which included modern horses, zebras and asses. It turns out that today's Equus is the only surviving genus from that once diverse family. Apparently, that horse emigrated northward, 2 to 3 million years ago, arriving in Europe, Asia and into Africa.

We continued around the museum, stopping at a glass enclosed chamber where a dozen or more archeologists were working directly in front of us, intricately cleaning fossils. The boys loved that! Next was an animated film in an air-conditioned auditorium.

Cooled down and refreshed, we ventured outside into the heat to view the outdoor pits. Our imaginations ran wild as we came upon the different sites and gazed at huge piles of random bones

Western Horse La Brea Tar Pits Fossil 13000 Years Old

protruding from the tar. To date more than 3.5 million fossils have been discovered.

We enjoyed our visit very much. On the drive home, the noise level in the car quieted as the boys fell asleep, giving me a chance to process what Eric Scott had said about the rich fossil legacy left for us. He had explained that horses had become extinct in North America due to climate changes and the arrival of humans. I pondered what I was learning, that across the many Ice Ages, Southern California was not always covered in ice, that about 15,000-25,000 years ago when the last Ice Age was ending, there was much vegetation from which large animals could feed as well as ample fresh water.

As we left Los Angeles behind and came into Orange County, I specifically recalled stories of large prehistoric animals wandering in our area. I recalled an *Orange County Register* article (February 27, 2006) which reported that near the Santa Ana Canyon, during the construction of the Foothill-South (241) Toll Road, 20,000 fossils were discovered. In 2015, construction workers using heavy earth moving equipment in Carlsbad, California discovered mammoths, horses, turtles and a prehistoric bison, as they excavated for new apartment buildings. One large fossil, Paleoparadoxia, of an ancient herbivorous aquatic mammal now extinct, is of particular interest to scientists as it lived in the Pacific coastal region during the Miocene epoch (23 million years ago to 5 million years ago during a time of global warmth). There's even a cast of it on display in San Clemente.

> "Equus was native to North America and flourished in past ages evolving over some 50 million years."
> Eric Scott

Eric Scott had explained that during the last Ice Age, horses were able to adapt and survive as they emigrated north because their hooves could be used to dig through the frozen tundra to find food. Sheep and other large animals then followed behind and foraged for food through the broken ice. He suggested that those grazing animals would have starved had the horses not cut through the hard ice. The star of his talk was Equus Occidentalis found in San Juan Capistrano; the same genus as the one on display at the Page Museum. The San Juan horse fossil is thought to be 190,000 years old, while the fossil record for other large animals found in Southern California extends back 180 million years! That span of time seemed like infinity to me. It was way too much to grasp.

I pulled my thoughts back to the idea of the horse as an instrument aiding the growth of civilization. Its strength and nature have allowed it to become our potent ally. I knew that its great strong spine, with its immense ability to carry loads, was particularly of value to humans. Horses, unlike many other animals, must depend on a hind gut for their digestion. The heavy hind gut requires a particularly strong spine for support. In addition to carrying goods, the horse increased humans' ability to travel across greater distances, to more easily trade, and to share culture and language. I understood why it can be said that civilization arrived on horseback.

A few years ago in Meknes, Morocco, I was lucky enough to tour the King's stables where His Majesty's legendary Arabian horses are scientifically bred. It was an incredible experience for me. I recall that as the magnificent animals, with their distinctive high tail carriage, were paraded in front of us, I was moved to tears by their beauty. Perhaps too, I felt a pang in my heart for that long ago time when my Arabian horse, Windy, took me sailing past the finish line. Arabians have always intrigued me. The breed is about 4500 years old.

On the grassy plains of Southern Russia many fossils of other equines have been discovered with bit marks on their teeth. This is especially true in the Ukraine and Kazakhstan providing evidence that those horses were domesticated as far back as 4000 b. c.

It's enough for me to consider some day traveling the famous Silk Road of Eurasia where our human relationship with horses began so long ago. I've investigated the many comfortable train tours that are now offered across the 6800 miles of Eurasia. In the meantime, I enjoy knowing that humans have benefitted from horses for 6000 years. Horses have been critical assets for herding, cultivating fields, waging war, sharing language and customs, providing pleasure, creating sport and even food as they proliferated across much of the planet. Horses have been valuable status symbols, prized gifts, and even companions.

Smiling to myself, I thought of my thoroughbred, Mr. T, and my other horses across the years, with their velvety soft muzzles and eager whinnies. They are always so happy to see me and their high pitched little sounds warm my heart. I get a big reaction when I bring them apples. I recognize that domestication was possible because of their calm nature and a social structure which allows for domination.

As we neared our exit on the freeway, I thought, I'm right to collect stories about horses and to capture some of the magic which surrounds them. San Juan's story begins with the Spanish explorers who came via horseback and mule to Alta California to colonize it for the Spanish crown. Of course they brought horses back to our part of the world. This is where the tale of San Juan Capistrano and its equestrian legacy should begin.

Chapter Three

Early Days – Saddle Up!

'Take care of the land and it will take care of you." *(Marguerite "Daisy" O'Neill)*

The congregation filling the beautiful Serra Chapel of the Mission San Juan Capistrano grew silent as we waited for Mass to begin. It was 7:00 a.m. on a warm spring morning. A sense of reverence floated between the ancient adobe walls. Anticipation seemed to grow as we awaited the religious processional. Once it began, I could see the cross as it was slowly moved down the center aisle. All had gathered for this traditional "Gibby's Mass" to bless the participants of the El Viaje de Portolá. As the first prayer began, we stood, my stomach knotting in excitement. I was surrounded by perhaps 150 men who seemed

1971 Portolá Ride to Mexico Lindo. Mayor Tony Forster Led Riders Up Camino Capistrano. Courtesy Tony Moiso

23

from my 5'2" perspective to be very tall in their heeled cowboy boots and Stetson hats. A shiver went through me. I never dreamed when I began to gather stories for this book that I would be invited to an event as unique as the send-off for the famous Portolá Ride, a symbolic 30-mile reenactment of the exploration of Gaspar de Portolá into Alta California.

I learned that the Ride has been hosted by the "Ranch" (Rancho Mission Viejo) for more than half

1971 Tony Moiso Standing, Tony Forster Seated.

a century in celebration of California's heritage. My interviews had brought me to Gilbert Aguirre, Executive Vice President of Ranch Operations for Rancho Mission Viejo, who welcomed me and shared stories from across some 50 years in which he has been involved as a leader at the Ranch. He knew that my research would not be complete without some sense of the legendary Portolá Ride.

As the Mass began, we again took our seats. My eyes were drawn to the hand-carved altar that had come all the way from Barcelona over 100 years ago. Its gold face caught the light and held my attention. I could not stop myself from imagining what California had been like so long ago. I thought about the thousands of years during which native stone-age people lived quietly along the coastal plains of what is now the West Coast of America. It is estimated that between 100,000-300,000 people lived in what was to become California before the Spanish arrived. I knew that in 1542 Juan Rodriguez Cabrillo explored the southern coast of California and claimed it for Spain.

I recalled, however, that the Spanish crown had little interest in doing much with it for the next 160 years. When other countries, especially Russia, began building outposts, Spain paid more attention. The Russians had been pushing south from the Bering Strait, establishing outposts, becoming enthusiastic over the lucrative Sea otter fur business. Fort Ross still stands in Sonoma County, a current day reminder of the most southern hub of their expansion into Alta California.

As I tuned back into the service, I thought about what these walls have witnessed; the centuries of Masses celebrated. They would have been in Spanish. I held that image for a moment and thought more about Spain during that era. Perhaps it was the pressure from the foreign crowns that caused King Carlos III to rethink the value of Alta California. In 1769, Spain, which controlled Mexico, began to push northward from Baja California to colonize it. An envoy divided into four units was sent via land and sea to explore the area with the intention of establishing a string of settlements along the coast. The master plan from Spain provided for two friars and six soldiers to create self-sufficient agricultural settlements depending upon a labor force consisting of Indigenous people.

The Expedition of Gaspar De Portolá

The initial expedition was led by military Captain Gaspar De Portolá, and the administrator for the Catholic Church, the President of the Missions, Father Junipero Serra. They left Baja California for San Diego in early 1769 tasked with mapping out potential sites in Alta California for presidios and missions. After experiencing great difficulty due to illness, the ships arrived in San Diego in April, with a very ill crew. Before long, the crew of 90 was reduced to eight soldiers and eight sailors. The land column having marched 300 miles, met up with the ships in May in much better shape. They had lost no men and their mule train with horses and 200 head of cattle was intact. Those cows would be the ancestors of some of massive herds that would roam the thousand hills of Alta California. [Later, with the Gold Rush, thousands more head of cattle would be brought in from the Midwest.]

By July of 1769 the Portolá company resumed the expedition north, carrying out its orders. The group of 64 men included Father Crespi and Father Gomez as spiritual advisors. The caravan consisted of 200 horses and mules for riding, as well as a large pack train carrying provisions for the trip. By 1823 the journey begun over fifty years earlier resulted in twenty-one Franciscan missions, four presidios, and several pueblos being established along Alta California, ensuring Spanish dominion over the land.

Inside the chapel, the final blessings were being bestowed, and my thoughts drifted once again to where I was; the birthplace of Orange County. I knew this chapel was the only remaining one in California where Father Serra, himself, had celebrated Mass. Our Mission was officially founded by

Mission San Juan Capistrano c. 1900. Courtesy Mission San Juan Capistrano Archives

Father Serra on November 1, 1776, and named for Saint John of Capistrano, a 14th Century Franciscan soldier priest whom Serra greatly admired. For the seventh mission, Father Serra chose a serene valley which boasted two creeks and three sloping hillsides where the natives were friendly. I knew that the first attempt at construction was met with difficulty. After about a week of work erecting a corral and some outbuildings, a courier arrived to tell of a violent uprising at the San Diego Mission. The soldiers mounted their horses and headed for San Diego, and they encouraged the friars to pack up their provisions and do the same. They all went back to help defend that mission where a priest and two others had been killed. It was not until a year later that they returned to complete the mission in San Juan.

First Site for Mission San Juan Capistrano

There is diary evidence suggesting that the first mission had to be moved "due to water failure" to its current location, and that the transfer was made on October 4, 1778. The location of the original site is a bit of a mystery, because some of the diary entries contradict each other. There is a brass plaque mounted at Reata Park, at Ortega Highway on the north side of San Juan Creek, which reads:

ON THE MESA ONE HALF MILE SOUTH FROM HERE THE ORIGINAL MISSION OF SAN JUAN CAPISTRANO WAS FOUNDED ON NOV. 1, 1776. Commemorated El Viaje De Portola, April 1968.
(The source of the above information is not documented on the plaque.
See Appendix B, Don Meadows' Article.)

Don Meadows, a respected Orange County historian, also believed the first site was on that same mesa which, for decades, was on Jean Lacouague's citrus ranch (today it is a housing development), not far from my backyard. I like that idea, for when I am gazing out of my kitchen window my view is of that mesa behind my home, I can imagine the early beginnings of our first mission under construction. Jean Lacouague allowed Mr. Meadows to view the many artifacts left behind from long ago on his property. It is possible, however, that it could have been elsewhere. (Again, See Appendix B for Meadows' explanation.) Today that mesa is home to a large housing development. Civilization marches on.

As the service closed and the recessional slowly moved past me, the old days once again grabbed my imagination as I contemplated what an indescribably massive effort it had to have been to convince the Native people that the new religion of the priests would be a pathway to heaven; that they would have

a better way of life, with an adequate food supply. What a herculean challenge it had to have been to take hunters and gatherers, and teach them new technologies. They would have known little of melting iron ore, creating metal tools, of crop techniques, nor wine making. I took a moment to think about that as each pew emptied in front of me. It was an awesome concept. Essentially, the missionaries built self-sustaining walled forts which became the bedrock of recorded civilization in California. Today it has the fifth most powerful economy in the world!

Mission Becomes a Successful Enterprise

I absorbed the fact that I was literally sitting within the walls of the beginning of something immense. It took my breath away. My brain felt like it wanted to explode! I mulled over the fact that within a few short years this Mission, along with the others, became successful business enterprises with a

Mission San Juan Capistrano – Interior Corridors. Photo 2018

workforce of Native people. The missions were able to provide not just for the individual missions, but for the military and civil government of all of California as well. Collectively, by the time Mexico defeated Spain, the missions owned 150,000 head of cattle, and massive herds of horses.

I respected a point made by Father Engelhardt, a celebrated mission system historian of the last century. He reproduced an August 2, 1796 Mission San Juan Capistrano economic report. It stated that "the harvest had been more abundant than was first supposed." That notation had followed a report that the Mission was sending 2600 pounds of white wool and 500 pounds of black wool to other missions and presidios (1922, p.36). The Mission was extremely productive. By 1806, Mission San Juan Capistrano had 11,000 head of cattle and 1400 horses.

Flourishing Mission San Juan Capistrano Made Wine and Brandy and Many Tools from Metal. Photos 2018

I was glad that we were moving to the next part of the ceremony. It would give me a break from pondering all that had come before. As our row slowly left the church, I noticed how subdued everyone appeared as we walked toward the Empty Saddle Ceremony. I had time to think about the lessons from my docent training. The Mission had controlled over 350 square miles of prime land, loaned by the Spanish crown. As we passed by the Mission's big grassy quadrangle, I visualized the Natives hard at work, weaving, shearing wool, making wine and tanning hides. I knew that about 1000 people once lived in or around the Mission. I thought of the Neophyte [baptized Indian] women cooking at the open fires, of others preparing tallow for candles and soap, while men labored in the fields, and newly-minted vaqueros tended to vast herds of cows, sheep and horses.

> By 1806, records show that Mission San Juan was in high gear with 1400 horses and over 11,000 head of cattle, 12,300 sheep and producing 11,000 bushels of wheat, in addition to corn, barley, beans. (Fr. Zephyrin Engelhardt. P 182).

The Empty Saddle Ceremony

The Empty Saddle Ceremony was about to begin. I could feel emotions running high in the crowd around me. We were in a corner of the Mission courtyard, Portolá Plaza, facing the bronze statue of the horse with an empty saddle. Many brass plates adorned the pedestal of the statue, the names of fallen riders engraved on their faces. Other name plates glinted, in the sun, blanks to be used in some future time. My friend, Laura Freese, and I found seats. Most of the Riders stood in silence at the back of the rows of seats where the women and families were seated. The program described the service "as a faithful memorial and in fond memory of the riders of El Viaje de Portolá herein honor their fallen compadres." As the speakers shared their favorite memories of their deceased friends, I felt the power of human connections. I soon understood how significant the Portolá Ride, and being a member of the group, must feel to those involved. In the months to follow, as I interviewed individual Portolá Riders I would learn even more.

Gibby's Mass and Empty Saddle Ceremony - Portolá Ride

When the Master of Ceremonies came to my friend Laura's husband, I reached for her hand. Tears glistened in her eyes. I saw how important this group was to her and to her late husband. As the stories about the Riders came to a conclusion, there was a closing prayer. The mood remained somber. We quietly adjourned to our cars. Laura was driving as we traveled the five miles or so to Amantes Camp on the Ranch, where a barbeque would be shared, and the awaiting horses would gain their riders.

The Modern Portolá Ride – Celebrating Western Traditions

As we left the traffic and houses behind and continued east on Ortega Highway through the rolling hills into the lands held by the Rancho Mission Viejo, my thoughts took me back to the Rancho days. Spain understood that it would take more than twenty-one missions and four military presidios to truly colonize California. Further settlement was encouraged through land grants. Between 1784 and 1821 Spain granted large tracts of land to prominent men to raise sheep and cattle. These grants became known as Ranchos. The Crown retained the title to the land and individual grantees were required to build a structure and use the land for grazing and cultivation. There were 21 Ranchos in and around what is now

Orange County. The head of each Rancho held the honorary title of "Don." I leaned back into the head rest as I recalled a description I had read of Rancho life shared by a descendent of the Yorba family [of Jose Antonio Yorba, a soldier in the Portolá Expedition]. She was Doña Felipa Yorba de Dominguez, a granddaughter of the Don. She was born in 1852. I smiled to myself as I recalled her words as captured by Father O'Sullivan.

> *"Ay those fiestas! – then was when your family, our cousins of San Juan Capistrano and Santa Ana Abajo, would come up with their vaqueros to compete with us in the corridas. –those were the days of bullfights, races, picnics and fandangos [balls]."*

It didn't seem like times had changed all that much; well, certainly there were no bull fights, but we were headed toward an outdoor picnic and I knew there would be music and merriment as the Riders

Empty Saddle Ceremony March 31, 2017

prepared for their three-day ride.

Another description came to mind of the glamour days of the Ranchos. It was a memory shared with Father O'Sullivan by a parishioner known as Doña Maria. She told of a large plaza in the front of the Mission in the old days. In her words:

> *"The dwellings along the boundary of the great plaza made an excellent vantage point from which to watch the bullfights and other functions held there."*

The Blas Aguilar Adobe at the eastern edge of what was the great plaza is all we have to remind us of the adobes that rimmed that plaza. It has been renovated and is open to the public. Doña Maria said that as a child she loved to perch on a high stool looking out the window in an adobe along there, watching the excitement on the plaza. In her words translated to English:

"On such festal occasions the corridors would be crowded with ladies in white mantillas, high combs and flounced skirts, admiring the horsemen in silk and velvet and glittering silver."

Doña Maria continued:

"The Californios, two or three generations ago, made a great account of silver, and were buttoned, buckled and spurred in it. In those days every ranch of consequence had its platero, or silversmith, whose handiwork adorned not only the hats, jackets and breeches of the riders, but the bridles, reins, bits and saddles of the horses as well. It was a brave sight when caballeros from far and near gathered in the plaza of San Juan and caracoled and galloped about it."

I loved that mental image of vaqueros and horses galloping about, adorned from head to toe in silver, parading around in front of the Mission. So many of those rich traditions are alive today. The Fiesta Association is doing its part to keep the old ways with us by organizing countless activities and events around Swallows Week; the big Western dance, the grandeur of the parade itself, the fun of releasing old time "deputies" garbed in silver spurs and ten-gallon hats onto the townspeople to be "arrested" if not in proper Western attire. There are many ways in which our city celebrates the past. I thought of the annual rodeo now held at the Riding Park which offers one of the biggest purses in the country and attracts elite rodeo cowboys and huge crowds for the two day event. Certainly the clients at The J.F. Shea Therapeutic Riding Center are pleased with their equestrian accomplishments, as they proudly demonstrate their skills at annual exhibitions under the covered arena in front of cheering audiences. I considered the countless trainers, teaching the next generation how to ride, the many equestrian competitions, and all the local stable owners who are perpetuating some of the traditions of those silver-adorned ranchero days. I thought of the large animal veterinarians available to help at a moment's notice, and the important, back-breaking work of the farriers. The Rancho Mission Viejo Riding Park at San Juan Capistrano hosts world class equestrian competitions, and is an Olympic training ground as well. I guessed that most San Juan residents had a stash of cowboy boots and hats secreted in their closets.

As we approached the Amantes Camp on the Rancho Mission Viejo, a guard ushered us into the picnic grounds where the welcoming lyrics of Dave Stamey singing, "If I had a Horse" greeted us. Soon we were swallowed into the crowd. I sensed the change in mood, from somber to celebratory. Tony Moiso, Chairman and Chief Executive Officer of Rancho Mission Viejo greeted everyone with a warm welcome. His sense of humor was contagious as he led the program. I noticed the crowd relaxing into the moment as Dave Stamey sang more western songs, I reflected on what Tony had shared with me about the Ranch and how his family was able to hang on to it.

In Tony's words: "It was my grandmother, Marguerite, known as Daisy O'Neill, who kept Rancho Mission Viejo together. In 1926, Jerome O'Neill, owner of the great Rancho Santa Margarita y Las Flores died; the Ranch was then held in trust. In 1944, the bank, managing the trust, was eager to sell it; administering liquid assets was far less complicated than running a big ranch. 'Ama Daisy', caught by surprise, vehemently disagreed! Her husband, my grandfather, Richard O'Neill, Sr., had died in 1943; she initiated legal action against the bank to stop any sale. She wanted to keep the Ranch for herself, her children; her son, Richard "Uncle Richard" O'Neill, and daughter, my mother, Alice O'Neill Moiso Avery, and for future generations. Daisy

O'Neill, 'Ama Daisy,' often admonished: *'take care of the land and it will take care of you.'* She
also reminded us, *'Never mortgage
your home, so you will always have a
place to live.'"*

And take care of the land, Tony did.
In 1967, he convinced family members to
purchase control of the Mission Viejo
Company, the Ranch's first developer, and
to develop the land themselves rather than
sell it off piecemeal. All the other Orange
County large landholdings were no longer
controlled by family members; the Irvine,
Moulton, and Whiting families. The loss of
historical ownership made it uncertain
whether the large tracts of pristine land
would remain and if the cattle businesses
would continue. Today, Rancho Mission
Viejo ranks with the largest privately held
landholdings in Southern California. Tony
believed that he and the family could better
control the quality of developments. He
formed development entities and purchased
land from the family landowners. In the
1970's, he established Santa Margarita
Company to develop the community of
Rancho Santa Margarita, opened in 1986.
Through other companies, he has continued
to develop award winning communities in
southern Orange County, including Las

Dave Stamey's Western Songs at Send-off March 2017

Flores, Ladera Ranch, and more recently, the communities of Sendero and Esencia within the Rancho
Mission Viejo. Tony professed: "Rancho Mission Viejo remains a ranch, a ranch where some of the
most successful large scale Master Planned Communities ever have been established." [See
Appendix D for Don Tyron's Article on 'Ama' Daisy.]

The music continued, and the audience was rapt. My thoughts came to another story Tony had
shared with me, this one about Larry Buchheim. Laughing, Tony explained that it was during a stroll
through the Historic Town Center Park construction site, when David Belardes, the Native American
monitoring the dig for any ancient artifacts, was examining an old bottle that had been found in an
excavation. David was leaning toward thinking that it was a real find, a leftover from the Rancho Period.
Suddenly, Larry, who was born and raised in San Juan, declared. "Why I know that bottle. In fact I drank
from that bottle right there under that tree!"

I stifled an inner chuckle and tuned back into the proceedings. There were presentations and more
welcomes and awards. The crowd enjoyed drinks, lavish amounts of freshly barbecued food, and lots of
laughing. I had a chance to touch base with some of my friends and verify various details of the horse
stories that had been shared with me.

Across the parking area I could see more than a 150 horses saddled and tethered to horse trailers waiting for their Portolá Riders. The long line of saddled horses reminded me of the Portolá Expedition of old. It, too, included a long procession of men and beasts. These current horses had an easy load compared to those in the first Portolá party. The Portolá soldiers of long ago, placed a heavy burden on their mounts. Because they could not count on reliable food and water sources, they had to carry (in addition to the rider and his saddle), water, food, cooking equipment, a musket, two pistols, shot powder, a leather shield and more. These waiting horses were to have far lighter burdens.

Horses Tethered Waiting for Their Riders

If the chuck wagon food we had just experienced was any indication, I knew that a delicious catered dinner could be counted on at the day's end as the Riders got to their camp. The afternoon passed in a blur. As the party was concluding and the men prepared to start on their ride, Laura walked me past the cars in the grassy area, to a serene tree-covered corner of the canyon and showed me the Ranch cemetery. The family plots are well tended. Several were adorned with fresh flowers. More than ever, I saw how self-contained the Ranchos were, and perhaps more than that, how well cherished were the old traditions.

Preserving the Traditions of Old

We drove away shortly thereafter, with Laura again at the wheel. I closed my eyes for a few minutes and marveled at what the O'Neill family had accomplished over the last hundred and thirty-six years; managing to hang on to much of the original 220,000 acres of the ranch, while being good stewards and preserving the old traditions. They were also key players in helping San Juan Capistrano to preserve its past, donating generously to preservation. It was astonishing.

I smiled as I recalled what Tony had told me about his growing up years in West Los Angeles. A city kid, his grandmother, Daisy, would bring him to the Ranch for special occasions, the round-ups, brandings and such. They would stay at her home on Balboa Island and spend the day at the Ranch. He explained, "When I was older, after the Army and all, one day, I was thinking out loud, chatting with Ranch Manager, Tom Forster. I remember that I was lamenting the fact that I had missed an opportunity by not working at the Ranch during school vacations, when I asked him, 'Why didn't I?' Tom looked me in the eye and said, 'You never asked.' I realized I hadn't. I had not thought to..."

I had so appreciated Tony Moiso's down-to-earth candor. As our conversation had continued he added, "When I came to work at the Ranch, my brother was telling me all about the Portolá Ride. It had been going on for two years, he'd said. 'It's a lot of fun and you *are* the quasi host.' That's when I started riding again. I had ridden from age ten with time out for college and the Army. I could fake being a cowboy and did fine in the saddle," he continued, chuckling, "but my Uncle Richard would have had you believe he was born in the saddle, when in reality he grew up in Beverly Hills!" We both laughed. As a beach kid myself, I knew something about getting used to the saddle.

Almost back in town, I thought once again about my good fortune in being invited to this send-off. It showed me more about the Portolá Ride and what it means to its Riders than all the books could impart. As we entered San Juan, it was time for me to shed my researcher mantle and focus on china painting lessons with my youngest granddaughter, seven-year-old Caroline.

Chapter Four

El Viaje de Portolá

Horse Advice: "Take life's hurdles in your stride, loosen the reins, be free-spirited, carry your friends when they need it." (quotesbae.com)

A few days after attending the opening ceremonies, I had a chance to sit down and write about some of the drama and fun that I had been hearing regarding the Portolá Ride. There were some pretty wild stories to jot down; naked-bottomed Tony Forster diving into the surf, or our former Orange County Sheriff knocked off this bunk, but first a look at how all this Portolá Ride business began. In my interviews with Tony Moiso, Chairman and Chief Executive officer, and Gilbert Aguirre, Executive Vice President of Rancho Mission Viejo, I was given plenty to think about. If you don't know how it started, here's a quick summary: it began as a business promotion in 1963 by the owners of the new Saddleback

1964 Portolá Riders on El Camino Real. Courtesy RMV

Inn in Santa Ana. The Inn owners thought that installing an El Camino Real bell in the front of the hotel would be a clever attraction, and a way to draw attention to the new facility. Of course they could not foresee that their idea would become the stuff of legends, and almost a mainstay of the equestrian story in San Juan!

El Camino Real Bell to Saddleback Inn

As the story goes, the idea of transporting the bell from Mission San Juan Capistrano along El Camino Real in a horse drawn cart, escorted by some riders, had a romantic note to it, and the promoters were all in. However, before long the entire concept began to grow as eight men: Bud Curtis, Ken Oliphant, Bill Riffle, Bill Shattuck, Fulton Shaw, Bill Votaw, Charlie Wheeler and Dudley Wright, (known as the "Big Eight"), planned the event in earnest.

Through their various contacts, they met Orange County historian Don Meadows who suggested that following a bit of the original Gaspar de Portolá's route up from Mexico would add a touch of nostalgia. Tom Forster, foreman at Rancho Mission Viejo (Tony's father), thought they could discover a riding trail from San Juan Capistrano through the various ranches to the future Saddleback Inn. It was he who came up with the name of the ride. Charlie Wheeler of the Irvine Ranch arranged for them to go up in the Goodyear Blimp to view the potential route.

Father Martin Blesses the Portolá Riders. Courtesy RMV

Painting of Portolá Ride. Courtesy RMV

From the outset, the Ride was accompanied by all kinds of fanfare and a blessing by the resident Priest at the Mission. For that first event, sixty Riders enjoyed a send-off at the El Adobe Restaurant. The horses were tethered in the parking lot behind the restaurant. Soon the processional began, escorted by two mules pulling a small cart on which the bell was perched, four white horses pulling a stage coach for the non-riders was next in line, behind that were the mounted riders. It must have been a fine scene as they marched up Camino Capistrano to the music of a six-piece mariachi band. The first night they camped at Trabuco Creek where historian Don Meadows shared stories of the original Portolá expedition. On the second day, the group passed through the other big ranches of Orange County and spent the night at the El Toro Marine Base. From there buses took them into Santa Ana where a party awaited them at the Saddleback Inn. Each of the Big Eight was in charge of seeing to their own guests. It was a hugely successful first ride, and as the years passed it grew in numbers and reputation.

The Portolá Ride Becomes a Tradition

When Gilbert Aguirre joined the ride in 1967, the send-off was from El Adobe and the horses were tied up in what today is Historic Town Center Park. It was a vacant lot back then. On that ride, there were about 200 riders who rode up Camino Capistrano and were blessed by the resident Priest. From the beginning the Mission was central to the Ride, celebrating Mass in the Serra Chapel in the early pre-Ride hours.

Tony Moiso (Right) and Gilbert Aguirre. Courtesy RMV

Gilbert recalls that on that 1967 Ride they went to the Irvine Ranch and stayed in upper Trabuco Canyon which they called "The Hilton" where the Arroyo Trabuco Golf Club is today. Gilbert remembers highlights of the Rides across the years, especially getting to ride on the beach in Crystal Cove. When Tony Forster got to bragging about the family holding the 200,000 acres, Gilbert would sometimes remind him, "Your family only held it for 11 years, and even then 'you stole it,' while the O'Neills had held it for 135 years!" Everyone would laugh. "The Rides continue to be so great because it is a time, when men can have fun acting like kids; when they have a chance to live out our Western heritage for three days." He concluded.

Across the years, the leadership has passed to others who have stepped up to become "patrones," [hosts] and more and more friends, sons and guests have been

Portolá Riders Across the Trail. Courtesy RMV

added. The Ride is a men-only group, and by invitation. [Of course I left my feminist hat at home!] It draws from a mix of cowboys, political leaders, business men, and sometimes even celebrities, such as Pro-Rodeo Hall of Famer, trick rider, Montie Montana and recently, actor, Will Farrell who also joined in.

Tony Forster Adventures

Later that day as I was slicing vegetables and looking out of my kitchen window, which has a long view of hundreds of acres of Rancho Mission Viejo, my thoughts carried me to more of the stories that the Portolá Riders shared that were appropriate to repeat.

Tony Forster, former San Juan Mayor, co-founder of the Capistrano Valley Boys and Girls Club, Santa Claus for a dozen or more years at the Christmas tree lighting ceremony, was the subject of many favorite stories told to me. My husband, Ken, and I always enjoyed Tony. Truly, he was a San Juan kind of guy. He played an important role in developing the Historical Society, was famous for his Santa Maria tri-tip, and was interested in all things San Juan. My favorite memory of Tony was when he brought his team of barbecue experts to our backyard and cooked up enough of that succulent tri-tip to feed the 320 guests we entertained in our backyard for our daughter Julie's wedding. Being a San Juan horse girl, of course, Julie had a Western-style wedding. The entire wedding party was dressed up in Stetson hats and tall Western boots. Tony's barbeque was a huge hit, and we were pleased to make a donation to the Historical Society's fund. His friends had much more colorful memories of his antics than I did. It seems that on one of the earlier Portolá Rides, when the group was still able to ride up through the Irvine Ranch, they rode down onto the beach at Crystal Cove, all 150 of them onto the sand. After the long dusty ride,

Former Mayor, Portolá Rider Tony Forster c. 2000

everyone was hot and tired. Seeing the azure blue ocean and the gently rolling waves, Tony dismounted, stripped off his clothing, and dived into the cool Pacific! I thought that was a great story. At the send-off picnic, I chatted with his widow, Ann, and asked if I could share the story. Laughing, she said, "that was

Tony! Of course you can. I have a photo somewhere of his behind in those waves, buff naked!" We were both smiling.

As I continued my interviews, additional pieces of that story emerged. His brother, Pat, added that Tony's pals stole his clothes, and in fact, threw them into the ocean, watch, wallet and all! When Tony came out of the ocean, of course all the guys were laughing uproariously. Finally, someone produced a yellow rain slicker and covered him up. I guess he rode like that all the way up to the night's camping spot somewhere near where Shady Canyon Golf Course is today. I could just picture Tony in that yellow slicker with nothing else on! They never did find his personal effects in the waves, but anyone who knew Tony, would know he would take it in stride with a laugh of his own.

Celebrating the Ride's 25th Anniversary

Another particularly colorful memory was shared by former Mayor Sam Allevato who has been a Portolá Rider for 30 years. It was the 1988 Ride into Camp Pendleton celebrating the Ride's 25th anniversary. They were met with a full military welcome. They bedded down the first night in the barracks as planned. At 6:00 a.m. the bugle sounded and a Marine Drill Sergeant, in immaculate uniform, marched into the quarters shouting, "You ladies rise and shine! What do you think this is? Get up!" As the story goes, Sheriff Brad Gates had been asleep and resented this intrusion, for he barked back, "Do you know who I am? I am the Orange County Sheriff!"

"I don't care who you are! Get up!" with that the Drill Sergeant flipped his cot over and Sheriff Gates landed on the floor.

Things got worse after that. They lined up for breakfast in the mess hall and the same Marine Sergeant came over to the Sheriff, "What's all that food?" You're too fat anyway!" Then he dumped his plate onto the floor. The harassing went on for a while longer, until finally the ruse was up and it was revealed that the "drill sergeant" was a paid actor, completing a prank on the Sheriff. The Riders all got a big laugh out of the prank, though I am not sure how funny Sheriff Gates thought it was!

There were more highlights to that Ride. The Marines were gracious hosts taking them in personnel carriers through the backlands of Camp Pendleton, sometimes showing off, doing wheelies and tricks with the vehicles. When they returned to where the horses were waiting, some of the young Marines asked if they could ride the horses around for a while. The Riders, wanting to return the hospitality, heartily agreed. Many of the young men having come from places like New York City, had never been near a horse before, so watching them mount up and often fall right off, or galloping across the field, hanging on to the horn for dear life, was another amusement for the Riders. Sam was laughing as he recalled that scene.

Colonel Jim Williams Recalls

As I continued to gather details about that 25th anniversary ride, I talked with Colonel Jim Williams, the second in command at the base, and in charge of the event. In addition, he was their host for the weekend. This was the Colonel's first encounter with the Portolá Riders and one he would never forget. Jim was the officer in charge and, therefore, had a whole different take on the goings-on. He described the personnel carriers as armored full-track vehicles, amtracks, that can transport up to twenty Marines from sea to land. He explained that the amtracks were being raced across the hills in a

41

demonstration for the horse riders. At one point, one of the vehicles was airborne to a height where the Colonel could see all the way underneath it and a Marine was dangling from the fast moving vehicle! It looked like a recipe for disaster to him. He was very concerned, and for good reason. A few passengers were jostled up and one man cracked a rib. In the meantime the antics on the horses continued, and there must have been some betting involved, because at the end of all this, one young Marine came up to the Colonel with a helmet full of money and said, "Sir, them guys are rich!"

The Colonel just shook his head as he said, "Son, just keep that between yourselves. Maybe have a little party!" The subject did not come up again, but the adventures that day did not end there.

1988 25th Anniversary Ride to Camp Pendleton Amtracks. Courtesy RMV

Later that morning after the excitement in the vehicles and on the horses, it was time to saddle up and head north back to Rancho Mission Viejo. They were in the far back country, when they came upon a huge white tent, in the middle of nowhere, with bouquets of white balloons streaming from its sides. Puzzled by such an elaborate sight, they tied their mounts, and entered the tent. A big band was playing Jimmy Dorsey songs, crystal chandeliers glinted in the light, and champagne was served in sparkling glasses. The men could hardly believe their good fortune. The food was outstanding. Everyone was having a wonderful time recounting the wild visit with the Marines. As lunch was winding down, suddenly the lights flickered.

It was the Ride's 25th anniversary, so when a glorious, five-foot long frosted cake was marched into the dining tent, no one was too surprised. The men lined up to admire the intricate design on it and to grab a slice. Sam Allevato recalled that Under Sheriff Raul Ramos, in a stage voice, warned him, "Sam, you might want to stand back!" At the precise moment that their leader, Bill Shattuck, one of the Big Eight, cut into the beautiful confection, out of no-where came another Portolá Rider, Dale Johnson, running at a fast pace. Dale sprang face-first into the middle of the thing, knocking it and the table to the ground! The crowd howled in merriment. The cake flew into pieces. To everyone's amazement and delight, the cake was made of horse manure! Colonel Williams added some more details. It seems that for years, Saturday night of the Ride included a big beautiful cake and that for several years in a row, Dale Johnson, known affectionately as "Guido" and "Guapo," had the habit of jumping into the cake. On this year, knowing in advance that he would jump into the thing like "a screaming banshee," they arranged for it to be manure. Johnson smelling the cake, immediately started throwing handfuls of the gooey stuff at his friends. A hilarious food fight immediately broke out as everyone joined in!

Colonel Jim Williams in Swallows Day Parade

Colonel Jim Williams – Portolá Rider

Fox Hunters and Hounds at Camp

Another colorful Portolá story came to me from long-time Portolá Rider and managing-owner of the Swallows Inn and El Adobe Restaurant, Steve Nordeck. Steve recalls that it was the year after the Camp Pendleton ride when Gilbert Aguirre pulled him aside one day and asked, "Can you get some of your buddies and their hounds at your fox hunting club to come and wake the riders up?" [There will be more about Steve Nordeck and the fox hunting later.] Smiling, Steve agreed that he thought he could, with that Gilbert organized another daring stunt.

Traditionally, on the third day of the ride, something crazy happens as a wakeup call at the camp. So on this morning, very early, fox scent was surreptitiously planted along the rim of the sleeping tents. Soon the hounds were let loose! You can imagine the wild uproar as 20-30 dogs caught the scent, racing around, barking, all about the camp with their mounted pink jacketed handlers following close behind. Also visualize the many dazed Riders as they stumbled, half asleep, from their tents! It was a well executed stunt. The fox club members eventually gathered up their rowdy canines and stayed for breakfast. It was a morning to go down in memory.

I couldn't help but laugh out loud at the idea of all the spectacular antics the Riders have enjoyed across the years as they've kept a taste of the Old West alive. There were other stories of when USC's marching band, at full volume, paraded into the sleeping camp, or another time when the men awoke to discover that elephants had invaded their site! I understood how the seriousness of the Mass and Empty Saddle Ceremony set against the playfulness of some of the other aspects of the Ride, illustrate the strength of tradition in the group.

Camaraderie on the Ride

Colonel Jim Williams shared with me that as he became more senior at the base, there were fewer of his old pals to socialize with. He had not fully realized how much he was missing the pure fun of male buddies. He became a member of the Portolá Riders as a result of that anniversary weekend. The relationships he built with the Ranch would allow him to be an important influence on the City of San

Portolá Ride Send Off Picnic Amantes Camp 2017

Juan Capistrano as he was hired as a liaison between the Ranch and the City. The Ranch and his friendships with his fellow riders have become a significant aspect of his life. Every Rider I talked with shared the same sentiment. It is meaningful in their lives, more than a fraternity, perhaps almost a way of life. It is easy to see why the institution of the Ride thrives across so many decades. It is so much more than just good times.

Sprawling Rancho Santa Margarita y Las Flores is now Camp Pendleton

In the days that followed the send-off, I continued with my routine. I enjoyed my docent tours at the Mission and my long hikes into the hills with the dogs. I had lots of time to think about that anniversary Ride and Camp Pendleton. As I write this, the concussive throb of mortar fire is vibrating though the sliding glass door of my home office. The Marines are preparing for war. I admire what it takes to keep us safe, sending our young people into harm's way. With another throbbing sound, I realized that such sounds have been with us since we moved-into our home in 1973. The explosions are a downside to being able to live next door to 125,000 acres of open land. Certainly, the sounds often frighten the dogs, but the beauty of living away from the bustle of city life, for us, far outweighs those vibrating noises. Our home is nestled into a small equestrian community adjacent to what was the Lacouague Citrus Ranch. During the first 25 years we were here, hundreds of orange trees grew next to our property. During the harvest, we would awake to the chorus of Mexican music and conversations in Spanish slipping through our open windows as dozens of braceros picked the oranges.

When one lives a bit away from the intensity of city life, it is easy to allow one's imagination to drift back to another time. My studies have taught me about the way of life on the great Ranchos, and the sprawling Rancho Margarita y Las Flores in particular, before the United States Government purchased it for defense purposes in 1942 and it became Camp Pendleton.

Time and the relationship between the present and the past fascinate me. It was no accident that Tony Moiso and the Portolá Riders chose to journey onto Camp Pendleton. In the scheme of time, it was not so very long before when Tony Moiso's great grandfather was the "boss man," of it.

Many of the traditions we celebrate in San Juan Capistrano have stemmed from those Ranchos of old. The fact that Tony Moiso and his family has been able to hold onto as much of the great Rancho Mission Viejo as they have, across the decades of development and heavy taxation, is a testament to their tenacity and forward thinking. The family's role in preserving our historic traditions has been significant.

Portolá Riders Blessed c. 1960's. Courtesy San Juan Historical

46

Chapter Five

Rancho Days and Horses

"Show me your horse and I will tell you what you are." English Proverb

In the weeks that followed my Portolá experience, my thoughts kept pulling me back to the old days before Rancho Santa Margarita y Las Flores was a Marine installation. I thought of the Ride's 25th celebration ride to Camp Pendleton. Symbolically, they rode into the past. That gala tent, for example, had been erected on what was once one of California's grandest Ranchos. Surely no fandango had ever been held way out where that tent was erected, but the land itself was once owned by their Portolá host, Tony Moiso's, great grandfather, Richard O'Neill. Certainly, the property had seen its share of horse riders. I imagined Mr. O'Neill on that Rancho. I could visualize him getting up from the breakfast table in the dining room of the old adobe home, where the Camp Pendleton Commander General resided for years at the Marine Corps Base. In my fantasy I could see him in his boots, walking out the front door to meet with his ranch foreman. Perhaps it was the end of the round-up or time to brand some of the thousands of cows. I loved thinking about this.

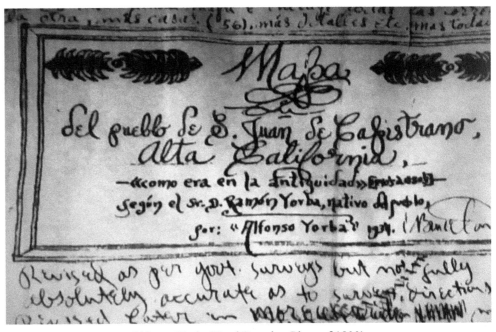

Alfonzo Yorba Hand Drawing Plaza of 1800's

The Past as a Time Machine

I thought about how each of us is a product of the past, whether we are aware of it or not. The other day I was leading a tour group of senior citizens at the Mission, and I was telling them that with the fourth graders, I have them imagine that we are in a time machine. One man kiddingly, replied, "We *are* the time machine!" We all laughed. He made a joke, but in some ways he's right. For many of us, the past is as close as our favorite memory, or the photos on our walls. My hallway boasts black and white images of all of my great-grandparents that lived around the time, the 1880's, when Tony Moiso's great grandfather was taking over the Rancho Santa Margarita y Las Flores. Two of my great grandparents, Lydia and Charles Lewis, appear fresh-faced in their photo. They seem familiar to me, though I never met them. In one of the old pictures, they had recently arrived in Los Angeles from Illinois via the train in the early 1880's, their suitcases filled with the stock for the pharmacy they would soon open in the City of the Angels. I marvel at how relatively young California is as a state, only a few generations old; young enough, that for so many of us, those pioneers are our fairly recent relatives.

I needed to further mull over the idea of a time machine. The Mission itself is a kind of time machine. I suppose in some ways our friends who have descended from the land grant families are as well. My husband and I knew Tony Forster (of the naked bum) for many years. It was his great great grandfather who bought the Mission and 44 acres around it for $710 in hides and tallow and then lived there for twenty years, while acquiring more land, [Rancho Mission Viejo, Rancho Trabuco, and eventually Rancho Santa Margarita y Las Flores] and becoming integral to the community.

To get a grip on this story, let's aim our own time machines back to when California was still a part of Mexico. If the dials on your machine do not want to stop here, just speed ahead to the next century.

Mexican Era

When Mexico defeated Spain in 1821, the missions of California began to lose their authority. The Secularization Act imposed by the Mexican government confiscated mission lands and gave or sold them to family and friends. It took quite a few more years before the actual death blow to the mission system was felt.

"Violent Hands Laid on the Priest"

According to Father Zephyrin Engelhardt, on March 6, 1823, a shocking event shook the world of the missions. In the report to the church hierarchy the situation was described as, "the most scandalous case that has been witnessed in California." One result of Mexico's defeat of Spain was an erosion of respect for the old structure of law and order. There were those Mission soldiers who lost respect for the priests. This unfortunate situation occurred when the Mission San Juan Capistrano priest, Father Barona, prepared to leave San Juan Capistrano to visit Mission San Luis Rey. The three soldiers at the Mission, commanded him not to go. With weapons raised, a gun, a lance and a saber, they ordered him not to get on his horse. The priest, with determination to fulfill his errand, climbed up on the horse. Again the lead soldier, Jose Cañedo, ordered him down. The priest persisted. Cañedo used force, pushing the horse so hard, that the horse fell, knocking Father Barona beneath it. He was not so much physically hurt, as psychologically. He was humiliated in front of the Mission Indians.

It was a serious offense and the three soldiers were arrested and excommunicated. Two of them repented. In the report to authorities, the incident was described as "violent hands were laid on the priest." Matters intensified for Father Barona when, not long after, there was a small uprising of Indians against him. It was quickly over, but added to Father Barona's angst. It was reported that his health was affected, and he retired to Mission San Luis Rey. On his deathbed, he requested that soldier Jose Cañedo be pardoned if he repented. Cañedo refused. Father Barona passed away before the case came to trial. [Note:

Hallan-Gibson on p. 30 states that this incident occurred in 1832. I believe she inadvertently inverted her dates.]

Some two years after the incident, a military court, (which did not invite the Indian witnesses to testify), released Cañedo. They found that he had already served two years in prison and had been following orders. Victorious, he moved back to San Juan Capistrano where he lived in the adobe which was torn down (around the early 1960's) and a Texaco Gas Station was built in its place, next to the Camino Real Playhouse.

In a Karmic twist of fate, Cañedo, who was considered a cruel man, ordered some of the local Indians to travel a great distance to fetch building supplies for him. In addition to bringing back building materials, they brought back the small pox virus. Cañedo soon died of the disease.

Secularization Act

The mission system was coming to a close, but even in light of changing laws, it persevered for some years and continued to be productive. When the Secularization Act was finally enforced in 1833, the Indians were emancipated and the missions were forced to surrender their lands. Hallan-Gibson in *Two Hundred Years of San Juan Capistrano* stated, "the mission system which once had charge of fifteen thousand souls, and thousands of acres of land, was already dead."

Andres Pico – Military Leader and Governor Pio Pico's Brother

Rancho Santa Margarita y Las Flores

Before Pío Pico became Mexico's last California governor, serving from 1845-1846, the massive 133,440-acre parcel of land that had been used by Mission San Luis Rey, was granted to him and his brother, Andres, by Mexican Governor, Juan Baptista Alvarado. Alvarado governed from 1836-1842. However, a conflict erupted between the Picos and Governor Alvardo. The result was a deal in which the Pico brothers were allowed to trade some land they had claim to around Temecula in exchange for more prime land along the coast. The coastal land had been earmarked for the Mission Indians who were displaced due to secularization. In the wake of this deal, the Picos' land grant extended from what is today northern San Diego County, encompassing present day San Onofre State Beach along the Pacific coast, and Camp Pendleton. They named it Rancho Santa Margarita y Las Flores. During Pío Pico's term as California governor, in 1845, he granted the lands around the Mission San Juan Capistrano to his brother-in-law, Juan Forster. Pio Pico was known for living large with flamboyant gold chains and over-sized rings that would glint from his person. In that vein, he gambled big too. A contract for a typical horse race described in Robert Glass Cleland's *The Cattle on a Thousand Hills* describes a quarter-mile race in San Juan in which Pío Pico bet $1,600 plus 300 head of cattle. This was at a time when a cowboy was content to make $15 a month. Eventually gambling debts and his high-living style gave way to

While life on the ranchos passed in a leisurely haze of parties for the wealthy elite, the demographics of the area were changing as the Anglo-American population was eclipsing that of the Californios. Estimates show that there were some 15,000 residents of Spanish descent in California before gold was discovered in 1848. Before European settlers arrived, an estimated 300,000 native people lived throughout the area. However, Old World diseases, poverty and bounties placed on Natives, reduced their population to about 30,000 by 1860.

The Ranchos were important because they established the basis of the agrarian society which ultimately led to California becoming the leading agricultural state in the nation. (Friess, Whispering Waters, 1998, from Cleland, 1922.)

financial problems. His brother, Andrés, had earlier deeded his share of the Rancho Santa Margarita y Las Flores to his brother Pio to protect it from creditors.

After a time, Pio Pico sold half of Rancho Santa Margarita y Las Flores to his brother-in-law, Don Juan Forster. As the monetary issues escalated, Forster loaned him more money. Eventually, through Pico's continued financial woes, the full title came to Forster. Pico claimed fraud and a trial ensued. There is a fine book about the trial: *Forster vs. Pico: The Struggle for Rancho Santa Margarita* (Gray.1998). Forster prevailed and held full title to the Ranch.

The Secularization Act allowed John Forster and his wife, Pico's sister, Ysidora, and their six children to buy Mission San Juan Capistrano and move into the former priest's quarters in 1845.

I came to know Ysidora Forster more fully through the stories found in Father O'Sullivan's *Capistrano Nights.* One of the accounts shows Ysidora offering marital advice to the parishioners, while other anecdotes reveal the important role that she and the Don played in pueblo life. Ysidora was known as a wonderful, gracious hostess and a person with a generous heart. When there were troubles, the townspeople often looked to the couple for solutions.

Ysidora was said to have lived a remarkable life for her era, being deeply religious and involved within the community. She was known for protecting her female servants by carefully locking them in at night, away from any nefarious vaqueros who might be about.

Sadly, Ysidora suffered a broken heart. Her beloved youngest son, Francisco Pio Forster known as "Chico," was killed in 1881. He was involved in a marriage dispute with actress, Hortensia Abarta, when she shot him. Understandably, Ysidora was devastated. Before she could recover from that horrendous loss, her husband, Don Juan also died. Within one year, Ysidora passed away.

The United States Returns Missions to the Catholic Church

In 1865, on March 18th, President Lincoln signed into law a declaration known as the Lincoln Document which upheld an 1851 petition to have all mission lands which had been illegally confiscated, returned to the Catholic Church. Private citizens living within the far-away California missions had to vacate the mission properties. After twenty years, the Forster family moved out of the Mission and took up residence at their sprawling Rancho Santa Margarita y Las Flores in a large adobe home built by the Picos.

The Mexican Era and Don Juan Forster

Don Juan Forster was one of the most respected of the great Dons. He worked hard. Samuel Armor states in his *Biographical Sketches of Orange County* that "John Forster became prominent among the ranchers, businessmen and political leaders of San Juan." He ran "5000 horses and triple that number of cattle. Fences then were unknown and the cattle and horses ran wild."

One reporter described Forster as an "epic worker," citing the fact that in one year alone, 1851, he sold 500 wild mares and 14 stallions to the California Stage Company at $20 a head. In addition, he sent great droves of cattle from San Juan Capistrano to Sacramento, and sizable horse droves to Utah, and cavalry mounts to forts in Arizona.

The Ranchos were independent, self-contained communities, each with a culture of their own, employing Indians and cowboys drawn by the guarantee of steady work. The Dons took advantage of the business routes that had been established by the missions and traded with mercantile companies which anchored sailing ships off the coast. The Rancheros became a wealthy class of businessmen.

Don Juan Forster

Floating Department Stores

Richard Henry Dana in his diaries described the arrival of a trading ship as a big event met with great enthusiasm by the wealthy Ranchero families from as far away as San Gabriel and San Fernando. A messenger-agent would be sent ahead to spread word that a ship would soon arrive. The Ranchero families would hitch up their wagons, carriages, and carts and aim their steeds toward Capistrano Bay for the arrival of the ship. Whole families would wait on the rocks to be rowed out to the vessel. Once aboard, they would proceed down into the ship's hold, where row upon row of merchandise in the "floating department" store awaited them. Available for purchase were books, linens, silks, porcelain dishes, fireworks, toys, guns, ammunition, furniture, iron made tools and so much more. Dana wrote, "There was everything under the sun, in fact everything you can imagine." The Rancheros used hides and tallow with which to trade. The hides were of great value in Boston where the leather was crafted into shoes, boots, saddles, and bridles. (This is from Smith and Stern's, *California: The Golden Land of Promise,* 2001).

Taking a break from my mental trip to early California, I took the dogs out into the hills. An hour later, they were stretched out for a nap around my feet. Back at my desk, I realized that the Ranchos could not be understood without a further understanding of the greater political picture. By 1821 California was exclusively under Mexican rule. Mexico was eager to increase its control over California and granted full title to those who had been vested in property through the Spanish crown. In addition Mexico ceded some 700 additional tracts of land to those who promised to work it.

The Gold Rush

During the Mexican Period, the economy of the Ranchos continued to flourish. The Dons became rich. When gold was discovered in the Sierra Nevada Mountains of California in 1848, there were even greater opportunities to make money as new markets opened up. Hordes of hungry miners streamed in from Mexico, Europe, and the Eastern United States. They required food and materials as they flooded into the mining fields of Northern California, and they developed an "enormous thirst" for the California wines and brandies. (Cleland, 1941). This influx of immigrants, the largest in America's history, (three hundred thousand of them), descending upon California in just ten years greatly changed the demographic from Mexican to American.

Near the time that gold fever was sweeping across continents, war broke out between the United States and Mexico. Manifest Destiny was ringing across the U.S. In 1846 the United States Congress under President Polk declared war on Mexico. The U.S. wanted to keep the disputed Texas lands (which had been annexed a year earlier) and to gain control of Mexico's northern territories which included California and New Mexico.

The majority of the California fighting took place in the north. However, two eruptions flared up at Mission San Juan Capistrano, both involving Don Juan Forster. American General John Fremont and his 200 men had been ordered to "pacify" the region and to capture the "most wanted" Californio, Governor Pio Pico, Don Juan's brother-in-law, and to execute Forster, a known Mexican sympathizer. When Fremont learned that Forster was hiding Pico, he and his men surrounded the Mission where Forster and his family lived, intent on preventing Pico's escape. Forster's loyalty to the U.S. was suspect, but, somehow he negotiated a talk with Fremont which cooled his temper (all the while Forster *was* hiding Pio Pico). Forster promised Fremont that he "favored any government, whether it be the present one or the United States, which could guarantee permanent stability for the area." (Stant, James.1977).

According to Forster's own writing, "Fremont was savage against me until we had an explanation…" Once Fremont understood Forster's loyalties were to a stable government; that he was trying to protect his family, Fremont relented. Pico, escaping detection, successfully fled to Mexico with mules, horses and supplies.

In another incident, suspicion again arose against Forster when four Californios, who had been injured in the Battle of San Pasqual against American forces, were discovered by American forces hiding in a house near the Great Stone Church. In the wake of that discovery, the American soldiers continued riding north to Alisos Ranchero to meet up with Forster and to confront him. The Don wisely and graciously supplied fresh horses and denied knowledge of the hidden men, but tipped off Fremont as to where General Andres Pico and his 600 Californio soldiers were lying in wait. Those actions supported a claim of loyalty to the United States, and he was allowed to stay free. Subsequently, Andres Pio obtained a favorable settlement for his followers from Fremont and the fighting stopped.

The Mexican-American war ended in March of 1848 with the signing of the Treaty of Guadalupe-Hidalgo. Mexico ceded California to the U.S. and within a short time it became the 31st state.

During my talks with many of Tony Forster's close friends, I was told that Tony was always particularly proud of his illustrious ancestors and their possession of thousands [320,000 at one point] of sprawling acres.

Ultimately, new laws were passed which forced Don Juan to fence some 212,000 acres of land. This depleted his capital, while severe droughts destroyed his cattle, and his attempts proved futile to attract colonists. By the time of Don Juan Forster's death in 1882, his widow, Ysidora, was forced to sell their vast holdings. According to a video-taped interview with descendent, Tony Forster, the sprawling ranch was cashed out for $250,000 in gold. (August 19, 2006, interview by Daniel Teyes.)

Richard O'Neill and Gold Fever

Our Southern California story might have been something else entirely without the gold rush. Young Richard O'Neill, the great grandfather of Tony Moiso, came to California from County Cork, Ireland to try his luck in the gold fields with his friend James Flood. According to the San Juan Capistrano Historical Society website, O'Neill and Flood met on the ship leaving Ireland for America. Both young men stayed on the east coast for a time, O'Neill, an experienced cattle man, started a meat business. That business was not growing sufficiently, so he and Flood headed west to find gold. Before long, the gold mining enterprise lost its luster. O'Neill went back to his original vocation, opening a butcher stall in a big market near the Mining Exchange in San Francisco, while Flood opened a saloon called The Auction Exchange with another Irishman named, William O'Brien.

O'Neill provided the meat for Flood and O'Brien's bar which served lunch and cocktails. It was the watering hole for the nearby stock brokers, a place to eat, drink, and talk business. Flood and O'Brien were within earshot of strategic financial information exchanged between the stock brokers. They learned a lot, and used the information to good advantage.

As I understand the account, two miners had a hunch about a mine known as The Consolidated Virginia Mine and were looking for financial backing to explore its potential, Flood and O'Brien invested. It's a get rich story, because by the time the mine ran out, it had yielded $136 million in silver, and was known as the Comstock Lode. The four men became known as "the Silver Kings!" It was the 1870's and they were said to be the wealthiest men in the world. Flood opened his own bank, the Bank of Nevada. Before long, the bank had to foreclose on a cattle ranch in the San Joaquin Valley. Flood needed someone to operate the ranch and turned to his trusted pal, Richard O'Neill Sr., who by this time, had wealth of his own, and was ready for a new challenge.

O'Neill managed that ranch so successfully that Flood's bank turned a significant profit. The experience taught O'Neill a love of cattle ranching. When the Forster ranch came up for sale in Southern California, he and Flood struck a deal. Flood would provide the cash and O'Neill would supply the brains and energy to run it. Flood promised O'Neill one-half interest in it if after twenty years all went well. It did and the Flood family made good on the promise. Richard O'Neill came to own half of the sprawling Rancho Santa Margarita y Las Flores.

Richard O'Neill Senior 1880's Courtesy RMV

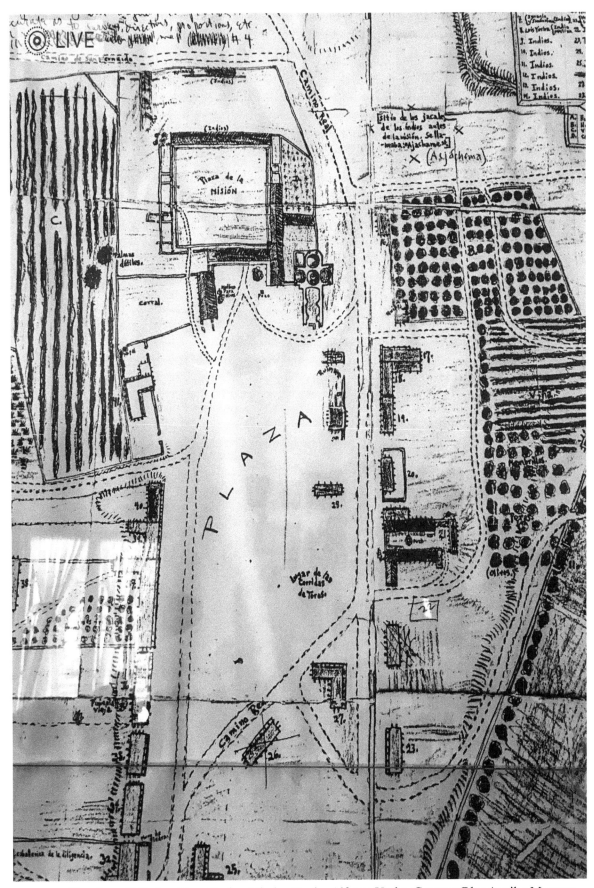

Drawing of Mission Plaza During Mission Era by Alfonso Yorba. Courtesy Blas Aguilar Museum

My granddaughter, Jill, runs marathons and frequently wears a tee-shirt that says: "Luck has nothing to do with it." Perhaps that saying applies to Flood, O'Brien, the Forsters, the O'Neill family, and so many who have pioneered during our state's short life span. They have nurtured California and helped to elevate it to become the most powerful economic force in the United States. In my view, their fortunes were the result of hard work, determination, brains, coupled with risk. It was a risk when Don Juan (John) Forster left the comfort of Liverpool, England and sailed to Mexico to become a naturalized citizen, and devoted himself to the mercantile business in Los Angeles where ultimately, he became a cattleman. When young Richard O'Neill had the courage to venture west from New Brunswick and then apply himself in his meat business, it took resilience, more hard work, and his application of good thinking. Those pioneers exemplify the type of people who have made California great, as well as the determined generations who have followed. Maybe luck played a part, but it was their personal character that allowed them the ability to think and to persevere, to not be too afraid to go for it. I see a lesson in this, one that has been acted out by Californians for the past 167 years or so, and is still being portrayed today.

However, it was not without its hurdles. While Northern California was rocked the hardest by the population explosion resulting from the gold rush, certainly Southern California felt tensions of its own. The power within this new state rested in the North. The northern politicians eyed the sprawling lands to the south with the idea of taxing the land for increased revenues. New laws were imposed on the Ranchos. One particularly onerous mandate demanded that the Ranchos be fenced. Angered by these demands, the representatives from southern counties got a bill through the California legislature that would allow the southern counties to withdraw from Northern California. Much to their dismay, the United States Senate did not agree and the bill failed. Southern California was stuck being a part of the North.

I had more on my mind, but the soft whinnies of my two Quarter Horse mares, reminded me that it was dinner time.

Rancho Santa Margarita y Las Flores Memories

The next day my friend, Christine and I took the horses into the hills, the very same hills once owned by the O'Neill family. My house sits on what was once the part of Rancho Santa Margarita now known as Rancho Mission Viejo. As my mare tromped up the trail behind my home, I imagined the same scene as it would have been in days of old, with cows and horses running free. My imagination began to drift to the most enthralling book, *Rancho Santa Margarita Remembered*. It was given to me by Tony Moiso. It is an oral history told by his cousin, Jerome O'Neill Baumgartner, Richard O'Neill's grandson. He lived on Rancho Santa Margarita during the last of the horse and buggy days, more than 100 years ago. It was told to his son, Jerome "Jome" Baumgartner in 1974. Born in1903, Jerome, the elder, tells of the days before cars, electricity, airplanes, and freeways. His experience growing up on the ranch, he was sure, paralleled life on the other great Ranchos.

I leaned forward onto my horse Blaze's neck to make her load easier as we trotted up to summit the hill. My thoughts fell to some of what I read of Baumgartner's childhood on the Ranch. He, too, had been thrilled by horses. He marveled at how many it took to get the work done. He reported that the Ranch needed: 100 work horses, 120 saddle horses, and a team of 42 side-stepping horses to pull the threshing machine.

Jerome O'Neill 1908. Courtesy RMV

As a little boy Baumgartner was fascinated by horses. The thresher machine itself was a complicated contraption of gears and paddles that knocked down the wheat stems while a conveyor belt carried the grain stalks into the harvester. This huge machine was pulled by between 32 and 42 horses. The threshing action was powered through gears off a main axle. For Baumgartner, the man who drove the team of horses was the real show. As he described it, there would be eight horses immediately in front of the driver and less in each successive row, and by the front, there were just two horses, so that the team created a triangular shape. He said it was magnificent to watch as they made the most exact, straight path through the grain. He tells of them side stepping to begin to harvest the next row. With the driver's lead horses nearly sixty feet in front of him, it took a great skill to manage the team. If a horse misbehaved, the driver would throw a rock from a coffee can of rocks he held for that purpose. The driver's target was the horse's rump and according to Baumgartner's memory, he never missed! I loved the idea of a single man in charge of a huge team of horses with just his reins and a can of small rocks! I wondered if part of the story had become a tall tale recalled from childhood. I could imagine the sight of 42 horses drawing the huge machine through the tall wheat fields. It must have looked like a ship at sea.

When I shared that story with my son, Dan, I could see that he had trouble believing it. I went on-line and found a half dozen such images of great teams of horses pulling harvesters. When I shared them with my son, he marveled at the thought of such a spectacular effort.

As our horses tromped along, I inhaled deeply of the fresh morning air and thought of another tidbit of ranch life that Baumgartner shared. It had to do with fleas. As a boy on the Ranch, young Jerome enjoyed a favorite sport of roping pigs, which he and his brother, John, did while pretending to be vaqueros roping calves. All this pig roping occurred around the barn area where many horses stayed. As he described the scene, there were: "dray horses to pull the buckboard or wagons, heavier dray horses to pull the farm equipment, regular saddle horses, cutting horses, roping horses- a lot of horses." The problem with hanging out at the barn around all the livestock was that he and his brother got a lot of fleas on them. A regular Saturday night involved him being dunked in hot bath water. He particularly recalled that when their "Aunt Jane" would be the one caring for them, they would be scrubbed. He recalled that when she would catch a flea, she'd snap it with her thumb nail and drop it in a pail of water. This was considered a normal part of the weekly bathing ritual. It delighted me to see such a specific detail remembered from childhood.

Horses Pull Thresher c. 1918

Fire at the Bean Farm

One memory that was particularly vivid for Baumgartner was from when he was five years old. This incident happened one night when he and his brother were being driven to Las Flores (a part of the ranch near present day San Onofre) in the buckboard with this same Aunt Jane (a close family friend). Brother, John, was asleep in the back. "Aunt" Jane grew beans out on the mesas along the shoreline. As the buckboard made its way out of the Santa Margarita Canyon and rounded the corner above the coast they could see a fire burning toward where their aunt stored her bean crops. Seeing the blaze, she became upset thinking the warehouse was on fire. She jumped off the buckboard, thrusting the reins into young Jerome's hands. He had never driven the buckboard alone. No doubt his heart was pounding in his chest as he held onto those reins and did his best to drive for the next few miles, while his aunt tromped behind the wagon. As she walked, she kept repeating her rosary. It was all very dramatic for young Jerome. When they got closer to the fire, it turned out that the farm workers were just burning the useless bean straw and had forgotten to tell her. Her barn full of beans was not hurt. It ended well, but it was a bit traumatic for the young boy driving that buckboard with his sleeping brother in back and seeing his aunt so upset.

Thinking of Jerome at five-years old, I recalled my own five-year-old daughter, Julina and a very

Thresher. Courtesy Bonanza Post Cards

scary horse moment she, too, would never forget. One afternoon, she was riding her Shetland pony, Connie, around the back yard enjoying herself when all of a sudden Connie took off with her! In those days our property wasn't fenced and within a very short time Connie had trotted off into the creek bed oblivious to Julie's struggle to get her to turn around. Soon Julie realized she couldn't stop the stubborn pony, and just grabbed onto her mane and held fast. When I realized what had happened to my green-eyed little girl, I mounted my own horse and gave chase. By the time I caught up with them, I was relieved to see that she was still mounted, but she eyes were huge with fear and her face was flushed. I was surprised that she wasn't crying. We got Connie to stop and I calmed Julie down. After a while I was able to lead Connie back to our corral. It turned out that the pony was in her season and probably thought there might be a boyfriend for her over at one of the local stables.

As with young Jerome and his attachment to horses, we were relieved that our daughter's love of riding was not deterred by that frightening experience. For many years she trusted Connie enough to ride her in the Swallows Day Parade, and then she graduated to our bigger horses.

Judas Day Pranks in Pueblo Days

As the horses brought us along the ridgeline above San Juan, my eyes were drawn north. The day was clear and I could see San Juan's Mission Basilica as it gleamed, bright white, against the landscape. I could also make out the curve of the garden wall at the front of the Mission. That wall reminded me that during the early days, the children of the tiny pueblo loved to play tricks. One of the favorites was on Judas Day, March 24th. It seems they would gather anything movable; outhouses, wagons, grindstones, buckboards, anything they could round up; using horses and mules; they would stack the sorry collection in front of the Mission. On top of the unsightly pile, they would place a gruesome effigy of Judas. All this in preparation for the next day when the townsfolk, stirred up due to their many confiscated items, would be pulled into the children's daring adventures. Ultimately, the troublemakers would attach the Judas effigy to a bull which would then dash around the plaza. Everyone would join in the fray, hissing and yelling at the Judas as the bull bucked and ran through town. The goal, it seems, was to force Judas to return to his tomb or roll over in his grave!

The children were not always up to mischief. A lot of times they enjoyed less rowdy activities such as barbecues, dances, bull fights, and perhaps even watching a horse race with their families. San Juan enjoyed a June farmer's fair called La Fiesta de Ocho Dias. For eight days produce booths were set up and prizes were awarded, not unlike the competitions at our Orange County Fair today. The town hosted a feast and people would come from as far away as San Diego and Los Angeles to join in the fun. The culmination was often a bull fight. In later years, the main event morphed into a "bull game" which spared the bull but made for a lot of excitement for the children; a bag of coins was tied to the bull's horn and the most intrepid of youth would try for the coins.

Doña Polonia the Captain of the Children

Father O'Sullivan shared an account illustrating how tightly knit the pueblo residents were. It seems that well before the turn of the last century, Doña Polonia Montenez, whose 1794 adobe is now open to the public on Los Rios Street, was an important person in the village. In addition to being the midwife, she was known as the "Pied Piper of San Juan" and as the "Captain" of the children, caring for them during the day. According to legend, a terrible drought fell upon the land in the mid 1860's. The ranchers, desperate for help, came to her and begged her to take the children out into the hills to pray for rain. She and the children created a portable religious dais and carried it into the hills for three successive days, walking in the bright sunshine, praying for rain. On the third day, they headed toward the mouth of

San Juan Creek, by the time they got to the beach, dark clouds had gathered. Soon strong winds and pouring rain began to pummel the children. Home was three miles away.

Back in town, the families were growing worried. They quickly organized a rescue party consisting of three large horse-drawn wagons which immediately took off toward the beach. An hour or so later the rain-soaked band of children led by Doña Polonia was safely returned. In the many years that followed, when prayers for rain were offered up, the old people in church would nod their heads and say to one another, "Do you remember the time when Polonia led the children out to pray for rain and had to be rescued from the floods?"

Dona Polonia Montenez, Captain of the Children, 1829-1917.
Courtesy Montenez Adobe and San Juan Capistrano Historical Society

As we headed back toward home, I nudged Blaze forward. She gathered up and stretched out beneath me. I let her have her head and she enthusiastically galloped up the next hill. As her massive muscles moved beneath me, I smiled and reciprocated, my body in tandem with hers. As her red mane flew in front of me, I grinned. Yes, much has changed across the last 167 years, but for many of us who love to ride in the hills, to hang out with our equines, and enjoy some of the simple pleasures, life isn't really all that different. Christine and I returned to my barn, unsaddled and brushed the horses. As we mucked the corral, I gave one last thought to what San Juan was like in the old days.

Doña Polonia Montenez Adobe. Courtesy Montenez Adobe

Horse Races and Big Money

By the 1870's the town boasted a school house, a hotel, a stagecoach stop, two stores, a post office, fifty homes, four saloons, and a resident priest, Father Mut. There was a lively society with traveling troupes coming through, as well as activities stemming from the school children. Horse races, however, were still the biggest of the attractions.

Even as the great Ranchos began to disappear and more Americans dominated the scene, horse races remained a passion. One of the most famous early races across California highlighted the rivalry between the Pico brothers and the Sepulvedas. In 1852 Pio Pico put his horse, "Sarco," up against an Australian mare named "Black Swan." She was primarily backed by the Sepulveda family's money. This race was a cross-country, nine mile event. According to Cleland, something like $50,000 was wagered in money, land, horses, and cattle! One can imagine how upset Pio Pico was when his horse lost! There were many other races, major ones which made the newspapers. and lesser ones, all of which provided ample opportunities to place lavish wagers.

Painting of Black Swan v Sarco. California's Most Famous Horse Race. March 21, 1852,
Courtesy of Irvine Historical Museum

Another notorious competition was between Don Pio Pico and his neighbor, Don Juan Avila, known as "El Rico" from the sprawling Rancho Niguel. Avila is remembered today because his home on Olvera Street is the oldest standing residence in all of Los Angeles. In 1860 those two Rancheros ran a series of well advertised races which had everyone talking and betting. It was between the most famous horses of the time; Juan Avila's horse "Coyote" against Pio Pico's "Azulejo." Cleland quoted a newspaper account, "popular excitement boiled over, Rancheros wagered recklessly-and often ruinously." The men even went so far as to run notices in the newspapers to round up additional bets! One of the races in that series took place in San Juan Capistrano. It required an entry fee of $3000 for each side for a 300 yard race. In that race, Pico's "Azulejo" won against "Coyote." It was reported that one backer won at least $8000 for his bet on "Azulejo!" Certainly the residents of old San Juan found exciting ways to entertain themselves!

As Christine and I finished up mucking out the corrals, I smiled to myself thinking of those horse races and of my mucking activities; we all find interesting ways to stay engaged in the world. We made plans for our next ride and said goodbye. We'd had a very good day.

Working the Fields. Courtesy Irvine Historical Museum c. Turn of Last Century

Chapter Six

Frontier Town – San Juan

"The years teach much which the days never knew." Ralph Waldo Emerson

A few days later, I awoke thinking about young Jerome Baumgartner and his memories of growing up at Rancho Santa Margarita y Las Flores. I understood those Rancho days were not just about fiestas, fandangos, and silver-clad cowboys strutting their skills. Southern California was a primitive frontier, complete with bad guys wrecking violence on the innocent. I thought of my own childhood as I'd been thinking of Jerome's. I grew up in the pre-television days of Los Angeles, and was a recipient of a rich oral history imparted by my own grandparents, early Angelinos. They specialized in enthralling me and my little sister with "true tales" of violent life in Los Angeles.

Criminals Bring Chaos to Southern California

My grandmother would gather my little sister and me in front of her. We huddled on the ottoman, while she leaned back in her easy chair and began weaving us into the world of *her* grandparents. Our grandmother's voice would slow as she introduced us to those pioneers, Catherine Mary Berry Mathews and husband William Mathews. They arrived by train in Los Angeles in the spring of 1883 with their eleven children. They were eager to leave the South due to a flu outbreak. [A deadly influenza pandemic in the late 1890's would kill a million people worldwide]. My grandmother's voice would drop another octave as she got to the part where Grandmother Catherine and her children began to disembark from the train. As Catherine began her climb down the steep steps, waiting to grab the hand of the child behind her, she heard a loud commotion. She backed up, holding the other children into the stairwell of the train as she witnessed two men engaged in a violent yelling match. Within moments she heard

Catherine Mary Berry Mathews Arrived on Train in 1883 to Shoot Out. This Photo Later in Her Life

gun shots. She could hardly believe her eyes. One of the gunmen was shot dead only a short distance from her feet! My sister and I would be holding our breath. We could only imagine such a scene. Our grandmother explained that her grandmother was wondering if she had made the best decision to come out West! I never knew for sure if that story were true or simply a family myth. It certainly spoke to the chaos of Southern California in the middle to late 1800's!

My grandfather, whose third grade Los Angeles City School photo from 1890 hangs on my wall, was also a great story teller. His specialty was stories of the old horse and buggy days, and of holdups in his pharmacy at 7th and Central Avenue in downtown Los Angeles, as well as on the city streets. We loved hearing about how he thwarted hold-ups. In one story, he was walking home in the dark, when suddenly out of the shadows came a masked gunman. Held at gunpoint on the deserted street, our grandfather, a very tall man, took command of the situation. He threatened the intruder with the parcel he held, inferring that it was a loaded gun. That warning combined with the parcel itself did the trick, he scared off the thug. For us, the fun of the story was that he was only carrying a bottle of milk! We were fascinated by the colorful outlaw stories, and the many robberies at his pharmacy. In one, he was ordered to lie down behind the counter at gun point, he refused knowing that a bullet might find its way to the back of his head. The robber ran off. My grandfather seemed to stand up to bullies and we loved hearing those stories. As an adult, I see that violence is with us always, all one has to do to verify that fact is to turn on the evening news!

1890 Los Angeles School 3rd grader RW Lewis, 3rd in mid row, right side

Notorious Juan Flores Gang Terrorizing San Juan Capistrano

Later in the morning I leashed up my dogs, and put on my walking shoes. I was still thinking of the bandits of old. My memory brought me to an interesting newspaper account from 2007 involving a devastating wildfire which swept through Santiago Canyon and the foothills of Orange County near the Foothill Toll Way. It reported a remarkable discovery. According to the *Los Angeles Times*, the flames burned away the brush that had long hidden a plaque that reads: *"Under this tree General Andres Pico Hung Two Banditos of the Flores Gang in 1857."*

While I am not sure of its origin, it is possible to hike in to view that sign. You recall just how important the Pico brothers were to early California history. Pio was the last Mexican governor of Alta California and his brother was a celebrated military leader. It is they who built the sprawling adobe ranch house at Rancho Santa Margarita y Las Flores in the 1840's. Later it became the military camp commander's home. Today the ranch house is a museum listed on the Registry of National Historic Sites and tours are available to the public.

That news article piqued my interest about the Flores Gang. It was easy to research the famous 1857 case. It involved a notorious outlaw crew headed by Juan Flores, age 22, whose girlfriend lived in San Juan Capistrano. Flores had just escaped from San Quentin and he and his outlaws had been wreaking havoc from Los Angeles to San Juan Capistrano. They frightened citizens as they robbed, and committed mayhem on anyone unfortunate enough to be in their path. In San Juan the gang robbed a local general store and after days of terrorizing the small community, killed the shopkeeper, and then blithely enjoyed dinner while his body lay on the floor. Needless to say, they were on the top of the 'most wanted' list.

As the story goes, the tiny pueblo desperately needed help from law enforcement. Answering the call, Sheriff James Barton from Los Angeles rode south with three deputies. He was prepared to capture the gang. The posse rested at the Rancho San Joaquin [today it is the area of the Back Bay of Newport Beach] where the Sepulveda family warned them that they were far outnumbered by the outlaws. They were told that it was simply too dangerous to keep up the chase. Nothing could dissuade Barton and his lawmen. They rode out and searched throughout the local hills, valleys, and canyons. In a tragic conclusion, they were ultimately ambushed and killed near Laguna Canyon. That bloody incident became known as the "Barton Massacre." When Flores was finally apprehended and hung, several thousand spectators came to downtown Los Angeles to witness his end. Others in the gang were rounded up and their ears were cut off and displayed as proof of their deaths. (*Los Angeles Times*. May 12, 2009. Mike Anton, "Hidden in O.C.'s Foothills, a Gnarled Reminder of California's Past").

Lynching and Trysting Trees

The idea of lynching trees and the discovery of the old plaque fascinated me. There's always been a tale around San Juan that the old sycamore tree at Junipero Serra in San Juan was such a tree. If not a lynching tree, a trysting tree for murderous gangs such as the infamous one led by the bandit Joaquin Murietta. My understanding is that in 1957 when the State Highway Department mapped out the new Interstate 5 freeway that was coming through San Juan, the residents put up much opposition. The town was unsuccessful in convincing the State to locate the freeway elsewhere. They were, however, successful in stopping a freeway off-ramp. Long time ranchers, Carl and Larry Buchheim, decided that the sycamore must be protected. They made a convincing case of its historical importance and state officials spared the tree by moving the ramp further south. Pam Hallan-Gibson points out there was never any proof that it was an historically important tree, but it proved that a convincing story might sometimes work. (Hallen-Gibson, p.144).

My interest in this aspect of history brought me to researcher Ken Gonzales-Day. Gonzales-Day has documented 350 such sites. He wanted to preserve the hanging trees of California through photography before they disappeared. His website is at: **www.kengonzalesday.com**. There one can find a

virtual tour of dozens of intriguing photos of such trees. His project grew as he learned more about the back story of the hangings. He discovered that deep racism permeated California and that much violence was the result. He has created an on-line self-guided walking tour of some of the places where the most notorious events took place in Los Angeles in the 1850's. The tour begins at Union Station and ends at historic Olvera Street. The tour reminds the visitor of the tumultuous beginnings of Southern California. I recommend you beware, as the virtual tour includes some pretty grisly details, such as the description of a gruesome item which was once on display in a downtown cantina, it was a necklace of "human ears!"

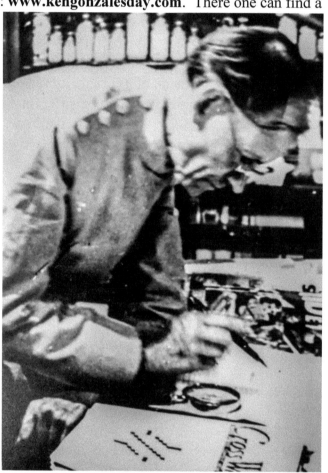

Pharmacist RW Lewis, Sr. Scared Off Robbers at His Pharmacy in Los Angeles in Early Days.
This Photo c. 1950

On this morning, my dogs and I had been out walking for some time when my attention was suddenly pulled away from the past. Three sheriff patrol cars drove from behind us with flashing lights. We halted as one sheriff slowed, rolled down his vehicle's window, and asked if I had seen a loose horse with no rider. I paused, looked across the way to Lacouague Street. My eyes immediately settled on a big horse, complete with saddle and dangling reins, calmly standing in the middle of the road. Pointing, I replied, "He's right there!" (I admit I felt very

helpful!) The three sheriffs' vehicles then proceeded up the street, surrounding the horse. I knew that my two lady friends, Diana and Deb, were riding in the hills and that one of them could have been thrown. The dogs and I power-walked up to the three lawmen who, by now, were, all three, standing a safe distance away from the animal. Pointing toward the nearby hill, I called softly to the sheriff closest to me, "Do you want me to get the horse for you?" I explained that the rider may be up on the trail. The sheriff answered me in stage whisper, clearly concerned about upsetting the horse. He explained that a call had just come through and that the rider was safe. No, they didn't want any help. There was nothing more for me to do. We left the scene.

Later, I learned that my friends had not been involved, but that yet another patrol car was dispatched as well as a helicopter! How times have changed! I could not believe that one lone horse could attract a posse of its own. Back in the day, Sheriff Barton and his three deputies, forced to hunt down a vicious gang, had to go it alone.

Violence Continues

The Barton case illustrates the contrast between the relatively peaceful years in Alta California when the missions with the presidios provided the structure for law and order. Once Mexico defeated Spain and the secularization laws were finally enforced, the mission system gave way to chaos. During the Mexican Era and after, pueblos such as San Juan were plagued by violence. Between the 1850's through the 1860's more and more discouraged miners, gamblers, fugitives, cattle thieves, out-of-work cowboys, and escaped criminals drifted through our village.

> Los Angeles had the ghastly distinction of having the highest murder rate in the state for its population.

San Juan has always been a convenient resting point for travelers between San Diego and Los Angeles. In those days it boasted having four saloons which were magnets for thirsty vaqueros and cowboys. Unfortunately, the bars also attracted highwaymen and other unsavory types. Travel between towns became unsafe, good people were terrorized. As seen in the Sheriff Barton case, lawmen were far away in Los Angeles. Outlaws did as they pleased with impunity. In a weak attempt to curb the chronic violence, citizens organized what they called "vigilance" committees, but the justice applied by those "vigilance" groups was ineffective and sporadic. Crime statistics are not available but newspapers, journals, and letters show the heinousness of the crimes committed from Monterey to the Mexican border. There are many newspaper accounts of the chaos in Los Angeles, for example in an article from the *Southern Californian* of November 16, 1854, according to Cleland in *Cattle on a Thousand Hills,* stated:

> "The week has been comparatively quiet; four persons have been killed is true, but it has been considered a poor week for killing; a head or two has been split open, and an occasional case of cutting; but these are minor matters and create but little feeling."

Another instance cited by Cleland, around this same time, had to do with the powerful businessman, Abel Stearns of Los Angeles. He was entertaining his friends with a lavish ball at his home when a group of unruly, uninvited rowdies, literally tried to crash through his iron gates to join the party. Unsuccessful, they took matters further by pulling a cannon up close to the home and firing several rounds into it. When the would-be intruders attempted to come in a second time, Stearns' guests were so angry that some of them shot into the unruly mob, killing two and seriously wounding two others!

The City of Los Angeles at one time held the ghastly distinction of having the highest murder rate in the state for its population. An interesting point to be sure, but one must also consider that Los Angeles, unlike tiny San Juan Capistrano, was large enough to have its own sheriff, and still crime was out of control. I couldn't help but think again of that lone horse calmly standing in the street while the helicopter hovered above. Oh how San Juan could have used some help in the old days!

Horse Raiders and Big Business

During those chaotic years, in addition to hold-ups, mayhem and murders, the Ranchos also suffered greatly at the hands of organized bands of desperados and Indians. Bands of raiding Indians sometimes including some outlaws would come through the Cajon Pass or across ancient Indian trails, killing unprotected cattle and making off with large herds of horses.

California Governor Peter Burnett, who served as governor from 1849-1851, listed stock rustling as one of the state's major economic ills and sought to have it made a capital offense. He wrote, "In some places whole herds of cattle have been stolen and farmers have lost their teams of horses and have been compelled to abandon their businesses."

The raids were so serious that ranch owners appealed to the people of Los Angeles for help. In just one such incident, cattleman Abel Stearns responded when Rancho Azusa was struck, by sending out a posse. The posse overpowered the Indian rustlers in the Cajon Pass, killing ten of the raiders and recapturing the stolen horses. Two of their own men were killed in the battle. In another case, the raiders were fifty men strong and the pursuers were only fifteen. The pursuers backed off when one of their own was hit by bullets. In this instance, they faced certain death but were saved by nightfall and managed to sneak away.

The *Los Angeles Star* ran a story in 1850 that the Rancho Santa Margarita y Las Flores was hit by a band of Paiutes which stole 500 horses. The article went on to state that:

"The mountain and desert Indians were on the warpath. Warner's ranch had been plundered, emigrant trains attacked and Antonio Garra, one of the leaders of the organized Indian rebellion, had boasted he would exterminate the white race in California...It is supposed that all the Indians are in a plot to massacre the whites."

The California-Indian Wars were a series of conflicts, massacres, and skirmishes between the United States and the Native people of California, lasting from 1850-1880. Some time you might want to

Mission San Juan Capistrano 1875. Courtesy of Mission SJC Archives

stop by California Historical Landmark 349 in the Owens Valley. It marks where the military installations at Camp Independence and later Fort Independence once stood. In 1880 the war ended when, perhaps, 1000 native Paiute people were forcibly removed to Fort Tejon.

These conflicts continued for some time, and not just between the Indians and the settlers. Abel Stearns and other wealthy ranchers put up $200 each toward the reward for the capture of Antonio Garra, the instigator of the threatened insurrection. He was finally apprehended and sentenced to death by shooting. Horse stealing was big business with many thousands of horses stolen across the years of 1850-

1853 and driven across to Texas, New Mexico, and into Utah. Some of the Ranchos were stripped of all their horses. In one letter written by the editor of the *Los Angeles Star* reprinted in Robert Cleland's *The Cattle on a Thousand Hills*, the editor speculates,

"Who that has lived in this county, for the past five years, does not recollect the magnificent droves of horses stolen from San Bernardino, San Jose, El Chino…and every rancho in the county?...In 1852 two cattle drovers alone lost near two thousand head by wholesale robbery of the Indians, who also attacked and murdered in their houses, at the Four Creeks six or eight Americans."

Conditions continued like that for years with rustlers meeting up on the Mojave River and driving their stolen horses and cattle up to Salt Lake City and other Mormon settlements. During this time the region between San Juan Capistrano and Santa Ana was riddled with robberies and murder.

1850's Population Explosion

With statehood, a feverish demand for land resulted in a significant population explosion. In 1850, California's population was 92,597. Just twenty years later, it had risen to 560,247 (Cleland: *History of California*, 440). It was thought to be the biggest land boom in the nation's history. Creative entrepreneurs in the East waged an intensive advertising campaign, touting California as a "Golden State," a virtual paradise. The federal government fueled the boom by offering nine million acres of public land at a fixed price of $1.25 per acre to people wanting to settle and work it. In addition, the railroads were given fifteen million acres of land to bring locomotives west. This cheap land, combined with the Federal Homestead Act, incentivized families to come west. At about the same time, gold mining began to decline, and thousands of miners, enthralled by the promise of California, retrieved their families in the East, and came to seek their futures in the Golden State. The Civil War ended and former soldiers were attracted to the possibilities of cheap, available land in California.

This explosion of settlers once again altered the existing social order. The sprawling Ranchos were negatively affected by crime, drought, and economic pressure; and most were sold off and divided into smaller enterprises. Over time as law abiding ranchers and farmers rose to dominate community life, crime began to decline.

The "Iron Horse" Crosses the Continent

In May of 1869 the Central Pacific and Union Pacific Railroads joined, completing the First Transcontinental Railroad. By 1885 the Santa Fe Railroad was able to bring settlers to Southern California. A cross-country ticket sold for the high price of $125.00. As the Southern Pacific Railroad grew, it needed more passengers and soon a price war broke out between the two competing giants. The Southern Pacific dropped its prices for a short time to just one dollar for a ticket from Missouri to California. The frenzied price rivalry continued for several months allowing even more settlers to move west. The cost of a ticket eventually went back up, but never to the high prices of the earlier days.

"The King of San Juan" Arrives in Town

The railroad made transcontinental travel feasible. It allowed all four of my of father's grandparents to come west as well as thousands of families wanting to carve out a new life. In May of 1869 a particularly important person to the future of San Juan Capistrano came to town. This man would be a force toward good for the next fifty years. His name was Richard Egan from Ireland.

A surveyor by trade, he purchased 600 acres near Trabuco Creek for $1.25 per acre and began to grow barley. His impact was so significant that he eventually became known as the "King of San Juan." He was elected Justice of the Peace in 1870 and served for the next 20 years, earning the title of "Judge," and "Alcalde," [mayor] in Spanish speaking San Juan Capistrano. Egan brought law and order to town.

My friend, and historian, Pam Hallan-Gibson points out in *Two Hundred Years of San Juan Capistrano* that historians have had a lot fun with the idea of Egan as "King" of San Juan. The thought took root through a request he once received addressed to the "Presidente of the Free and Independent State of San Juan Capistrano" asking for the extradition of a local criminal to Baja California. As it was, Egan complied with the request and sent the lawbreaker packing back to Mexico. A colorful story for sure, illustrating how independent the folks in San Juan held themselves from other population centers.

Judge Egan also served as the County Supervisor for Los Angeles. He held the fifth seat, representing the people of what was then known as "the Santa Ana Valley of Los Angeles County," before it was separated from Los Angeles County in 1889. It took dedication and determination for Judge Egan to attend the frequent Board of Supervisors meetings in Los Angeles. He had to travel by the Seeley and Wright stage coach to Santa Ana, from there, he boarded the Southern Pacific Railroad for the next leg of the four hour trip into Los Angeles.

Judge Egan Elected to Justice of the Peace in 1870.
He Was Instrumental in Repairing the Mission. Courtesy Griffith Family

When Orange County was created, it was Egan who was the commissioner, working to achieve that county separation.

Egan's leadership was seen in yet another important endeavor. Sadly, by the close of the 19th Century, the once prosperous Mission had become a dilapidated ruin where only rats and mice thrived. Judge Egan threw his energy into helping restore it. When Charles Lummis, and the members of the Los Angeles based Landmarks Club committed their financial support toward trying to save what was left of Mission San Juan Capistrano, Judge Egan was all in. He supervised much of the restoration, working alongside tradesmen. The effort resulted in some 5000 feet of sidewalk being paved with asphalt and the placement of tiles on the crumbling roofs of the buildings in the quadrangle, which were still standing.

Judge Egan's Harmony House: Residence and Court House

As Judge Egan prospered, he was able to build a beautiful Neo-Victorian home one block down from the Mission on Camino Capistrano. He named it Harmony House. His living quarters were upstairs and he eventually placed a large window in the north-facing wall, giving him a clear view of the front of the Mission. The rooms downstairs served as the local court house and gathering place. One of my favorite historical photos of old San Juan is of a carriage standing in front of Harmony House with a team of four white horses waiting at the ready. There is a town myth about a tunnel under the street that once ran between Harmony House and the El Adobe Restaurant to a jail cell. However, the is no evidence of

Egan's Harmony House Served as Courthouse. Built 1883. Courtesy Griffith Family

the tunnel. The jail cell part is true as it is available downstairs in the El Adobe Restaurant for diners to enjoy. A party of up to ten can be served behind the bars of the cell.

Across the decades of the 20th century, Egan's Harmony House fell into disrepair. In fact, in this century, it sat empty for eight long years until William and Chris Griffith had the vision and desire to protect it. They purchased the property, taking on the herculean job of restoring the iconic Victorian building. Dan Friess served as the Development Manager, while their son, Jake Griffith, worked as the Project Analyst. Judge Egan's landmark building was listed in the National Register of Historic Places in 2016. At the grand opening of the newly rehabilitated building, Ilse Byrnes was awarded a plaque to honor her work in registering such structures, including this one. The Egan House is open for business today as a restaurant called Ellie's Table. It is a popular attraction along San Juan's weekly walking tour of the historic downtown.

Judge Egan's Team at Harmony House Placed on National Registry of Historic Places by Ilse Byrnes 2017.
Courtesy Griffith Family

Chapter Seven

Nearing the 20th Century: An Agrarian Community

"My horse has saved me in ways no one could ever imagine."(Pinterest)

In today's world, just thinking of struggling through clogged northbound freeway traffic from South County is enough to keep many a resident at home in the Capistrano Valley. Los Angeles County, with its ten million plus folks, the most populated county in the entire United States is chock full of cars. When one adds in the 3.3 million others residing in today's Orange County, it can be an over suggestion to venture out onto the streets. It takes a bold imagination to conjure up the old days of horse and buggy when San Juan was an isolated little farming community.

Los Angeles County Originally Included San Juan Capistrano

The *Los Angeles County Directory for 1875* cited in Robert Cleland's *The Cattle on a Thousand Hills* shows that Los Angeles County, which included what is now Orange County, had a population of 33,000 back when Judge Richard Egan reigned as "King of San Juan." In his day, the greater population of the county supported 43 blacksmiths, 30 boot and shoe dealers, 28 wagon and carriage makers, 27 saddle and harness makers, as well as 22 livery and feed stables. Horses were a vital element to the economy, providing many livelihoods.

Even though Judge Egan was successful in bringing the California Central Railroad through to San Juan in 1887, the little town of 376 residents was content to enjoy the virtues of a pastoral existence. As technological inventions and world politics moved

> *Make your handshake your bond.*
> Richard O'Neill, Sr.

forward across the globe, and new businesses opened up in San Juan, the village's character remained much as it always had been. The bloody chaos of marauding horse thieves and criminals of the mid-19th Century had given way to a cattle frontier. While taxes and droughts forced most of the great Rancheros into decline, Richard O'Neill and Don Marcos Forster, son of Don Juan Forster, continued to fill rail cars with vast numbers of livestock and crops for markets in Los Angeles, San Francisco, and San Diego. At one time, O'Neill produced more wheat than any of his competitors. In time, the cattle and sheep industry yielded to crops of walnuts, then oranges, wheat and barley.

Sixty miles north, in Los Angeles, an enormous population explosion was taking place. Due to heavy advertising, the 1892 population of 50,000 burgeoned within just ten years, to 150,000. Continued dependence upon the Los Angeles River for water became impossible. In addition to 100,000 thirsty new citizens, the city suffered the effects of a ten-year long drought. They needed water. Long time water engineer, and Superintendent of the Los Angeles Water Department, William Mulholland, knew he needed to find a solution.

One September morning in 1904, he and his well connected, business-savvy, friend Frederick Eaton, rented a mule-pulled buckboard wagon and set out ostensibly to go camping. In reality they made the rugged trip north via Mojave to search for a water source. Eaton had been telling Mulholland about the lush Owens River for years. With water shortages becoming critical, Mulholland was finally listening,

The men were successful in figuring out a feasible plan for bringing the Owens River water to Southern California (against much push back from the Owens Valley farmers.) Their journey resulted in the Los Angeles Aqueduct which set the stage for Los Angeles to grow into perhaps, the most glamorous, iconic city in the world. (Krist, 2018). I highly recommend, Gary Krist's, *The Mirage Factory: Illusion, Imagination, and the Invention of Los Angeles, 2018.*

As all this was taking place a short distance to the north, and much of the world began to modernize, San Juan Capistrano slumbered contentedly for the next fifty years much as it always had. Wells were dug, rail service came through, a national Depression would be suffered, Ortega Highway would be constructed, but still, people mostly depended upon animals for working the land, for transportation, and in some cases, for entertainment.

Marcos Forster, the son of Don Juan, continued his father's tradition of hosting town-wide parties, the highlights of which were horse races down Camino Capistrano and on the old road [El Camino Real] in front of Mission Hill. In those days, Mission Hill was pasture. At the bottom of the hill was a swamp. The lobos [wolves] lived on the side of the hill. According to Karen Wilson, the great-granddaughter of Nathaniel Pryor, an American pioneer who came to California in 1823, "Mission Hill was a great big hill behind the Mission, practically a mountain." Her testimony was taken on August 28, 1975 as part of California State University, Fullerton's Oral History Project. Construction of homes did not begin on Mission Hill until the mid-1920's. Clearly, the area was a great place for horse racing.

Daily Life c. 1920 Often Included a Horse

Horses and mules were very much a part of daily life. There is a delightful account focusing on a frequent antic of school children and their horses. My co-author of *Whispering Waters: Historic Weesha and the Settling of Southern California*, and dear friend, Janet Harris Tonkovich, tells it. Here are some tales from her grandfather and great uncle around 1900.

Lunch Time Horse Races
Four Horse Wagon as School 'Bus'

In 1898, Janet's great grandparents, John and Anna Launer, began ranching in La Habra. [I have three beautiful Swamp Lilies growing on my patio from the original plant which Anna brought to California in 1898 on their move west from Highland, Illinois, with their four sons. The lilies are precious to me because during that trip, John and Anna's freight car filled with stock for their new ranch was

Baling Hay 1910 Fullerton. Nelson Launer Feeding in Hay, Albert Sitting on Hay Baler

demolished in a train wreck in Arizona. Much was lost as the chickens and horses scattered about. The Swamp Lily survived. A plant from the original is also growing at the entrance to the La Habra Historical Museum, with an inscribed plaque explaining its origins. Later, the horses were rounded up.] One of Anna and John's boys was Janet's grandfather, the others were her great uncles. This snippet allows a tiny peek into school-boy life in Orange County in 1904. Surely the boys and girls of the nearby Capistrano Valley enjoyed similar activities. This excerpt is from California State University, Fullerton's Oral Documentation Program. I appreciate it because it is in Janet's great-uncle Albert's own words. Here is Albert Launer's testimony taken December 11, 1964.

Regarding school: "We would occasionally have horse races at noon-time. A number of the boys came in to school on horses….the horses would be tied out back of the school and staked out too. At noontime, occasionally, the young fellows would have a horse race between twelve and one. I graduated out there in 1904.

When Janet's grandfather, Nelson Launer, whom I knew, began high school in 1907 there was an area along Lemon Street on the east side of Fullerton High School where the students let their horses graze while they were in class. Janet remembers riding with her grandfather as he enthusiastically pointed out where his black stallion, Ben, once liked to graze.

In the 1909 *Pleiades*, Fullerton High School Yearbook, Albert Launer described the "school bus." "Our high school is the first in the state to institute successfully a system of free transportation that is maintained at the cost of the district. 85% of our students come to school on wagons to Fullerton High. It would be impossible for many of these to go to school above the grammar grades if they did not enjoy the advantages of free transportation."

"At present there are six wagons in use bringing in the students from the districts composing the [Fullerton] Union. One wagon comes from Buena Park, a second from Brookhurst via Orangethorpe, a third from Placentia, another from La Habra, a fifth starts in East La Habra and takes in the Randolph district, while a sixth, a four-horse wagon, comes from Olinda via Placentia. The wagons start from home about 7:30 a.m. and leave the school for the return trip at 3:45. (A. O. L. 1909)

Family Wagon Waiting for Babe c. 1915

78

1930 Visiting the Barn and Horses - A Common Experience

Farm Animals Were Essential to Farmers' Livelihood 1915

Surveying Future Ortega Highway 1928. Courtesy O C Register

Mission San Juan Capistrano in Ruins c Late 19th Century.

French Colonists Settle

Around 1910 a group of French colonists came to settle in San Juan, led by Father Quetu who was attached to the Mission. He purchased 500 acres on both the north and south sides of what is today Ortega Highway and set about raising ostriches and horses. Quetu's endeavors continue to illustrate the importance of horses to the agrarian lifestyle. One of his horses, Champlain, was a massive draft stallion weighing in over 2200 pounds. Champlain was so sensational that he took first place, against 159 contenders, in a special horse show held in Salt Lake City.

Ultimately, Father Quetu closed his horse and ostrich business and the French colonists moved away. However, Father Quetu's contribution to life in San Juan was important. He made an essential connection to the future of San Juan. In 1909 while traveling in Arizona, he met a young priest who would forge an indelible imprint upon the Mission, and would come to be known as "The Great Restorer." The young priest was suffering with tuberculosis when Father Quetu invited him to come to California, to the Mission San Juan Capistrano.

Father Saint John O'Sullivan Arrives in San Juan

On July 5th, 1910 Father Saint "Sin-Jin" John O'Sullivan, the young priest who met Father Quetu, stepped off the train in San Juan. It was reported that he walked the short blocks to the Mission and cast his eyes upon it, falling in love with the ruins. He, whose own body was in decay, felt an immediate affinity for the Mission, also in decay.

In spite of the Landmarks Club and Judge Egan's earlier efforts, the Mission was again uninhabitable for humans, while rats and spiders lived in contentment. It had not enjoyed a resident priest since 1886. O'Sullivan studied his new home, learned of its illustrious past, and dreamed of its future possibilities. He was impressed by the history held within its walls, and amazed that time had not eroded it into complete devastation. He set up a tent among the arches by the Serra Chapel and began the work of restoring it. He envisioned bringing the Mission back to life through intensifying the preservation process which had begun some years earlier with Judge Egan, Charles F. Lummis, and the Landmarks

Father St. John O'Sullivan c. 1910. Courtesy San Juan Capistrano Historical Society

Club. Not only did O'Sullivan labor: carving, plastering, and nailing with his own hands, he also enlisted the help of others. Coincidentally, as the Mission grew strong, so did Father O'Sullivan.

Father O'Sullivan faced many challenges, among which was his lack of tools and equipment to carry out his vision. The day that I sat with Gretchen Stroscher Thompson at the Historical Society's luncheon was when she shared this second horse story. Her Stroschein grandparents were next door neighbors to the Mission and some whom O'Sullivan tagged for help. Gretchen recalled a family story. It seems that because Father O'Sullivan owned no horse, nor wagon for hauling in materials, he somehow persuaded Gretchen's grandmother, Frederika Stroschein, to loan him her horse and wagon. He could be seen on many occasions hauling great loads of lumber and supplies with her horse and wagon into the Mission grounds. Gretchen is proud that her family had a hand in revitalizing the Mission. She also wondered if the horse pulling one of her grandparents' wagons was one of the famous race horses.

Mission San Juan Capistrano as Tourist Attraction
Automobiles and Movie Producers

As the Mission began to take on its former glory, it became something of a "must see" tourist attraction. The invention of the automobile began to take hold. In the beginning, cars, known as "machines" were nothing more than toys for the wealthy. In 1908 Henry Ford produced the Model T. During the first year of production, he turned out 1700 cars. By 1910, there were 8000 "machines" on the roads across America with just 144 miles of roads being paved. Between 1908 and 1927 Henry Ford would build an astonishing 15 million Model Ts.

Mission San Juan Capistrano Becomes Tourist
Destination c. 1928

While automobiles were becoming a more common sight, horses remained the mainstay of transportation. One morning in 1911, my maternal grandmother, Gertrude Borwick, loaded her two-year old daughter, my aunt Marjorie, into the family wagon to go shopping. Sitting high on the wagon seat, she shook the reins and called, "Git up!" The horse would not budge. This was the family's finest, most cooperative mare, Babe. My grandmother could not imagine why Babe would not move. She tried again. "Hah! Git up!" As she more vehemently shook the reins. Nothing. Annoyed, she climbed down from the wagon and walked around it, only to discover that young Marjorie had somehow fallen down off the wagon. She was quietly lying in the dirt in front of the heavy wagon wheel. Had the horse proceeded, certain death awaited the little girl. Once the small child was secured in the wagon, Babe immediately responded to my grandmother's command and took them to market! My mother tells me that this was one of her father's favorite stories, as it validated what he had always known about Babe; that she was a fine mare.

All four of my grandparents had memories of horse drawn green grocers and milk wagons coming through their neighborhoods of old Los Angeles. Such wagons existed in major population centers even up through the 1930's. In quiet San Juan, most families had a cow for milk and butter, grew their own vegetables, while the chickens and turkeys ran across the yard.

Recently, I encountered our long-time neighbor, Marie Lacouague, who arrived in San Juan Capistrano, as a bride in the 1940's to live on her new husband's family citrus ranch. Standing in the produce section of Trader Joe's we chatted. I could not resist asking her about the early days as I explained my horse project. She said that her husband, Jean, never depended upon animals to plow, however, she recalled that his parents, Pierre and Bonisacia, worked the land with a team of mules.

Mare Babe with Borwick Family c. 1915

Henry Ford's Model T and Social Change

Though people continued to depend heavily upon horses, the next ten years would see one million of Ford's cars driving around the USA. Paved roads sprang up, electric power, and telephone service became available. Life as it had been lived for decades began to change.

The automobile was a significant innovation that led to social change for that era, much as the train had been a generation before. In the decades to come, airplanes would allow people to travel even further, and finally when the technology of the Digital Age would erupt, information and possibilities never before considered would be a reality. But back in the early years of the 20th century, it was the automobile which allowed Americans real mobility. It became possible to venture out toward new discoveries. As a child in the 1920's in Los Angeles, my mother recalls that a typical Sunday activity after church would be "going for a drive."

The same year that Father O'Sullivan arrived in San Juan, so did the pioneer movie maker, David Wark Griffith, known as "D.W." He arrived with his entourage and three railroad cars. The train pulled the cars alongside the Depot. Among the luminaries with Mr. Griffith was the starlet, Mary Pickford. The film, "Two Brothers," was a period piece where the outlaw scenes were filmed in the local foothills. However, a scene filmed in downtown caused a problem. During one of the scenes, the actors moved in a processional toward the Mission. A crowd gathered to enjoy the filming, but before long the locals believed Griffith was belittling a funeral procession that had taken place the day before. The crowd grew disgruntled, throwing rocks. It was only after some cajoling through the negotiations of the hotel proprietor that the crowd settled down. Griffith's peace offering was a rodeo and roping show to be performed by the professional cowboys in his troupe. That 1910 production was the first movie filmed in Orange County. In the ensuing years, another famous Western film, *The Mark of Zorro* would bring national attention to the tiny pueblo. That movie was adapted from a magazine story entitled, *The Curse of Capistrano*. The 1920 pre-talkie film takes place in the village of Capistrano. Zorro became a celebrated character, a vigilante heralded as a warrior, riding his horse up and down the highways of California defending commoners against evil. A soldier in the film asks, "Where is Zorro?" The printed response on the screen, "He was in Capistrano. He could be anywhere!"

Henry Ford's Invention Changed America. Only 144 miles of paved roads in 1910

c. Late Teens Dirt Roads   c. Teens. Tire Trouble Was Common

Horses Continued to Serve Through the 1930's – Milk Wagon

c. 1920 Donna's Great Grandfather's Paint Co. Truck

Mission San Juan Capistrano Becomes a Parish Church Once Again

In 1918, the Mission San Juan Capistrano was given parochial status, becoming a recognized parish by the Catholic Church with Father O'Sullivan as its first modern pastor. During the 1920's Father O'Sullivan began the tradition of celebrating the return of the swallows on Saint Joseph's Day each year. That tradition ultimately combined with a village-wide Heritage Festival which, by 1936, evolved into a celebration known as the Fiesta de las Golondrinas. That year, a popular NBC radio show was broadcast from the Mission hosted by Clinton Twiss. The show announced to the world the return of the swallows. Today that celebration includes two weeks of fun, culminating in the magnificent Swallows Day parade. The parade is hailed as the largest non-motorized parade in the West. This year, 2018, we celebrated the parade's 60th Anniversary. In 1925 the Mission was touted by *National Geographic* as an important place to visit, "a shrine linking the present with the past." (Hallan-Gibson, p.101). O'Sullivan's broad vision included rehabilitation of the Serra Chapel. To help fund the project, he instituted a ten cent entry charge to the Mission's many visitors. He was also responsible for the construction of the Sacred Garden fountain (1920), the Front fountain (1924), and the Central fountain (1930), among other features. His foresight helped the little pueblo of San Juan Capistrano to become a tourist attraction. One travel writer declared, "It's not for what it has become, but for what it has been."

San Juan Capistrano is worth bragging about. It was the start of mighty Orange County. It has the oldest church in the county, as well as the oldest continuously lived on street in the State. While San Juan was being written about in travel magazines, new attractions were springing up down the road. In Capistrano Beach, a resort at Doheny Beach was being built which boasted a train stop. Further south, the Spanish Village By-The-Sea, known today as San Clemente, provided more impetus for travelers to visit the area. One of my favorite family photographs is of my great grandfather, the pharmacist turned State

Donna Friess' great-grandfather, Senator Charles Lewis visits Mission 1928

Senator, Charles H. V. Lewis, standing in the Mission courtyard in 1928. As I lead my tour groups across the tiles where he stood, I sometimes feel a flicker of joy as I imagine him possibly having a chat with Father O'Sullivan.

San Juan Capistrano continues to be proud of its past as it embraces the future. The City motto is: "Preserving the Past to Enhance the Future." History has come to know Father O'Sullivan as the "Great Restorer." Without Father O'Sullivan, perhaps none of this would have been possible.

Before we leave the first decades of the 20th Century, I think this excerpt from Hallan-Gibson's Conference article is worth noting.

"World War II brought an end to the Depression and the formation of many volunteer organizations to help the war effort. Spotters were trained to watch for planes on old Mission Hill, the volunteer fire department, organized in the early thirties, received special training for possible disasters, and most households sent someone to join the armed forces. Like elsewhere, Japanese farmers in the valley were rounded up and sent to internment camps. Most did not return to the area, but relocated elsewhere after the war." ("San Juan Capistrano the Second Hundred Years and Beyond" excerpted from *Proceedings of the Orange County History Conference of 1988*.)

Father O'Sullivan. Courtesy Engelhardt, 1922

For more on old San Juan, I highly recommend the well written and interesting book *Two Hundred Years of San Juan Capistrano* by Pam Hallan-Gibson as well as the Conference Proceedings described above. I find Hallan-Gibson's work to be remarkable and I have relied heavily upon it.

The Western Movie is an Enduring Theme

As the months of interviewing San Juan residents and horse enthusiasts came to a close, I realized that many who had something to share for this project, have been greatly influenced by Westerns on televisions and the movies. My interviewees frequently described themselves as "wanna be" cowboys or cowgirls. Sometimes they would define themselves against others who were "real" cowboys. As a child, I knew that I was enamored of Roy Rogers, and then with that kiss on my cheek, Hopalong Cassidy had stolen my heart. As I collected stories, I came to see that many of my friends and neighbors shared that deep cowboy connection. I have been aware that my generation is the first one to grow up with a television in the living room.

I was awakened out of a deep sleep one night, realizing that many of us enjoying the presence of horses in our community have been influenced by the Western traditions portrayed in movies and on television. I will share some of my contributors' specific remarks later.

From the early years of the 20th Century until the 1930's audiences across the globe enjoyed the invention of the new "Moving Pictures" or "Silent Movies." Music was used to set the mood for the silent action taking place on the screen and organs were a common feature in theaters. [Today, in some historic theatres, an occasional organist will still play before the screening. We have recently enjoyed such music at the Casino Theatre in Avalon.] The Western was a common genre for those early Silent Movies as the plot and actions were self explanatory. **"The Western movie, [is] the single most enduring theme in the history of American films. From the silent era to the present…the Western movie occupies center stage of the American myth."** (A. Hoffman, 2003).

It fascinates me that the "Wild West" theme stems from a relatively narrow band of American history, 1870-1890, the time of the great long cattle drives. Those drives have become the stuff of legends, *Wyatt Earp* and *Gunsmoke* come to mind. Tom Mix was a famous American actor who appeared in 291 films, mostly silent Westerns. He was Hollywood's first big Western star and helped define the genre as it found its way into modern cinema.

From September of 1948 through 1949 the United States television network began its first season in which all four networks, then in operation, were offered. There was a television in my house in 1948, and I recall the great disappointment I felt when I turned it on, only to see the black and white station logo showing on the screen. It meant there was no programming available. On June 24, 1949 *Hopalong Cassidy* became the first network Western television series. The series turned William Boyd (Hoppy) into a star. Early television hits were *The Ed Sullivan Show* and *Howdy Doody*. *Howdy Doody* touted a Western theme for kids. By 1951 Roy Rogers and Dale Evans thrilled boys and girls across the country, while Hank Williams sang to their parents. Gene Autry was a big hit as a singing cowboy and rodeo performer. *The Lone Ranger* was a popular Western drama on ABC Television which aired from 1949-1957. Roy Rogers was known as the "King of the Cowboys" and he appeared in over 100 films as well as *The Roy Rogers* television show which aired its 100 episodes on NBC for six seasons between 1951 to 1957, plus shows like *Bonanza* appealing to adults.

My travels have taught me that it is not uncommon for foreigners to think about the "Cowboys of the Wild West" when they think of American culture. However, more recently when I explain that I am from Orange County, California in America, the response that comes back in broken English accompanied by a knowing look, is: "Oh yes, *Real Housewives of Orange County!*"

Roy Rogers TV Western Hero

A War Horse of No Equal Returns Home
"Courage under Fire"

In August of 2017, I attended a lecture sponsored by the San Juan Capistrano Historical Society. The guest lecturer was Barbara Greenbush of the Rancho Santa Margarita y Las Flores Docent Society.

Staff Sergeant Reckless War Hero, Courtesy Rancho Santa Margarita Historical Society Lecture

We gathered in the Boy Scout Hut in the Mission Flats District of San Juan, where this beautiful story was told. In 1950 the Korean War broke out pitting Capitalism against Communism. American troops fought a violent three-year war in the mountainous terrain of Korea. In the wake of that conflict, a famous soldier emerged, focusing international attention on our corner of the world. The amazing soldier was a horse, Sergeant Reckless. She was honored with the Purple Heart for her valor under fire. She became a national celebrity. Known as "America's greatest war horse," she led parades, was the subject of news headlines and even a book. She appeared on the *Art Linkletter* television show and was the highlight at Marine celebrations.

Sergeant Reckless was a mare of Mongolian descent, purchased in 1952 at a racetrack in Korea by a member of the United States Marines. She was trained as a pack horse for the Recoilless Rifle Platoon, Anti-Tank Company 5th Marine Regiment, 1st Marine Division.

Sergeant Reckless was a war horse of no equal. One of her most famous accomplishments was in the Battle of Outpost Vegas in March of 1953. Reckless was in the middle of a savage fight "where twenty-eight tons of bombs and hundreds of the largest shells turned the crest of the hill into a smoking death-pocked rubble." According to written reports, she could easily be seen by enemy soldiers during this five day battle. On one day alone, she made 51 trips from the Ammunition Supply Point to the firing sites.

On ninety-five percent of those trips she was all alone. No one was leading her. Across the days, she carried almost five tons of ammunition, and walked over 35 miles through open rice paddies and up steep mountains with enemy fire coming at her. Often she would carry wounded soldiers back down the mountain to safety, unload them, get reloaded with ammo and go back up to the chaos. Once she even provided a living shield for Marines who were trapped. Though she was wounded twice, she never stopped. Indispensable to the Marines, she was beloved, a symbol of heroism in a difficult war. Her military decorations are many and she was promoted every chance the men could get. Her last promotion was to Staff Sergeant, conferred by General Randolph McPate, the Commandant of the entire U.S. Marine Corps.

Reckless' bravery was legendary. She is the only animal given an official rank in the U.S. Marine Corps.

Reckless retired to Camp Pendleton with her men where her bravery and antics in the field became legendary. Marines told of how she would wander in and out of the Marines' tents on cold nights. On very cold nights she would stand next to the tent's stove, sometimes she would even lie down next to it. She would chomp up anything in sight, including poker chips! The men repeated stories of her love of beer or how she would amble down to the mess hall and eat pancakes with maple syrup. At home at Camp Pendleton, she led military parades and presided over exhibitions. She birthed two foals, Fearless and Dauntless. After a long full life, 1947-1968, she was buried with full military honors. She is immortalized in bronze

SS Reckless Memorialized Camp Pendleton

at Camp Pendleton.

"Old War Horse to get Deserved Recognition," this is the story title on the front page of the *Orange County Register*, Tuesday May 8, 2018. The story is about Camp Pendleton's own Staff Sergeant Reckless. She is being further immortalized in a bronze statue at the Kentucky Horse Park which honors "the best horses in history." Reckless is the only animal given an official rank in the Marine Corps. Her statue sits in the center of the park. World War II Marine veteran Ted Bassett is the President of the Marine Corps Coordinating Council in Kentucky and a horse lover. When, *Reckless* book author Robin Hutton, approached him about a statue in the educational horse park, he needed no persuasion.

Bassett said, "She [Reckless] was a legend; fierce determination, undaunted courage, zest to succeed and defiance of danger. One of the most important things to those who served with her was that she embraced the Marine Corps code of never giving up. She will reside among the pantheon of famous horses, there are lots of race winners, but there is nothing in the category of military heroes like Reckless."

Staff Sergeant Reckless - War Hero
Courtesy Rancho Santa Margarita y Las Flores Historical Society

Part II

"Any view is better from the back of a horse." (BRL Equine Nutrition)

Bringing Goods to Market. Courtesy Irvine Historical Museum

Chapter Eight

San Juan Capistrano Becomes a City

"There is No San Juan without Our Equestrian Community." (Mayor Sergio Farias)

Sometimes current events occur that reinforce our connections to the past and the importance of horses to our way of life. During the annual restructuring of our City Council in 2017, the newly elected Mayor, Sergio Farias, opened his acceptance speech with this observation, "Our equestrian lifestyle is at risk now, and I think this Council will move forward in a way that will ensure that it [equestrian lifestyle] will always be a part of this city…there is no San Juan Capistrano without our equestrian community." Dec. 5, 2017.

There it was, what I had been working toward, coming from the newly elected Mayor: the importance of horses to the people of San Juan Capistrano, and an acknowledgement that a serious threat is facing the existence of horses for the future in San Juan.

Horse Country Sign at Tar Farms

The Mayor's declaration reminded me of the heated political scene which greeted us upon our arrival in town in the summer of 1973. We soon learned that it was by no means the first such fierce battle. San Juan Capistrano had incorporated in 1961 with a population of 1,130 in the wake of two bitter battles with San Clemente and neighboring areas. The first clash was over the selection of a new high school site and the School District's order to demolish the historic Capistrano Union High School located in San Juan Capistrano. The second fracas was in regards to the issue of importation of public water. Historian, Pam Hallan-Gibson in *200 Years of San Juan Capistrano,* reprinted the headlines of the *Coastline Dispatch* from July 21, 1960 which read: **"Capistrano Valley Shocked by Sneak Incorporation Move."** Five residents had taken out incorporation papers to allow for further study and a cooling down period of 90 days over the high school issue. As incorporation become more feasible, there were disputes over boundaries. Thirty years before, such incorporation talk had included Dana Point and Capistrano Beach. This new 1961 effort included more of Dana Point and Capistrano Beach than those entities were willing to give. There was much pushing back. Ultimately, the Orange County Board of Supervisors set the boundaries and San Juan Capistrano became incorporated on its own on April 11, 1961. The first five council members were Bill Bathgate, Carl Buchheim, Ed Chermak, Don Durnford, and Tony Olivares, with Carl Buchheim becoming the first Mayor.

As a teen in the late 50's, I recall bumper-to-bumper traffic on El Camino Real when we would return home after a day of surfing at San Onofre. I have a particularly vivid memory of inhaling the fragrant pine scent when our automobile would slow to a crawl in the narrow part of the two lane road which I was to learn was next to the Bathgate and Williams Ranches. In those days cars were not air conditioned so all the windows were open. That memory has always stayed with me. When I got to know Pat Bathgate later in my life, I treasured the old image and its piney fragrance even more.

In the mid 1960's during the early years of our marriage, when Ken and I frequently traveled on the Interstate 5 Freeway and Ortega Highway to visit his grandparents, who lived in Lake Elsinore, San Juan came more into my consciousness. We made the frequent trip to Lake Elsinore because we loved showing off our new baby, Ricky, to his great grandparents. The Freeway was only a few years old, and still a novelty as it allowed much speedier travel south than in the old days when one had to fight the traffic on the old two-lane road (El Camino Real) that bisected San Juan Capistrano.

What impressed me the most from those long-ago weekend trips, was the forest of "Acreage for Sale" signs that dotted the orchards hugging the sides of Ortega highway.

"10 Acre Parcel: Buy Now;" sign after sign set against dying orange trees. The land was too valuable to continue to simply raise oranges, plus taxes were catching up with the value of the parcels. At the time, I had no idea, that one day, in the not so distant future, many of our good friends would live in the tract homes which would replace those trees.

The Interstate Freeway not only allowed us a short trip to visit the grandparents, it also provided a route for commuters in job centers in northern Orange County cities. Soon families, disillusioned with the chaotic urban life of the 1960's, with the war protests, inner city riots, and racial violence, looked south. Tiny San Juan Capistrano with its historic roots began to look attractive. Perhaps people felt that the small town atmosphere was a safer, more peaceful place to raise their children. Following the City's original General Plan, tracts of condominiums sprang up along Camino Capistrano, homes were built off Ortega Highway and San Juan Creek Road, and mobile home parks continued to open up along Alipaz Street.

Following its incorporation in 1961, residents of the new City of San Juan Capistrano struggled for nearly ten years to set the tone for the City's future development. Begun in 1962, and added to until adopted in its final form in 1970, the first General Plan was guided by an intent to "protect the historic treasures of the past, the Mission, the Adobes, and the architectural attempts of the early residents." (P. 3 of the General Plan Adopted June 8, 1970).

These sentences were juxtaposed with the planning that projected the City to a growth of 85,000 people. The adopted plan of 1970 included the following nine development goals:

1. **Protect and enhance San Juan Capistrano as a residential community giving priority to facilities and services for local residents.**
2. **Provide facilities for the continuing influx of visitors in a manner designed to minimize interference with the use and enjoyment of the community by local residents.**
3. **Protect the present character of the foothill and mesa area of the City.**

4. Protect and enhance the "combined Mission District" of the City, San Juan Capistrano's greatest economic resource for the benefit of all.
5. Encourage diversified residential, commercial, industrial and recreational development in appropriate locations.
6. Discourage heavy traffic from entering the "Combined Mission District."
7. Provide adequate parks and playgrounds throughout the City for local residents and way-stops and picnic areas for the visitors to the City.
8. Provide adequate school sites in relations to the population generated.
9. Continue to strive to improve the appearance of the City with respect to rehabilitation of structures and the undergrounding of utilities.

By the early 1970's, the rapid growth began to look like over-development. It alarmed many long-time residents, as well as the newly arrived. Old and new residents cherished the village atmosphere. Certainly our little family was no exception. As I mentioned earlier, when our dog Max barged through the block wall fence trying for the mail man, we knew we had to make a change; Huntington Beach tract living was not a good fit for us. Our home search took us to a four-year-old home off a dirt and gravel road on the way to a citrus ranch. It was so far out from the main center of town, that there was no mail delivery, natural gas service, trash pick-up, newspaper delivery or sewers. It seemed we had purchased a property that was far out in the country. Even though the home was fairly new, it had no fireplace, as the insurance company considered the distance from a fire department to be a liability. Today, you might laugh, as our equestrian development is nicely placed between Hidden Mountain, Juliana Farms, and Hunter's Creek. A bit further down San Juan Creek Road there is a big housing development built by Warmington Homes on some of the land that was once the Lacouague Ranch.

The wave of rapid development that came to San Juan required the demolition of many old buildings. In my interview with preservationist, Ilse Byrnes, she told me that what mobilized her into action, to save old buildings and to preserve the equestrian life-style, was seeing the two-hundred year old Cañedo adobe torn down at the southeast corner of El Camino Real and Ortega Highway. A Texaco gas station was to take its place. (You will remember Cañedo as the Mission soldier who assaulted Father Barona). Byrnes was further upset and frustrated when in 1965, the historic Capistrano Hotel was demolished on Camino Capistrano across from the Mission. Soon a new concrete commercial center, where Hennessey's Tavern is today, rose where the old thirty-four room hotel had been.

A new sentiment began to emerge in town. Citizen groups began to develop that questioned the direction the City was taking. Remarks by the newly formed San Juan Capistrano Historical Society with Les Remmers as their representative, sum up the new spirit growing in town. These are Les Remmers' comments before the City Council.

"We of the newly formed Historical Society ask each other what has happened to the present citizens and property owners of this City? Are we destroying something priceless, our heritage, that cannot be replaced---to become another rubber stamp community?"

A campaign was launched in San Juan, to save the City's heritage. The original 1965-1970 General Plan with its growth build-out to some 85,000 people, became suspect. In response to growth concerns, a group formed calling itself the Town Hall Association of San Juan Capistrano, Inc. It was a non-profit political action group, describing itself as, "a citizens group dedicated to controlled growth and the preservation of a rural, self-contained, village-like community."

The *1974-1978 Town Hall Report,* referring to the original General Plan, states: *"In 1961 the city dwellers incorporated and joined the trend toward urbanization. Its leaders adopted a plan for growth and development that would complete the urban transition and allow San Juan to grow to a population of up to 85,000 people."*

The *Town Hall Report* continued: "In 1972, there began to arise a feeling of uneasiness among new residents. They began to ask; was this urban density for San Juan responsible? ... There arose a crescendo of political interest and action to bring about a change in these plans." Later in the same report, the point was made that "San Juan Capistrano is probably the only city in Orange County to adopt ordinances to preserve significant and historic buildings and trees. Furthermore, the City's sign ordinance is one of the strictest in the county and encourages small signs to protect the rural character."

In 1972, new Council members were elected on the platform of "Preserving the Village Atmosphere." The 1972 Council consisted of Dr. Roy Byrnes, James Weathers, Josh Gammell, James Thorpe, and Edward Chermak. By 1974 a new City Council majority of Roy Byrnes, Doug Nash, Yvon Heckscher, and John Sweeney was firmly in favor of controlled growth.

In 1974, my husband, Ken, was appointed to the Planning Commission, and recalls many late night, heated community-wide sessions regarding the new vision for San Juan. The result was a revised General Plan which became law in 1974, with a build-out to only 42,000. The City Council of 1976, supporting the new General Plan and protection of the hillsides and open space, included: Kenneth Friess, Richard McDowell, Yvon Heckscher, Doug Nash, and John Sweeney.

At this writing San Juan's population is under 40,000. The revised plan provided for parks, open space, and the guarantee that the equestrian life-style would be protected.

> *The City of San Juan Capistrano's General Plan Vision for the Future*
> **Growth in San Juan Capistrano should be a cautious evolutionary process that follows a well-conceived set of general guidelines and specific controls. The underlying growth philosophy should be to preserve the present character of a small self-contained village-like community with abundant open space. (p. 1)**

The Revised General Plan adopted in 1974 included the following important provisions as related to horses. This is excerpted from that revised plan, page 28:

Equestrian Facilities: In considering the future of San Juan Capistrano's rural environment, careful consideration has been given to the role of the horse. Horses have been an integral part of the economics of the Capistrano Valley for hundreds of years. Most recently the horse has come to be very important as a source of recreation and learning for adults and children alike.

The relationship between children and horses is a very special one. As further development impacts the Valley's life style, care must be taken to perpetuate the role of the horse and to continue to provide opportunities for people to experience the healthy psychological and physical effects of horses.

Central to the survival of horses are boarding stables. The stables in San Juan Capistrano exist primarily for two purposes: one of which is to house, care for, and protect horses which belong to persons who do not have adequate space or time to provide these animals, and to provide a healthy atmosphere for children in this community who may otherwise seek less constructive pursuits.

Since the majority of horse owners in San Juan Capistrano are indeed children and a large number of these children are responsible for all or part of their stable fees, the economics of boarding must be kept within their reach. If they are not, an association with nature through the caring of a horse may be denied to the young person who may need it the most. Future planning provides a means for keeping stables economically feasible by acknowledging the above factors and by giving due consideration to them in the development of zone districts and construction regulations. Equestrian trails are a part of the General Plan and are discussed fully in the Parks and Recreation Element.

1982 Council From Left Friess, Hausdorfer, Buchheim, Bland, Schwartze, City Manager Steve Julian

During those years, one of the leaders in the movement to protect the village-like character of San Juan Capistrano was Dr. Roy Byrnes. During the tumultuous time of changing the direction of the City, he served a four-year term on the City Council, two of those years as Mayor, 1972 and 1973. He was again elected to City Council in 2012. Upon his retirement from the Council in 2014, at age 90, he was interviewed. In a 2015 article in the *Capistrano Dispatch*, Dr. Roy Byrnes explained how proud he is of having had a hand in shaping the future of San Juan and helping to preserve open space and initiating the developing of parks. [His 2012 City Council approved plans for the 18 acre Reata Park, a public open space.]

In that *Dispatch* interview, I noticed that Dr. Byrnes deflected his very important work toward preserving the village-like character of San Juan Capistrano by shifting the subject to his wife, Ilse's contributions. Roy Bynes is an unassuming, humble man who made a lasting contribution to the San Juan Capistrano we have today. Certainly, shifting the conversation to his wife, Ilse's effort is well deserved. He said, "Ilse, is the one who is responsible for creating the trail system and for the preservation of historic structures."

Ilse Byrnes - A Warrior for Preservation

In the way that Judge Richard Egan, Don Juan Forster, Father O'Sullivan, and the O'Neill family have left their indelible handprints on San Juan, so, too, has the extraordinary woman, Ilse Byrnes. Ilse's work has been foundational in helping preserve San Juan's equestrian way of life, as well has having statewide influence in terms of making parks and trails important. Ilse is the person most responsible for laying out the City's forty mile trail system for horses and hikers. She is the subject of frequent news stories which often refer to her as *A Warrior for Preservation.*

Kathy Holman, owner of the Ortega Equestrian Center, shared with me that when the development of the Ortega Cottages was under way, the new owners gave notice to all seven of the stable owners who were operating along the north side of the creek. They all had to leave. This was a brutal punch to the horse industry. Those stable owners turned to Ilse. Ilse went to the City Council and requested that some of the city land along the Creek be set aside for horses. She was heard and the result was that the City agreed to lease a portion of land at the east end of Cook Park for the purpose of a stable. Mission Trails Stable was begun. Kathy explained, "It was Ilse who championed us."

Kathy Holman Enamored with Horses Since Childhood

Everywhere I went, interviewing those in the horse community of San Juan, I heard the same sentiment repeated. "If not for Ilse Byrnes our equestrian way of life would have been lost." Her leadership on the State level, as well, has been instrumental in preserving horses, parks and trails beyond San Juan Capistrano.

I met Ilse at the Montenez Adobe one spring morning. As we sat on the porch, the birds chirped sweetly around us. She shared her story with me. Ilse Byrnes moved to the area in 1958 with her husband, Dr. Roy Byrnes, who, as discussed earlier, has been a major force in his own right. In the beginning, she kept her horses at Weddel's place, a large stable at the corner of what is now Del Obispo Street and Stonehill Street where the Albertson's Market is in Dana Point today.

"The population was only about 1000 people in the valley back then. In the 1970's San Juan started to be developed and the many places we used to ride soon disappeared. In 1976, I asked the City Council to establish an Equestrian Commission which would help to design and establish multi-use trails through and around new developments, such as the Hunt Club."

Ilse Byrnes Preservationist for Trails and Structures in San Juan Capistrano

The Council granted her request to form a commission, ensuring a course toward preservation. Governor George Deukmejian appointed her to the State Trails Committee, where she served from 1983-1995. That committee provides trail professionals, advocates and users with up-to-date trail management skills, to help ensure trail stewardship for generations to come. She is a founding member of the California and Greenways Foundation, and has served since 2000. In addition, for the past twenty years, she has worked as an appointee to the California State Round Table for Parks and Tourism. With a proud smile, she confessed, "San Juan Capistrano was the first city in the State to have a separate commission for horses." Ilse has been a member of the San Juan Capistrano Trails and Equestrian Commission for decades.

> "Ilse Byrnes' work has been foundation in preserving our equestrian way of life."
> (Dr. Roy Byrnes)

Ilse continued, "The biggest battle I had was over Casper's Park as there was heavy pressure to develop it into houses. I managed to finagle a park! As a preservationist of buildings, I saw my work as going hand in hand with preserving horses, if we were going to preserve our lifestyle." She continued: "When I first nominated the Los Rios District to the National Registry of Historic Places there was a great uproar. I got terrible trouble over it. They kept saying 'you have no right to do this.' I nominated it anyway, and the State said 'yes'. Once it was on the Registry, then the residents were very proud to be on it and even bragged about it. I started preserving in 1976 when I asked the Council to take action to protect the horses. My life work is preservation and I am happy that it happened."

At this writing Ilse Byrnes is credited with preserving 13 historic homes and buildings in San Juan Capistrano. I was present at the ribbon cutting for the Egan House in 2016 which Ilse is credited for having gotten on the National Register of Historic Places (The official listing was January 26, 2017.) She was honored that day with a plaque acknowledging her important work. She is known in town as our "preservationist" and is highly lauded and honored for her local work, as well as her state-wide efforts to maintain trails for future generations. Ilse's impact on the future of California is undeniable. For the record, Ilse rode her horse on the trails well past her 90th birthday.

I love Ilse's concluding statement: *"Preserving homes and buildings just goes hand in hand with horses and preserving our lifestyle."*

During those contentious growth years, when our family first came to town, the blue print for San Juan was being sculpted to allow it to bloom into the vibrant small town that we have today. In the 70's and 80's, (while my husband, Ken Friess, served four back-to-back terms on the City Council,) protecting San Juan's ridgelines, open space, as well as agricultural preservation, were hot issues. Ken explained that the battle to save the ridgelines from development would have probably been lost "had Ilse not been working so hard to preserve old buildings and open space. She was a vital force to achieving those goals."

Ultimately, it was through a political exchange, that both objectives were accomplished. In 1976 City fathers adopted an Agriculture Preservation Program that was designed to preserve 220 acres of active agricultural operations. In order to gain unanimous support for agricultural preservation, Council members agreed to General Plan and zoning measures that would protect the ridgelines forever. Eventually, in the years that followed, although agricultural operations disappeared because of industry changes, approximately 120 acres of former agricultural lands would be purchased through Open Space

Bond measures approved by more than 70% of the voters, and would be protected as open space into perpetuity.

As the City was working hard to preserve open space, America was celebrating its bicentennial, once again reminding the residents of San Juan Capistrano about the importance of their heritage. An **American Freedom Train** toured the U.S.A. with a special exhibit of Americana. Each train had its own special red, white and blue paint scheme and its own itinerary and route around the continental United States. The 26 car train carried more than 500 precious pieces of Americana, including George Washington's copy of the Constitution, the original Louisiana Purchase, even Dr. King's pulpit and robes, as well as replicas of Jesse Owens' four Olympic gold medals from 1936. The tour lasted from April 1, 1975 to December 31, 1976. More than 7 million Americans visited the train and millions more stood near the tracks to see it go by. The train traveled to Southern California and the crew spent Christmas 1975 in Pomona decorating the train with a large Santa. For 1976 the train traveled from Southern California eastward through Arizona and beyond. (American Freedom Train *Wikipedia*). The hype for the big event had the school children in San Juan in a state of exuberant anticipation. On the actual day the train stopped in our town, hundreds of us gathered at the Depot. It was a moment in history to remember, and underscored the deep commitment the townspeople hold toward protecting our traditions.

Community Support for Stables

As the City looked to building more soccer fields, the subject of the stable created on City land next to Cook Park, subsidized through a low cost lease, (a result of Ilse Byrnes' work) came up for consideration. Should the City renew the stable's lease or turn the property into an extension of the park? Ken thought having a public hearing on the subject was in order. A meeting was called. The neighbors in the homes adjacent to the stable spoke up. Ken and his fellow Council members were astounded when a large contingent of neighbors overwhelmingly asked the City to extend the stable's lease. "We like for our kids to be able to look at the horses." "We enjoy the rural feeling of having horses nearby." "We want the horses."

The council extended the lease and Mission Trails Stable is still operating today, in 2018, as a reasonably affordable place for local residents to keep their horses.

Residents want the stables

Another issue was rearing its head around 2004 regarding water run-off and the stables. Federal Water Quality Regulations threatened closures to stables near water ways. City Engineer, Ziad Mazboudi, organized a task force to study the problem which included both private and public entities from Orange and San Diego counties. It included Dr. Julie Ryan Johnson, President of the San Juan Capistrano Equestrian Coalition, Patty Harris, owner of Rancho Sierra Vista Stables, Parks and Recreation Commissioner Ilse Byrnes, and others. (Please refer to the text box for full membership.) The result of the task force was a document entitled: "Equestrian-Related Water Quality Best Management Practices." Those guidelines became the standard for water management as related to stables. However, pressure continued to build regarding the City's adherence to the federal watershed regulations. The concern, once again, was the run-off of contaminated water from the stables into waterways. In 2008, Councilman Sam Allevato, an equestrian himself, considered the concerns of the City's Engineering Department. He requested that the Mayor, Joe Soto, with the Council, appoint a subcommittee to study the subject.

The Equestrian Subcommittee was formed, including stable owners, residents, and City staff. It consisted of eight members and was led by Sam Allevato. The members were Dr. Lon Uso, former Mayor Ken Friess, Kathy Holman, Joyce Hoffman, Patricia Harris, Ron Hanson, and Planning Commissioner Ginny Kerr. The goal of the subcommittee was to review the City's existing Land Use Code regarding equestrian stable standards and make written recommendations to the City toward regulatory improvements. The earlier water quality document was relied on heavily. The job of the subcommittee was to focus on horse density standards, building set-backs, water management, water quality, stable sanitation, and more. The end result was a plan to ensure the equestrian way of life continues as a cherished and essential part of San Juan Capistrano.

The committee drafted specific recommendations which were sent to City staff for input from the City Attorney and put into a legal format for consideration by the City Council. Recommendations and standards were implemented, and the stables were allowed to continue provided they conformed to the guidelines. For a decade the stables were generally free from major water quality issues. At this book's writing, several stables are again struggling with *new* water quality challenges launched by the

"Coastkeepers" an environmental protection non-profit. Because of economic and land use issues, the fight to continue offering affordable stables is still an issue. Since 1984, 28 stables have closed in Orange County. At this writing, stable owners and concerned professionals continue to hold monthly meetings as the Equestrian Coalition, organized by veterinarian, Dr. Julie Ryan Johnson. The goal of the group is to resolve current challenges and to conform to legal watershed standards to ensure the continuation of equestrian life.

John Berney, the current Coalition President, recently addressed the City Council to inform them of upcoming fund raising events to bring awareness of the need to protect our horses, as well as to raise monies to that end. Mr. Berney shared with the Council the activities which the Coalition was sponsoring to celebrate the upcoming Kentucky Derby Day, May 5, 2018, which included a "Fancy Hat" contest, showing the live television coverage of the big day in

Equestrian- Related Water Quality Best Management Practices Contributors: Joe Ames, City of Laguna Hills; Matt Rayl, Serrano Creek Ranch; Julie Ammel, USDA natural Resources Conservation Services, San Diego County; Tom Anderson, Equestrian Coalition of Orange County; Robin Borders, Cinnabar Ranch; Ilse Byrnes, Parks and Recreation Commissioner, City of San Juan Capistrano; John Carrol, Rancho Sierra Vista Equestrian Center; Dean Daggett, Camp Cookie; Vincent Fortuna, Leisure World Stables, Laguna Woods; John Frank, Camp Cookies; Whitney Ghoram, San Diego Regional Water Quality Control Board; Kim Gould, Las Vaqueras; Patty Harris, Rancho Sierra Vista Equestrian Center; Karen Hauptly, County of Orange; Leigh Ann Howard, San Luis Rey Downs Thoroughbred Training Center; Cookie Hubbs, Camp Cookie; Jason Jackson, USDA Natural Resource Conservation Service; John Loerfscher, City of Orange; Steve Mayville, Santa Ana Regional Water Quality Control Board; Andrea Richard, County of Orange; Erica Ryan, City of Rancho Santa Margarita/City of Los Alamitos; Dr. Julie-Ryan-Johnson, President of the San Juan Capistrano Equestrian Coalition; Mike Settipane, Leisure World Stables, Laguna Woods; Sandra Verrall, City of Laguna Woods; Kathy Weldon, City of Encinitas

Louisville, and a special screening at the Regency Theater of the film *Dark Horse* after the race. He also invited the community to a regulation Chili Cook-Off to be held at the Swallows Inn. John explained, "All proceeds to fund the San Juan Capistrano Equestrian Coalition will be used to preserve and enhance our equestrian lifestyle and industry in San Juan."

Stables are a Mainstay of Equestrian Life

San Juan's commercial stables are the mainstay of its equestrian life. Perhaps one hundred horses are stalled in backyard barns. The bulk of the horses in town are housed in eight professional stables which serve approximately 2500 horses. Hundreds more come to town for big special jumping and dressage events at individual stables and the Rancho Mission Viejo Riding Park at San Juan Capistrano. Equestrian activity is an important economic engine for San Juan. Competitors and their families, judges and support personnel, fill up hotels and restaurants, and frequent local businesses as they purchase supplies for their sport.

The stables allow private residents not only a place to keep their horses, but a place for children and adults to learn how to ride, how to rope, barrel race, how to jump, and the art of dressage. English as well as Western riding lessons are available for beginners or competitors. The many trainers provide opportunities for both horses and humans to become more skilled.

Community Trails Committee

Another important community group working to protect the equestrian way of life was the Community Trails Committee. Councilman Sam Allevato, Renee Ritchie and Shelly Barker were among the organizers. Across the years, some of the Community Trails Committee members also served on the Parks, Recreation, Youth and Senior Services, Trails and Equestrian Commission, the San Juan Capistrano Equestrian Coalition, and as board members for Las Vaqueras Women's Riding Group. Renee Ritchie explained that the Community Trails Committee advocated for the equestrian staging area at Reata Park and was responsible for getting the pens at the San Juan Hills Golf Club where equestrians could corral their horses while stopping in for breakfast or lunch.

Renee Ritchie and Her Beloved Horse, Rosalyn

One of the accomplishments of the team of Renee Ritchie, Jana Adams, Shelly Barker and Julie Ryan-Johnson was naming and describing the trails. For many years there was a Virtual Trail Tour on the City's website explaining the characteristics of the many different trails and their level of difficulty. It was taken down because some of the trails described went through private communities and there was some push-back from those communities.

Ortega Equestrian Center

I had the pleasure of talking at length about horses with Ortega Equestrian Center's owner, Kathy Holman. Some thirty-six years before, she worked as the Center's manager. In the early days, her sister Dee Dee Gates and brother-in-law, Brad Gates, developed the Center. That was in 1982. For ten years Kathy was the manager, until her sister and brother-in-law opened Creek Side Stables, Blenheim, in 1992. At that time Kathy and her husband, John, were able to purchase Ortega Equestrian Center. It is a fully certified training and events center. During my conversations with Kathy, I observed the life of the center buzzing around me. I noticed several eager young women grinning, as they followed their leader and walked past me, joyfully anticipating their time with the horses. In the main arena I saw a trainer coaching a client. In another corner, horses were being groomed, and still others were being tacked up. I felt a warm vibe spilling across the air, just by being there. I discovered that many different kinds of groups come for "horse therapy," from the faith based, to those in homeless shelters, to special needs people, to people in recovery, and many others.

Stable Friendly San Juan Capistrano

Among Kathy's many important activities is the founding of a volunteer California non-profit horse rehabilitation program called "Otra Mas," [meaning 'another one']. As president of the organization, she and the group raise funds for medical treatment for aging performance horses that would otherwise be put down. One such horse is Demi, a former champion on the cow working circuit. When severe arthritis attacked her ankle, veterinarian, Mark Secor of Mission Equine Hospital, volunteered his surgical skills to implant a bone plate and screws into her ankle. Otra Mas raised the funds for Demi's medication and maintenance. Demi went on to have a career at Ortega Equestrian Center as a therapy horse. Family therapist, Carol Caddes is working with her clients through Otra Mas to help them deal with emotional issues. By connecting with a horse, many clients are able to stay grounded in the present.

> **Stables operating in 2018:** J.F. Shea Therapeutic Riding Center, Sycamore Trails Stables, Ortega Equestrian Center, Mission Trails Stables, Rancho Sierra Vista Equestrian, Tar Farms, The Oaks and Blenheim Farms. Many professional trainers work at these centers, and Rancho Mission Viejo Riding Park at San Juan Capistrano hosts important riding events.

As we talked about how Kathy came to spend her life among horses, I learned that as a small child, she too, was enamored with Hopalong Cassidy. At a young age she was allowed to walk to a nearby neighborhood stable on Camino de Estrella in the Palisades area of Capistrano Beach, where Steinmart and Whole Foods are today. There, she earned the right to sit on a horse by brushing it. That was great fun and only whetted her appetite for more contact with horses. Her military father was stationed at Camp Pendleton, which gave her access to a string of riding horses at the base. For a few weeks one summer, she was staying at a Major's house near the stables when, during a trail ride, a horse bit her on the leg. She kept the bite a secret, fearing that she would not be able to continue the ride. Later that day, the Major's wife saw the deep laceration on her leg. The Major had to report the injury to the Colonel, who was Ace Bowen (who also founded the Padre Junipero Serra Riders now known as Las Tortugas, a men's riding club). The Major got into a lot of trouble with his wife for allowing the injury to happen! I enjoyed her interesting youthful story, and was surprised, when suddenly, she reached down and lifted the fabric on her pants and showed me the scar. I nodded in agreement, understanding that she was allowing me to be privy to her triumphant badge of courage!

Neither bites nor scars would deter her great enthusiasm for riding. As a teen, she worked at Luigi's Restaurant, which today is where the Denny's across from Doheny Beach is located. The goal was to save money to buy her own horse. Finally she was able to purchase a half Arabian/ half Quarter Horse, mare named Pepper, from a man at Rosenbaum Ranch for $125. To visit Pepper, she had to ride her bike from her home in Capistrano Beach across the valley to the Rosenbaum Ranch. For just $35 a month, Pepper grazed on the lush irrigated grasses in the two- acre pasture. She found a cheaper pasture that appealed to her small budget. For only $20 a month a horse could graze on a large open range, where the

Kathy Holman Founded Otra Mas to Save Aging Performance Horses. Courtesy *The Capistrano Dispatch*

Mission Hills Ranch development is today. Smiling, she said, "But, if I had kept her there, catching her would have taken too much time. I had to bike home before dark; and I would not have had as much time to ride."

Another favorite horse story Kathy shared was the time when long-time cowboy, Dusty Otero's horse decided to take matters into his own mouth. It seems that one night Dusty rode his horse home to his house in the Mission Terrace tract (the homes across from Ambuehl School). It was late, so Dusty just put him in his back yard. Apparently those accommodations did not meet with the horse's approval, because he maneuvered the gate open, picked the grain sack up by his teeth, and headed across the Creek. Kathy discovered him the next morning at her stable, grain bag and all. Later, when she saw Dusty, she exclaimed, "Dusty, that horse wants to live here!" The horse had the final word.

As we talked about old time horse stories, I realized that Kathy had spent time at Camp Pendleton in the stables and I wondered if she had met our famous equine war hero, Staff Sergeant Reckless. I asked about that. "I did meet her. She didn't really look like much, but the amount of respect she garnered by all who came near her left a big impression on me. I was a young girl, but I knew reverence when I saw it. I'm proud that I got to meet her."

It was time for Kathy to get back to her horses and for me to continue to think about the huge positive impact the stables and trainers have on the community. Driving the mile back to my home, I recalled something Ken had shared with me. "Donna, our friend Bruce Taterian, who lives in Hidden Mountain, is not a rider, or a horse man at all, but he told me he just loves looking out of his windows to the horses at Tar Farms. They give him great pleasure just seeing them." The horses offer our community something intangible, perhaps something magical.

By far my biggest take-away from my time with Kathy is that she is a truly remarkable woman. She is outstanding in so many areas, yet remains humble. On top of everything else I learned about her, she also rescues horses! She says, "I have too many horses." I am certain that not one of them is going to go without breakfast. I am deeply impressed by Kathy's strength of character, her compassion toward her clients, her friends, her horses, and her devotion to the preservation of the equestrian life-style in San Juan Capistrano. It takes a massive effort on the part of many, as we have seen, for horses to continue as a mainstay of tradition in San Juan. Kathy Holman is at the center of that effort.

Chapter Nine

Dreams Grow to International Renown

"There is something about the outside of a horse that is good for the inside of man."
(Will Rogers and Winston Churchill)

Recently, my friend, Christine, and I were chatting as our horses ambled along the trail adjacent to The Oaks Stables. It was a spring day and the occasional bunny would dart in front of us, all the while; the horses were keeping a hopeful eye toward the fresh bamboo growing recklessly along the edge of the trail. As we clomped by The Oaks Farms home development, Christine started laughing. "Donna, do you remember a few years back when the food truck arrived here every day in time for the construction workers' morning break? It always sounded that really raucous race track bugle song, the call to line up at the starting gate?"

Becoming more animated, she settled into her memory. "I was riding Mr. T (Our former race horse, once known as "Short Timer") when that loud bugle sounded. As the ancient memory overcame him, he'd raise his head up as if to say, 'Whoa…' With ears perked to attention he'd start prancing. Then he'd begin tossing his head, maybe looking around for the others heading to some long ago starting gate. I swear, he'd shed about twenty-five years and he'd strut all the way back home!" She paused for a long beat. "He was such a wonderful guy."

Sharing the sweet thoughts, I responded, "I do. It was also a bit scary as we worried that a few more bugle trumps and he might have run off with you!" We didn't say anything for a long while, visualizing a sprightly Mr. T. We both missed him as he'd crossed the Rainbow Bridge in July of 2017.

Joan Irvine Smith's Horse Farm

Later that day, once again at home working on this story, I thought about The Oaks and the remarkable accomplishments of its owner and founder, Joan Irvine Smith. This led to my ruminations about another woman whose vision, too, has left a timeless legacy in San Juan. This woman arrived a few years before Joan, and our story would not be complete without telling about both of them. Both have changed the face of San Juan.

Fran Joswick and The J. F. Shea Therapeutic Riding Center

In 1978, Fran Joswick, a social worker, brought her vision to a rented open space by Trabuco Creek. She had been learning about the nascent therapy using horses known as "hippotherapy." As a rider herself, this new kind of therapy inspired her. She dreamed of helping disabled people in a new way. She had been working with a young boy, Michael Lewis, who was born with cerebral palsy. Together with the boy's parents, Derek and Nancy Lewis, she decided to pioneer with this cutting edge hippotherapy. With the Lewis' funding and Fran Joswick's skills as an equestrienne, they embarked upon a journey. They began a therapeutic riding program. It was a humble beginning. In addition to Fran as the instructor; they had one horse, one rider, two volunteers, two trailers and one port-a-potty.

Dana Butler-Moburg

Dana Butler-Moburg took over as Director of The J. F. Shea Therapeutic Riding Center more than twenty years ago. Back then it consisted of two construction trailers, a dozen pipe corrals, an old tack shed, a dirt lot and a small arena. Even though the beginnings were humble, it was a vibrant place, where magic happened. They had eighty clients and ten program horses. Dana had worked for the American Heart Association as Director of Communications. She did fund raising and development for them. Early on, at the beginning of her time with them, she had seen an advertisement for Director of the Fran Joswick Therapeutic Riding Center. She was interested, but she was too late, the position was filled. Seven years passed before she once again learned that the Riding Center was looking for a director. This time success was hers! She explained, "I feel called to this work. The universe had me learn all the things I would need to know, and then I got to put them to work. My work at the Heart Association was a tremendous boot camp for me. It taught me so much. This work at The Shea Center allows me to combine my love for non-profits with my love of horses and children. It is a perfect fit."

Shea Center

Forty years later, from its meager beginnings, the Center has blossomed into one of the top five such centers among 800 Professional Association of Therapeutic Horsemanship, International (PATH, Intl.) centers in the U.S.A. The J. F. Shea Center is a state-of-the-art facility with covered arenas and classrooms. Th Center services more than 1100 clients, both adults and children. The Center's name was changed from the Fran Joswick Therapeutic Riding Center to The J.F. Shea Therapeutic Riding Center when the national developer, The J.F. Shea Company, Inc., donated the ownership of the organization's eight-acre property that it currently occupies.

Across Dana's tenure at Shea she has been privileged to have taken the Center through the transformation stage to become the world-class facility it is today. It is supported through philanthropic donations and a huge team of volunteers. Volunteers log in 31,000+ hours per year working with clients and the 23 highly trained therapy horses. The philanthropic support comes not just from the equestrian community, but from the larger community as a whole. "Our world is so much stronger for the support of our many families and partners. Local supporters include: The O'Connell Family, the Gilbert Aguirre Family, Rancho Mission Viejo, the Klein family, The Rotary Club, veterinarians Richard Markell, Mark Secor, and Julie Ryan-Johnson, Olympic jumping coach Robert Ridland, and many local horse professionals. The stable owners, Patty Harris, Kathy Holman, Mark and Molly Talla, and Ron Hanson, have also been good friends to the Center. So many people help to support us."

A year or so ago, I was present at one of the Center's gala BBQ performance events. I still get goose bumps when I think about the dozens of adorable children walking, and gliding in their wheeled chairs past us, many with joined hands as they strolled by, singing. I pushed back tears, as their lyrics thanked the donors for their support. It was clear, looking into those sweet grinning faces, the triumph they felt; little boys and girls, some with autism, some with physical limitations, and others with a variety of learning disabilities. They were jubilant! Their pride was written across their faces. I could feel their sense of newly-found independence and mastery.

Courtesy of J.F. Shea Therapeutic Riding Center

Earlier, in addition to the children showing their equestrian skills in the large arena, there was a featured rider. He was Kevin Whitney, a Navy veteran, who had sustained a spinal cord injury in a skydiving accident. After two and a half months of in-patient care, he returned home in a wheel chair. He had lost the use of his legs. He came to The Shea Center in a wheelchair and left walking. In the videotaped testimony played later in the evening, Kevin explained that when he got on the horse, connections were made between his brain and his hips. He said, "I felt tall again."

As he continued a rigorous workout routine on the horse, he began to rebuild the circuitry to his legs. "I felt so independent and strong…I felt a surge of my confidence coming back." Smiling for the camera, the young man, concluded, "I got here in a wheelchair and I am now running." Today, he is married and has just welcomed his first baby. He is headed for a business degree at Chapman University.

During another visit to The Shea Center, I was privileged to watch a demonstration by two Shea clients working on horses. The first was a six year-old boy named Reid. He executed multiple turns around the arena, both walking, trotting, and stopping his horse, "Rushmore." His mother explained to the listeners that when Reid was three years-old he was diagnosed with Autism and ADHD. They struggled to find a sport for him. When he began on the horse, he "could barely hold himself up." She explained. "He has motor delay. Now his fine motor skills have improved, just working holding the reins has helped him to better hold a pencil. He is happy to be here and our entire family has a positive outlook." Next the physical therapist explained that hippotherapy is a three dimensional movement in the pelvis; the gait of the horse is used as a physical therapy tool because the horse's movement replicates the back and forth, side-to-side movement of humans as they walk. As the movement of a horse replicates the human walk, the rider's hips are rotated up to 3,000 times, in a 30-minute session, building core strength and balance.

The next demonstrator was Mary, a 70 year-old woman, who walked around the arena on her horse (with side walkers supporting her.) She told the audience that she suffered from multiple sclerosis and has been scooter bound for some time. In her words, "the world has been looking down at for me. During physical therapy, here at the Center, we have been working on my muscle strength. Through 'gentle' persuasion, the therapists have gotten me up on this horse, two other times. I am in a pilot program using hippotherapy for multiple sclerosis, trying to improve my strength and balance. It really makes a difference. This is my third time up on the horse. I love that I can look at you, eye-to-eye!"

The Shea Center is proud to consistently earn premier accreditation certification from PATH, Intl., and draw interested professionals from across the globe. It is a world class hippo-therapeutic center, and an institution which enriches our City.

"Horse of the Year" - Rushmore
Eileen Caldwell

During that same visit to the Center, I asked Eileen Caldwell, Editor and Community Relations Associate for one of her favorite "horse" stories. She shared this:

"Rushmore" is a favorite horse in The Shea Center barn. Born in 2008, "Rushmore" arrived at the Center at the age of 18 months as a gift from The American Gypsy Horse Angel Foundation. He is calm and extremely well behaved, qualities for which this breed is known.

A black and white Gypsy Vanner gelding, "Rushmore" is gentle, easy to work with, and loves people. His even temperament and wonderful gait make him an outstanding horse for the quality of the treatments provided to the children who ride him. The physical, occupational and speech therapists design many treatment plans utilizing the horses' movement to help clients make progress.

At 13.1 hands tall, "Rushmore" is small, yet sturdy. He is versatile and can carry a variety of small and large riders. Some riders need constant hands-on assistance and corrections to stay in position on the horse; "Rushmore" stands perfectly still during the adjustments. He also has a lush mane and tail, which helps many of the kids who have sensory processing issues. Children love grooming him, especially braiding his long flowing mane and brushing his feathers (the long hair on his lower legs). This activity becomes part of their therapy treatments at Shea.

In 2017, the Center's staff, volunteers, and clients chose "Rushmore" as "Horse of the Year." He is a valuable, patient, and loving partner to our many clients.

Dr. Carol Daderian

When I asked popular San Juan dentist, Dr. Carol Daderian, former Rotary Club President, for her horse experience, she vehemently replied, "Oh no! You don't want to hear about my one experience. Oh no! It lives in infamy!" Well of course I did. She explained that it happened when the Shea Center was giving a thank-you tour to the Rotarians for their donation. The tour included the classrooms, meeting Emerson, the therapy dog, and then the riding arena. At the ring, a smiling young girl, arrived in a

Rushmore - Shea Center Horse of the Year

wheelchair, and then proceeded to demonstrate a perfect exhibition around the arena. She was in complete control of her horse. Carol explained they were told that when the young girl arrived at the Center, that she was permanently wheelchair bound. No one expected her ever to walk again. Carol observed that upon completing her ride, the girl got down from her horse and she *walked*. It was inspirational.

However, that was not to be the end of the demonstration! Someone in the Rotary group suggested that the President, Dr. Carol, also take a spin around the arena. Carol reiterated, "It was not a pretty sight; it's a day that lives on in infamy!" She paused, took a deep breath, and began. "It was ugly. I got up on the horse with the Shea volunteers supporting me on either side. With each forward motion of the horse, my terror intensified. I was wobbling from side to side and holding on for dear life. The volunteers walking along next to me, kept me upright in the saddle. Of course my friends were all laughing hysterically from the sidelines. I now call it 'Rotary Club president hazing'!" Laughing she added. "I'm never getting on a horse again!" She paused a moment longer, smiling, before adding, "Of course it was just the gentlest animal ever…"

Volunteers: Jillian Friess and Jacqueline Miller

The Center provides an especially appealing opportunity for high school volunteers. My granddaughter, Jill, very much enjoyed the two years she worked with the riders when she was in high school. Our friend, Jacqueline Miller, a San Juan Hills High School senior, has been working with a fourth grade boy, Tommy, for almost a year. She explained that the Center makes a policy of keeping the volunteer with a specific client. She says, "I have developed a real relationship with Tommy. Keeping that stability for the kids enables us volunteers to create a closer bond. This helps the kids even more. I am able to see his improvements as riding helps him feel more confident physically and socially." Jacqueline went on to explain, "I thought it was really amazing to make a difference in someone else's life and to be able to see—for myself, those changes."

The Story of Cash

As I learned more about the clients at the Center, I also learned about a very grand Quarter Horse named Cash. Dana told me this story. "He belonged to Ann Forster, and he was the sweetest horse. He came to live with us in his golden years. He knew the difference between disabled riders and others. He particularly understood one little girl with cerebral palsy. Her condition was very involved; she was wheelchair bound full time. Her muscles were very tight and she required a smooth walk. Cash seemed to know what she needed. Each day he would greet her by nuzzling her cheek. After their ride, he would again nuzzle her cheek and he then would nibble at her fingers. The horse and girl seemed to adore each other. It was heartwarming to see that special bond."

Cherylin Von Aldenbruck

Another talk I had for this project was with professional horse trainer Cherylin Von Aldenbruck with whom I have had a long friendship. She explained that, "one of the crowning moments in my life was helping paraplegic, Jerri Gardner, to become a qualifier for the Para-Olympics."

In Cherylin's words: "I became involved with the Center when I was asked to judge a dressage competition. The first competitor into the ring was Jerri Gardner, I knew her, but had not taught her. She had lost the use of her legs in a devastating car accident. I watched her on my friend Emma Cuzack's stubborn horse. Jerri was bareback on a pad with a vaulting surcingle that had handles. She was able to get the horse to move in ways that professional trainers with crops and spurs could not. Then out came Ken Granger, a 62 year-old former fighter pilot who was blind as he tested in dressage. Next came "Ziggy" Zigler, an 82 year-old blind man, also competing in dressage by depending on the sound of "living letters," people who called out letters so he would know where to ride the different movements. My jaw dropped open. It was so beautiful. This was a defining moment in my life."

During Cherylin's teen years, her brother had broken his neck. Through physical therapy and a miracle, he went from being a complete quadriplegic, to becoming an incomplete quadriplegic where he is able to walk. Cherylin, inspired by what she had seen of the disabled competitors' abilities, asked to help at the Center. Before long, she went from intrigued event judge to an active staff member under the leadership of the Center's director, Dana Butler-Moburg.

Cherylin began working with Jerri, who dreamed of qualifying for the Para-Olympic Riding team. Ultimately Jerri realized her dream and did qualify for the U S. Para-Olympic Equestrian team, and she did it on her own horse, "Simplicity Itself," also known as "Leah," a beautiful grey Irish Sport Horse." Qualifying was a major victory, although, due to illness, Jerri was not able to compete in the actual Para-Olympics, she has held this victory in qualifying close to her heart.

The many beautiful stories I heard at The Shea Center inspire me. They illustrate the multitude of satisfying ways in which a person can work with horses while helping others. Perhaps they model the best in us, serving others.

Ten Facts about the J.F. Shea Therapeutic Riding Center

1. **245 + riders each week. The youngest is two, the oldest is 98.**
2. **Physical and cognitive disabilities comprise more than 75 diagnoses seen each year.**
3. **Autism is the # 1 diagnosis; Cerebral Palsy is the # 2 diagnosis.**
4. **More than 75 cents of each dollar raised goes back to programs and services.**
5. **There are 250+ volunteers each week from the community and 13 different schools.**
6. **Every family does pay to ride at the Shea Center, and there is a financial program to help those families in need.**
7. **The annual expense budget is $4 million.**
8. **Benefits of the riding program: increased strength, balance, coordination and learning to speak.**
9. **There are 26 full time staff members, 16 part-time and contract staff.**
10. **We have a variety of horses, but the Quarter Horse is the most popular breed for therapeutic riding.**

Horse Country

Chapter Ten

One Woman's Vision Leads to World Class Outcome

"The nail supports the hoof, the hoof the horse, the horse the man, the man the world."
(Arabian Proverb)

A few years after Fran Joswick began her Therapeutic Riding Center, another influential woman brought her dreams to San Juan Capistrano. She is Joan Irvine Smith. She staked her claim on a property along San Juan Creek.

We met one afternoon during an American Cancer Society Relay for Life event at the Sports Park when she was honored for her service to the community. At the event, I presented long-time championship ultra-marathoner, Bill Ramsey, with a painting I had done of him. Understanding that I was an artist, Joan invited me for a visit at The Oaks. She wanted to show me some of the paintings in her plein aire collection. During my visit, we had an enjoyable conversation. She sent me home with a huge stack of books she had written. They are heavily illustrated with California plein aire paintings. I enjoyed looking through them and placed them on a book shelf. They sat there until recently, when at a San Juan Hills High School track meet, I met up with her son, Morton Smith. I asked him for some horse stories, old family anecdotes from his mother's horse days. He looked me in the eye, and said, "Donna, just look in her books!"

Joan Irvine Smith's Farm

That was all it took. The five books she had given me are a treasure trove of history, as well as a record of her accomplishments; and her life-time adventure with horses. I had known she was fascinating, but the books illustrated just how wide-spread her contributions have been.

In 2004, the California State History Museum in Sacramento honored Joan Irvine Smith as one of California's Remarkable Women. Her accomplishments on the State as well as the national stage are significant. Her testimony before the House Ways and Means Committee and the Senate Committee on Finance in support of the Tax Reform Act of 1969, helped to get the new legislation passed into law. Her personal tenacity in insisting on a master plan for the Irvine Ranch, resulted not only in the creation of a master plan, but also in her being the first woman to be named "Orange County Press Club's Man of the Year." She was instrumental in bringing the University of California campus to Irvine, as well as helping to save Crystal Cove for the public. She is credited as cofounder of the Children's Hospital of Orange and established the Irvine Museum. Her accomplishments are many. I encourage you to read her book, *A California Woman's Story*. (2006, Irvine Museum.)

The focus of this work, however, is on Joan Irvine as horsewoman. Growing up on the sprawling Irvine Ranch, the daughter of one of the wealthiest families in the State, I suppose she could have lived a life of leisured entitlement, instead she became an activist and a visionary. At a young age, as she followed her grandfather, James Irvine, around the Irvine Ranch she fell in love with animals, especially horses. She became an accomplished equestrianne. Her autobiography includes a photo of a favorite childhood mare named Donna. I, of course, appreciated Donna's presence in the beautiful table-top book written by Joan. Ultimately, Joan Irvine's devotion to horses would lead to the establishment of three world-class horse facilities. The 22 acre property in San Juan Capistrano is of interest here.

In 1985 with her mother, Athalie Richardson Irvine Clarke, Joan began acquiring the property that was to become her private equestrian training facility. In her autobiography, she states that The Oaks "is located directly across San Juan Creek from the Lacouague Ranch, the original site of the Mission San Juan Capistrano from 1776-1778. A beautiful oak grove on my property was once an Acjachemen Indian campground that existed centuries before the arrival of Portolá and the padres." (Smith, 2006, p. 127).

Joan applied herself to breeding horses. Her goal was the development of an American Sport Horse capable of competing against European horses. At the height of breeding production at The Oaks Farm, 50-60 American Sport horses were bred each year. Prior to bringing her equestrian operation to San Juan, she established two other equine facilities, The Oaks in Virginia and The Oaks Indian Hill Ranch in California. Over-all, her efforts have been recognized on a grand scale. Her sire, "South Pacific" is one of the most prolific Jumper sires in American history. The United States Equestrian Federation's leading Jumper Sire trophy is called the South Pacific Award in his honor. Joan's son, Morton believes that the first ten or so winners of the award were all offspring of "South Pacific", a feat unmatched by any other sire. Morton travels to Kentucky each January to present the award during the annual USEF conference. USEF is the United States Equestrian Federation, the national governing body for most equestrian sports in the United States. It began in 1917. He told me that, "the trip is a double blessing for me as I get to visit my father. He is Morton W. "Cappy" Smith, a 1991 inductee to the Show Jumping Hall of Fame." [He is a legend in the world of Jumping.]

In addition to "South Pacific's" recognition, Joan Irvine Smith is the recipient of the U.S. Equestrian Federation-Performance Horse Registry Silver Stirrup Leading Hunting and Jumper Breed Award. (Whew!) She has hosted equestrian competitions such as The Oaks Classic, an Olympic style grand prix jumping event, and other such competitions.

The Oaks became a booming enterprise. On several occasions, Ken and I were honored to be among her guests at events, dining under the shade of ancient oaks.

R. J. Brandes

One of the competitors at The Oaks was Katie Brandes. Joan became friends with Katie's father, R.J. Brandes, a horse lover from Argentina. R. J. and Joan became partners, putting on elite competitions as Oaks-Blenheim in the leased property which today is the RMV Riding Park at San Juan Capistrano.

The Oaks to Rancho Mission Viejo Riding Park at San Juan Capistrano

In 2011 Joan decided to sell the Farm and dial back her activities. In a newspaper statement at that time she said, "The Oaks in San Juan Capistrano has brought me great joy over the years and the creation of this lovely farm has been one of my greatest accomplishments." The bulk of the farm was sold to Bill Davidson who, at this writing, is just finishing the sale of the last three of his luxury, equine-themed homes. Mr. Davidson was the subject of a *Wall Street Journal Article:* "How One Developer Learned Not to Put the House before the Horse." The story explains how the boutique builder cleared the hurdles to develop the California site known as "the equestrian Capital of the West Coast." The houses could be built, but the horse training and breeding facility along the creek had to stay. (C. Kirkham, Aug 9, 2016).

The success of The Oaks, with its many competitive equestrian events, paved the way for an equine park that would achieve international stature. When the City of San Juan Capistrano used new Open Space Bonds to purchase and annex 132 acres of Rancho Mission Viejo holdings in 2010, a 40-acre parcel of that open space was set aside as a riding park. The park, known as the Rancho Mission Viejo Riding Park at San Juan Capistrano is adjacent to the former Oaks Farm, (the Davidson homes) and Blenheim Farms. The park was designed by world renowned course designer Robert Jolicoeur, and features a manicured grand prix field which stretches across a space of 500 feet by 900 feet.

Blenheim Equisports

The City owned Riding Park is operated by Blenheim Facilities Management. Blenheim Equisports is the entity that hosts the elite competitions. Melissa Brandes, Senior Vice President of

Marking at Blenheim Equisports, and eldest daughter of R. J. Brandes, talked with me to discuss the organization. During our telephone interview, she explained, that for the past 18 years, since 2000, Blenheim Equisports has hosted a variety of high level competitions. Those events include Olympic Trials. In addition to the San Juan facility, they also host competitions in Del Mar, California, and Las Vegas, Nevada. When I asked Melissa about Joan Irvine Smith's role in putting San Juan Capistrano on the map as an world class equine center,

World Class Events

she responded. "Joan has been a huge influence in bringing in elite competitions. We have named the main arena, 'The Oaks International Grand Prix Field' in her honor."

Melissa Brandes, as Blenheim Equisports, is partners with Robert Ridland, President of Blenheim Equisports. Mr. Ridland is a former member of the United States Equestrian Team. His career includes victories on four continents, including the American Invitational, the Grand Prix of New York in Madison Square Garden, and the Grand Prix of Switzerland. In addition, to his personal wins, he has been involved in the governance of the sport, including important board positions, and is an experienced course designer. He is the United States Olympic Coach for Show Jumping.

Today, the Riding Park, a result in part of Joan Irvine Smith's great vision, is a world class facility routinely hosting U. S. Olympic Equestrian Selection Trials, World Cup events, as well as jumping and riding competitions. The Riding Park is also home to soccer tournaments, dog shows, concerts, kids' camps, kids' riding lessons, barn dances, the RMV annual rodeo, and more. It is open to the public during events. There is currently a public perimeter trail in development.

On warm summer nights, upbeat strains of music stream in through our windows from the concert producers who rent out the venue. The Park is a highly used aspect of open space for the City of San Juan Capistrano. The Park's website describes it as "a hub of equestrian and other competitive sports throughout Orange County." Perhaps, that is an understatement. A hub for sure; on many weekends one can see hundreds of RV's, horse trailers, trucks, and cars parked on the decomposed granite parking lot next to the show fields, as families wait for the next event. The sheer volume of use which the Riding Park is enjoying, speaks to its importance as a valuable community asset. Dr. Julie Ryan-Johnson described the Riding Park as "hallowed ground in the equestrian world." Certainly its presence combined with the many stables and miles of trails, is why San Juan Capistrano is so often referred to as "the horse capital of the west coast."

Jumping Competitions
Hilary Powell

Recently my friend, Hilary Powell, and I took our golden retrievers for a hike. When we came upon an open field, we let the dogs run free and our conversation turned more serious. I had attended the Jumpers and Hunters competition at the Riding Park earlier in the week. I mined for more information about the actual competitions, knowing that her daughter, Allison Powell, now Dupont, had competed during her high school years. What I did not know was that Allison was a champion, having earned a four-year varsity letter through IEL, the Interscholastic Equestrian League. Her big 17 hand high horse [68 inches tall], "Willie-B-Jammin," took her through her high school career.

By scouring the Internet I have learned that there are three such California leagues and seventeen across the US. Youth from both public and private high schools compete through the League. She also pointed out that many young people also participate through private club programs, in addition to going through the schools. Hilary explained that it is a very demanding sport, requiring dedication and a lot of travel. A few days later, she emailed me the St. Margaret's Episcopal High School newsletter headlines and team photo. *"ST. MARGARET'S EQUESTRIAN TEAM FINISHES AS RESERVE CHAMPIONS".* "St. Margaret's Equestrian team finished the 2017-2018 Orange County Interscholastic Equestrian season as Varsity Reserve and English Novice Reserve champions." (4/20/2018).

Partial List of Southern California Interscholastic Equestrian League Schools: St. Margaret's Episcopal, Cathedral Catholic, J. Serra, San Dieguito Academy, The Bishop's School, Chadwick School, mater Dei, Unified Christian School, Peninsula HS, Tesoro HS, Thurston Middle School, Aliso Niguel HS, Canyon HS, Our Lady queen of Angles, Classical Academy, Capo Valley Christian, Ladera Ranch Middle School, Valley Christian HS, Laguna Beach HS, St Mary's, Saddleback Valley Christian, Corona Del Mar HS, Marina HS, Newport Harbor HS, San Clemente HS, Rolling Hills HS, Tarbut V'Torah, Fusion Academy, Serrano Intermediate, Rancho Santa Margarita Middle School, Waldorf School, Mission Viejo HS, Foothill HS, and many more.

Jumping Competitions
Allison Powell Dupont

Some time later, I had a chance to ask Allison about her years of competition and what it meant to her. She explained, "Riding horses is very different than playing a team sport. For me it really taught me patience and compassion. At the end of the day, you are riding an animal and the animal has given you the privilege of building a trusting and meaningful relationship with it. The years of competition were life changing for me."

Champion Allison Powell DuPont. Courtesy Allison Powell DuPont

Mechelle Lawrence-Adams

One warm April Saturday in 2018, I hiked over to the Riding Park to observe one of the jumping competitions from the sidelines. My research had brought me a heightened sense of interscholastic competition. I was impressed by the vast number of judges and stewards who were facilitating the smooth operation of the event. Multiple arenas were in use, sprawling across the 40 acre park. The quiet orderliness of it all, particularly interested me, so did the grace and dignity with which the youthful riders comported themselves. The rigorous practice schedule, and the demanding competitions, must empower the young competitors toward a heightened sense of self-mastery. Surely, the demands of a sport such as this yields a confidence and self-esteem which serves in the future. My friend, former City Planner, and long-time Executive Director of Mission San Juan Capistrano, Mechelle Lawrence-Adams, is the first to point out that for her daughter, Lisa Lawrence, the many years of competitions, and exhaustive training regime brought her a deep sense of self, and a confidence which is serving her well, as a university student.

In Mechelle's words: "My daughter Lisa Lawrence was humbly shaped by the San Juan Capistrano's equestrian community of trainers, grooms, and veterinarians, as well as being formed by the preparation for hundreds of rounds of competitions at the Riding Park. Lisa seemed to be born with a love of horses. When she was only three years-old I negotiated with her to wait until kindergarten to begin riding lessons. She rode in the Western tradition for five years and later, seven years in the Hunter Jumper discipline at Orange County Horse Show Association and Interscholastic Equestrian League shows (IEL). Lisa found deep joy and success in her emerging teen years as she thrived in the dusty show jumping arena.

While winning many champion ribbons during her time on the Dana Smith Show Team, Lisa learned how to work hard not only during the shows, but more, during both the preparation and clean-up times. Lisa "showed up for work" five to six days a week for many years to ensure that her horse was exercised, her tack was clean, and everything was in order for her furry partner. When classmates were at the mall, or having slumber parties, she was at the barn.

As a mother, I had a hunch that horseback riding would shape her, and so I supported it with my time and my funding. When Lisa approached high school she was given a choice of attending private school or having her very own horse. She took the horse. He was a faithful and valued friend during the sometimes challenging high school years of social and academic pressures. Despite all that, she never wavered in her commitment to her horse. As a mother, I was rewarded handsomely as I saw her master new courses and difficult jumping patterns that would, in one championship show, result in her having an arena named after her horse, "The Quito Arena," Lisa became a lettered athlete in the IEL, in public high school, and a featured champion hunter in *California Rider Magazine.*

Lisa also won something ephemeral, she learned how to take criticism and feedback in a healthy way, how to win gracefully and to lose kindly to good friends. She learned how to overcome serious fears as she "got back on the horse" after recovering from frightening falls, bucks, bites (too many to count), and changing circumstances, intense pressure, in wind, in rain or sun. She learned to love and care for an animal and to understand that love requires work every day.

I am awed by how the equestrian community shaped our now 19 year-old daughter. In San Juan Capistrano people like Dana Smith help raise our daughters to be the best of women through example. Equally, I am deeply grateful to the hard-working grooms who ensure our children's safety. Today, Lisa shines bright and confident as a successful costume design major in college. As a former show mom, it is critically important to me that as we celebrate the history of horses in San Juan, we celebrate how the San Juan Capistrano equestrian tradition shapes our children."

Champion Lisa Lawrence. Courtesy Mechelle Lawrence-Adams

Professional Horse Trainers

Going the Extra Mile
Kerilyn Stewart

I thought more about the important role of trainers. Last year, two of my high-school age granddaughters, Elizabeth and Emily, decided to learn how to barrel race. They took lessons with Kerilyn Stewart at Ortega Equestrian Center. One day, Elizabeth had ridden our horse, Dancer, over for her lesson. As evening fell and it was getting dark, she wasn't back yet. I began to worry. I started mucking the corral as an excuse to keep an eye out for her. After a while, I looked down the lane and saw her coming. Relieved, I was surprised to see that she was escorted by Kerilyn, who was not about to let a young girl ride alone for half an hour in the dark. I appreciated that Kerilyn went the extra miles (literally) for her students. When I asked her about her career as a trainer, she said, "I don't have words for what teaching these girls has meant to me. I wish I could keep teaching forever to work with these lovely young people. I have been blessed with a talent to connect with the students. It makes my life complete."

"Eesh, my brain!"
Molly Oehlert

As I was purchasing some bags of grain and pellets at American Horse Products the other day, I asked the woman helping me for a horse story. Molly Oehlert explained that she is a long time trainer at Sycamore Trails. "Oh I remember working with a four year-year-old girl who talked like she was thirty! I would get her up in the saddle and she would exclaimed, 'Eesh, my brain.' It always made me laugh. One day, I set her up on a particularly tall pony, more than 14 hands. She got up in the saddle and said, 'Uh oh! Something is wrong. Something is too high!' I fixed the stirrups and she had a nice ride around the arena. I worked with her for a long time and I always remembered her saying, 'Eesh, my brain.' It was so cute, coming from that little tiny girl."

Ron Hanson and Cherylin Von Aldenbrock

There was another occasion when our family needed horse help. About nine years ago Ron Hanson, owner of Sycamore Trails Stables, decided to give us a horse. Ron and my husband, Ken, had been friends for years, and Ken had asked Ron to keep an eye out for a new horse that I could ride. Ron's idea was to *give* us a beautiful horse.

It was a win-win situation. We got a big Quarter Horse mare named Lucky; a gorgeous paint with a serious leg injury that was not healing, and she got a roomy corral in which to recover. In Ron's words, "it's a good deal all around."

I smile at the mental picture of Ron riding up in front of our house on his horse, Big Blue, and right behind him followed Ken on Lucky. We were thrilled with the addition of this stunning animal to our family. Before long, her leg did improve, however the lounging about had caused her to become skittish. My young granddaughters were afraid of her, and she was a handful for me, plus she was hard to catch. We hired Cherylin Von Aldenbrock to work with her. I spent a good part of a year watching Cherylin stand completely still waiting for the stubborn Lucky to come to her. I admired Cherylin's patience, knowing that in no way could I have managed the patience to stand in the corral for those long stretches of waiting!

The routine was that once Lucky came to her, we would take to the hills. I would ride Mr. T while Cherylin drilled some manners into Lucky. During those months of riding, I came to appreciate the important role of the trainers at our local stables. Perhaps there are 100 of them. If not for their dedication, I doubt our equestrian industry would be as strong as it is. They are some of the unsung heroes working in the background to make it all happen.

Ron Hanson and his wife, Rowena, were pioneers in the development of commercial stables in San Juan Capistrano, and set a high standard for quality care and instruction. Ron is well known for his quiet philanthropy. My husband, Ken, who spends a lot of his time volunteering with youth likes to tell stories about Ron.

Ron Hanson and Ken Friess Bring Lucky

Ron used to drop in unannounced to visit at Ken's office near Vons on Camino Capistrano. Around 2007 Ken was telling Ron that he had started a youth wrestling program at the Boys and Girls Club the year before, and was trying to raise the money to buy a wrestling mat. The mat would cost $10,000. Mission Hospital had already donated $5000 toward the purchase. Ron got up, walked out to his car, got his check book and wrote a check for $5000. That mat is still in use.It turns out that Ron did a lot of good things for our community with that checkbook over the years, mostly unsolicited. Ron is the embodiment of the notion, "All for one and one for all." He exemplifies "Riding for the Brand;" his brand being San Juan Capistrano.

Jillian Meets Lucky - Gift From Ron Hanson 2009

Ron Hanson on Big Blue 2009

Chapter Eleven

Swallows Day Parade

"The horse with beauty unsurpassed, strength immeasurable, and grace unlike any other, still remains humble enough to carry a man upon his back." (Wise Old Sayings)

Within a year of moving our family to San Juan Capistrano, we joined the spectators lining the curbs along the downtown streets, eager to view the famous Swallows Day Parade. Our first time was in 1974. We had already fallen in love with the rustic little town, but the parade, billed as the largest non-motorized parade in the western United States, seemed an endless strutting of fabulous horses, and colorful marching bands. Our family was hooked.

Swallows Day

In the 1920's Father O'Sullivan began the celebration of the return of the swallows to the Mission on Saint Joseph's Day. As the years passed, a radio show was broadcast from the Mission which helped spread the word of the little flitting migratory song bird which showed up each spring from South America. There is a vintage photo exhibit currently on display at the Mission which shows a March 19, 1936 NBC Radio announcer Clinton Twiss with Father Hutchison in a live broadcast of Saint Joseph's Day and the return of the swallows.

The parade portion of the festivities grew out of a school carnival. The children wanted to ride their horses through town. As a tribute to the swallows returning to Mission San Juan Capistrano, Leon Renee wrote a song," When *the Swallows Come Back to Capistrano.*" It was released in 1940, with Bill Kenny and the Ink Spots. It reached #4 on the

March 1936 Clinton Twiss and Father Hutchison Announce St. Joseph's Day. Courtesy Mission San Juan Capistrano Archives

Former Mayor Sam Allevato on Blaze 2018 Parade

U.S. music charts. The same year, Glenn Miller also recorded it and it reached #2. In the years to follow it would become a favorite with other artists recording it as well. Swallows and San Juan Capistrano became household words across the nation, and the annual celebration continued to grow.

As the parade and collateral festivities grew, the City of San Juan Capistrano officially authorized the volunteer Fiesta Association to take the lead in planning all things for the celebration of Las Golondrinas. In March of 2018, the Fiesta de las Golondrinas celebrated its 60th year. This year the activity schedule included: Kick-off party held at Zoomars; The Fiesta Orientation and Membership Mixer; The Hairiest Man Sign Ups; Taste of San Juan at the San Juan Hills Golf Club; Kids' Pet Parade; El Presidente Ball at El Adobe; Fiesta Grande held at Swallows Inn; Frog Jumping Contest held at Mission Grill; Hoos' Gow Day held on the streets of town; all culminating with the famous 60th Annual Swallows Day Parade and Mercado Street Faire.

The parade itself is a grand spectacle encompassing two or more hours of equestrian showmanship, staged banditos skits, marching costumed Native people, dancing children, legions of clubs and groups showing off everything from over-sized dogs to miniature horses. The parade is a colorful, musical, spectacle. It has something for everyone, attracting huge crowds which fill the downtown.

Spectators begin saving vantage points early in the morning, laying down blankets and metal chairs. They come to enjoy the 120 floats and entries cruising through down town streets. Newspaper accounts for the 2015 parade put the crowd at 40,000 [that year attracted a larger crowd as Father Serra had just been canonized.]. Most years attract crowds more in the 20-30,000 range. (O. C. Register. Matt Fleming. 3/21/15).

As I collected horse stories from anyone in town who offered one up, many revolved around the parade. Former Mayor Sam Allevato smiled as he recalled riding in the parade with his Portolá friends and then doing a quick turn-around to join the Tortuga Men's Riding group. As he recalled this next incident,

Rick and Dan Friess in Pony Cart c.1979

he was chuckling, at the memory of his son, Sammy, who was with my son Danny. The boys were around age nine (nearly 40 years ago) when they had this big parade trauma. For weeks they planned to ride our pony cart in the parade as a "chuck wagon." Dan constructed a covering around the frame of the pony cart and attached pans and skillets to the sides for authenticity. On parade day, Sammy arrived at our home, and the boys drove the pony cart, aka chuck wagon, to the staging area which was behind the Mission inside the San Juan School grounds. Apparently, when our pony, Connie, arrived in the area with all the other horses and ponies she became "hyper frisky", as Sam put it. She took off running with the boys and the cart, causing the pans to bang together, adding to the pandemonium, spurring her on to running even faster, all around the staging area. As the boys struggled to take control of her, she lost the pans, skillets, the covering, and then finally, she lost all of the elements that made it a chuck wagon. When Sam and Ken arrived to check on the boys, they were sitting, reins in hand, on the seat of the cart with the most stunned and disappointed looks on their faces. Once the parade began, they stuffed away their great misery and bravely marched the headstrong Connie with the ramshackle pony cart in the parade. They put on brave faces, but those of us along the parade route who really looked at the boys' slumped shoulders and sullen expressions understood their great frustration.

Wagons and Horses Swallows Parade 2018

Native American's Pony Dressed for Parade 2018

2018 Heading to Parade. Rancho Viejo Road

American Cowgirls Pose Before 2018 Swallows Day Parade

Swallows Day 2016 Donna and Grand Girls

Emily and Ella Friess Swallows Parade 2018

John and Sherry Clifton – Cross Country Horse Race

I talked with John Clifton to refresh my memory about the cross-country horse races of the 1970's. John has explicit recall. As we chatted, his wife, Sherry, sat next to him, filling in even more details. This is their story.

It was in the mid-1970's when horsemen, John Clifton, and his pal, cowboy Jimmy Jackson recreated a San Juan tradition after the Swallows Day Parade by organizing the cross-country horse races in the creek, which were described earlier in this book. It began innocently enough with a huge barbecue at the Cliftons'. Neighbor, Don Shaw and farrier Jimmy Jackson were happy to pitch in. The men brought in five kegs of beer and five carnitas pigs. They roasted the pigs for twenty-four hours in a pit in the field

First Cros Country Race c. 1975

in front of John and Sherry's home. They invited the whole neighborhood. It was great fun. I recall filling my plate with succulent carnitas, rice and beans, served from an impromptu wooden plank functioning as the food bar. They were marvelous parties. The kids ran around playing tag and enjoying themselves, as the adults laughed and talked about the parade. John and Don hosted this pig roast for a few years, and each time the crowd grew larger. One year Jimmy Jackson had the idea, "Hey, since there is such a crowd, let's give them a friendly neighborhood cross country horse race."

135

The first race included about fifteen entrants who put up a fee, so the purse was about $250 for the winner. The riders raced down into the creek bed, across to the berm, headed east along the dike, and then turned back and dashed across the riverbed to the finish line. The race went well. Ken rode our horse, Windy, and took first place, and I was on our huge Appaloosa, Paiute, and came in second, with others strangling in behind us. The event was a big hit.

Because that first race was such a success, the next year Jimmy had the idea to invite more racers. He went around to all the stables, and tack and feed stores, putting up flyers about the race. I remember on Swallows Day, opening our draperies that morning, seeing our little hidden valley filled with horse trailers. There were trucks, trailers, and cars, parked every which way on any open dirt lot. Apparently, Jimmy's flyers attracted interest!

That year, riders trailered in from distances as far as Bonsall, and the Leisure World Stables. John recalls that about 30 riders lined up for that race. He said that some of them considered their mounts to be *real* race horses! The purse grew to over $600. This time, I was on Windy and Ken was on Paiute. For weeks before the race, Windy and I practiced every afternoon after school. Windy, being an Arabian, had racing in her blood; she started shivering with pleasure, each day when I just showed up at the barn. She burned to race. John and Sherry reminded me that Sherry and I also had a side bet which I had forgotten about. She challenged me. "Donna if you beat me. I will cook you dinner!"

In the 2018 version of that memory, John and Sherry tell me that Sherry thought the finish line was somewhere else and slowed down toward the end, while I galloped full speed ahead of her, to the actual finish line, winning the race. She did cook me dinner. I remembered that.

"John," I asked, "don't you remember, the look-out posted along the creek, was shocked that I was winning. Wasn't everyone?"

"No Donna. Not at all, we had all seen you ride!" He answered.

Hmmm. It's interesting how memory works. Across all these years, I thought everyone was surprised that I could beat real cowboys. Maybe the only surprised person was me! (I'm still surprised!)

Kids' Cross-Country Race

Our son, Rick, also found those cross country races to be important moments. Rick recalls that Jimmy also organized a race for the kids. In the weeks leading up to the event, Rick explained that the kids talked of nothing else. Rick said, "I

Hidden Valley Kids Head to Cross Country Race

trained Paiute for weeks. I was cocky about it, telling the other riders that Paiute would easily bring me a win. In those days, our valley had lots of young riders, many of whom were also practicing after school." Some of the others were not so inclined to believe that Rick's victory was a sure thing. At race time, Rick recalls, "I got to the starting line, and Paiute starting jumping around. I couldn't control him. I didn't even finish the race! I definitely learned something about the danger of bragging after that day!"

As my conversation with John and Sherry Clifton continued, they reminded me that the race got too big, and certainly, now, I realize, it also became too dangerous. Anyway, my victory day was also the end of the Hidden Valley Cross-Country horse races. It has gone down in our memories as one of the most special times, raising our kids and enjoying the neighbors, our big group of Valley kids, and of course, the horses.

The Hidden Valley Gang

John remembered that Dan and Mary Doyle helped organize all the Valley kids into an entry for the parade. The kids brushed their horses, donned clean pressed, long sleeve Western shirts and marched proudly in the parade. There was a big group of them, maybe 25. I remember sitting on the curb across from El Adobe when our mounted gang came by displaying a big banner, "Hidden Valley Gang." It's a sweet memory.

John had more to tell me about Jimmy Jackson's operation. "Jimmy kept a string of rental horses which intrigued the young Marines down in Pendleton. The Marines would come up from

Hidden Valley Kids c. 1970's

Pendleton and ride off on the horses. Ortega Highway wasn't so busy back then. The Marines would saddle up and cross down into the riverbed. Often times the horses, delighted by the water, would roll in it, and then head back up the hill to the barn." John was laughing when he recalled, "Many times the horses showed up without their riders! Eventually the young men

137

would be coming along, soaking wet, and out of breath from their hike up the hill. Life was more relaxed in those days. No helmets, instructions, nor guides," reminisced John.

Horses Ride through the Swallows Inn

Tony Moiso recalled some of his favorite parade moments. For many years the Ranch joined in the parade, riding on a big wagon filled with Ranch people. More recently the Portolá Riders represent the Ranch. When I asked Tony, if the story about Larry Buchheim riding his horse through the Swallows Inn during Swallows Day was true or not? He smiled and replied, "Yes, for sure. I rode my horse through there as well!" We laughed.

Later, I was to find a photograph of Tony on that horse in the Swallows Inn. When I asked for permission to use it, he offered me this advice, "Please remember: if you have the right horse-very calm, anyone can ride through the Swallows!" [I am amused at the notion that anyone might have of *me* riding my horse through the Swallows Inn. Well, maybe it's not that crazy, considering those cross-country horse races!]

Tony went on to explain that for some years, the Portolá Riders erected a big tent in the open field

Tony Moiso Rides into the Swallows Inn. Courtesy Tony Moiso

behind the Esslinger Building to house the after-parade party. One year a group of rowdy Marines came in to crash the party. Fred Love, who is not of large stature, confronted those Marines and got them out. Smiling at the memory, Tony concluded, "he is great, he'd fight if he had to!"

The parade has become an iconic symbol for San Juan, that celebrates the Mission, the swallows, and our equestrian life. The events surrounding La Fiesta de las Golondrinas are not only classic and traditional, they are also a way of binding the community together. While serving as a powerful economic engine, they are in many ways a cultural experience. People love parades, missions, animals, and just plain being together. An important by-product for our City is that when people gather they also spend money that supports the community's everyday economy.

Hidden Valley Gang - Swallows Parade c. 1970's.
Courtesy Hill Family

Hidden Valley Kids Swallows Day Parade 1970's

1982 Parade, Council from left, Tony Bland, Ken Friess, Phil Schwartze.

Donna and Ken Swallows Day Parade 1970's

Hidden Valley Kids Swallows Day Parade 1970's

Chapter Twelve

Rodeos and Adventures on Horseback

"Fortune favors the bold!" (Latin Proverb)

Sitting in the bleachers on a warm August day in 2017, I was watching the stunning Rancho Mission Viejo Rodeo. It is considered one of the richest two day Rodeos in the country with a purse totaling some $225,000. This rodeo, sponsored by the Ranch, has enjoyed 17 years of packed stands and eager crowds. The Ranch has been able to donate over $2 million to local charities over its long run. In my talks with Gilbert Aguirre and Tony Moiso of the Ranch, I learned that across the years, other rodeos sponsored by service organizations such as the Lions Club, have come and gone. Tony said that, "back when 'Uncle' Richard O'Neill ran the Ranch, he was asked, 'Shall we put on a rodeo?' He answered,

Uncle Richard O'Neill (Left) with Nephew Tony Moiso
RMV. c. 2000

'Sure why not, the rodeo demonstrates daily life on the Ranch. The value of the rodeo is that it shows kids what the Ranchos were about. It preserves our Western heritage.'" Tony concluded, "The Ranch is one of the last Ranchos left. It is still a cattle ranch, and it will always be, though avocados and citrus are grown as well."

Rancho Mission Viejo Rodeo

The RMV Rodeo draws the best competitors from across the world. The top 30 in each event compete for cash prizes. They hope to get to the grand prize at the Nationals Final Rodeo held in Las Vegas. The categories are Saddle Bronc, Bareback Bronc Riding, Tie-Down Roping, Steer Wrestling, Bull Riding and Team Roping. It is a much anticipated highlight in South Orange County. The marketplace attached to the rodeo is well attended and the post rodeo dance is a big draw.

Gilbert Aguirre

From my top row seat, I could take in the entire event. I was intrigued to see Gilbert Aguirre, Executive Vice President of Ranch Operations for Rancho Mission Viejo, and President and General Manager of the Rancho Mission Viejo Rodeo, proudly riding his horse in the ring. I knew that he had joined the Ranch in 1964. He is a man among men, a cowboy among cowboys. He won the Oscar of the ranching world, the prestigious Live Stock Man of the Year Award in 2015 given by the California Chamber of Commerce. The award recognizes leadership, achievements and professional service of an outstanding and deserving individual in California. Mr. Aguirre was honored at the Cow Palace in San Francisco during the Grand National Rodeo, Horse and Livestock Show Cattlemen's Day.

It was he who had seen to it that I was a part of the Portolâ Ride send-off. As I watched his strong

Gilbert Aguirre Cowboy Hall of Fame. Courtesy of University of Arizona

2017 Rodeo - Gilbert Aguirre

silhouette mounted on a big paint palomino horse, my thoughts drifted to an on-line newspaper story I had read about his bravery.

The year was 1969 and Orange County suffered a 100 year flood. I remembered canoes paddling down the streets of our tract homes in Huntington Beach. I had been worried that my son's preschool might be threatened as we lived near the Santa Ana River flood control.

Southern California had more water than it could handle, and the waters of San Juan Creek were no exception. The creek rose so high that it took out the bridge at La Novia, known then as the "Ganado Bridge." The creek was treacherous, with swiftly moving tree trunks and huge chunks of brush floating toward the ocean. That was the situation when Gilbert Aguirre learned that an infant was deathly ill on the Ranch, stranded by swift moving waters, which were impossible for a vehicle to cross. The child had to get to a hospital. Thinking only of saving the child's life, he mounted up, and carried her across the raging waters on horseback. He saved the child, got her to safety, and admitted later, "It wasn't smart."

He's that kind of hero.

Gilbert Aguirre - A Cowboy Among Cowboys. Courtesy of University of Arizona

During my interview with Mr. Aguirre, he shared many interesting aspects regarding the Portolá Ride and the Ranch, and not once did he let on about his remarkable life accomplishments. There was no hint from him that he is a highly celebrated and respected leader in the ranching industry. In 2013 he was honored by the University of Arizona as *Alumnus of the Year* for the College of Agriculture and Life Sciences. In the University's video honoring him, I learned that he was elected to the *Cowboy Hall of Fame Board*, and to the *California Rodeo Hall of Fame.* Shane Burgess, Dean of the College of Agriculture and Science at the University, described Gilbert Aguirre as "an innovator in the ranching industry with a passion to preserve the cowboy way of life."

As this book went to print, I learned from a friend that Mr. Aguirre was awarded an Honorary Doctor of Science Degree from the College of Agriculture and Life Sciences on May 11, 2018, by the University of Arizona. The University included a very long biography of accomplishments. This is excerpted from the information.

"Gilbert Aguirre is responsible for the daily land management of the 23,000-acre mixed-use-master planned community in Southern California. Rancho Mission Viejo is the largest family-held landholding in Orange County and is the last remaining cattle ranch in the region...He has participated in all major land-development decisions for more than 40 years."

Truly, the man is a legend, a great man. I am privileged to have had a chance to become acquainted with him.

Gilbert Aguirre Executive Vice President Rancho Mission Viejo

Lacouague Sisters

As I continued enjoying the rodeo drama playing out in front of me, my memory stayed for a minute longer on the idea of the rush of San Juan Creek during rainy seasons. One year my husband and oldest son floated down the creek on their surfboards. Another year, also with big waters, which was so unusual that it stayed in the memories of the Lacouague sisters, Denise, Michelle and Renee. They shared the memory with me. It was of one of their grandest horse adventures as they were growing up. It seems that a deep pond formed in the creek near the golf course. It was deep enough for the horses to swim across. The enthusiastic teens invented the sport of holding onto the tails of their horses as the horses pulled them, giggling and laughing, across the pond! Free rides! They were still laughing about it as they told it to me, decades later!

Quick Sand Traps an Arabian

I recalled one of my own riverbed adventures. It happened in the late 1970's, after the winter waters had stopped flowing. I was riding my horse, Windy, in the mostly dry creek bed when suddenly she stepped into an innocent looking sandy spot and became mired. She was stuck in a huge hole filled with something like quick sand. As it filled in around her legs past her knees, to her belly, I knew to get off, fast! This was decades before cell phones. I had no choice but to try to figure out how to get her out. I surveyed the five foot pit and considered my options. If I ran for help it would be too late, she would sink deeper into the pit, past her chest, and then even her lungs could fill with sand. I could see nothing to do but try to remain as calm as I could possibly be. I remember lying on my stomach, pulling on her reins and crooning to her. I worried that if she struggled, she would sink more deeply into the sand. I talked to her, forcing my voice into a rhythmic pattern as I kept a steady pressure on those reins, while digging as fast as I could. I dug, and dug, hoping it was enough. Over and over again I repeated, "You are okay girl, come on." I began to stand up to obtain more leverage. I pulled steadily, forcing her attention on me. I admit to feeling waves of panic washing over me, but I kept up what I was doing until I could see some movement at her front right leg, then her left. I backed up a bit and put more strength into my pull. Slowly she began to move forward and up and then somehow, she found a footing and managed to stumble out of the pit. As she shook herself off, I sat on the ground to catch my emotions. After a long while I mounted her again and we made our way home. Forever after, to this day, when I must cross a sandy place in the river, I do so with extreme concern! I have never written about that day before, but I also have never forgotten it.

Ginny and Ward Kerr Run into Trouble

My friend Ginny Kerr and her husband, Ward, were coming back from a nice trail ride one day. Ginny and her young horse had just crossed the shallow water of San Juan Creek east of the La Novia Bridge when she heard thrashing and splashing behind her. She turned around to see that her husband and his horse were in trouble. Ward was off the horse holding its head up out of the water; somehow the horse was stranded in a sink hole and was turned almost on its side. As Ward pulled firmly on the reins, he kept saying, "Don't quit on me! Don't quit on me!" He, too, was sinking into the deep sand as the horse struggled. Finally, he managed, somehow, to get himself out. He kept pressure on the reins until suddenly the horse lunged and caught its footing and just popped out. They were shaken up, and of course, drenched. Ginny and Ward walked their horses back home to the Ortega Equestrian Center, where everyone who saw them looked confused, as water dripped off Ward and his horse, and asked, had they been swimming!

Bucking Bulls

Still enjoying the rodeo, I turned my attention back to what was going on in the arena in front of me. A huge grey, and apparently very angry bull, was let out of his holding pen with a cowboy clutching the strap around the bull's waist with all his strength. As the bull bucked and ran, and bucked again, swiveled and charged, the young cowboy held tight with his right hand while his left remained raised above his head. The bull jerked again attempting to rid himself of the cowboy! The clock was ticking. The crowd held its collective breath. A few more bucks, and finally the bull managed to rid himself of the rider, but not until a good score had been earned for the competitor. The crowd exploded in applause as the mounted cowboys corralled the bull and managed to usher it into the pen across the arena. Whew! I thought about the danger of it all. Certainly riding horses cannot compare to bull riding, but still there is risk.

I continued to watch the spectacle of the rodeo, holding my breath during some of the most daring events. When it was over, my daughter-in-law, Jenny, four of her girls, and I, wandered into the Rodeo's Marketplace where we bought the girls tee-shirts with their favorite horse sayings on them, and I got a new cowgirl hat. It was a perfect day.

Round-up RMV. Courtesy RMV

Unforeseen Circumstances on the Trail

The next week my thoughts revisited some of the possibly unforeseen circumstances which can prevail when one is enjoying the horses. Ginny Kerr and her husband began boarding their horses at Ortega Equestrian Center in 2002 and she has seen a lot of drama regarding horses. One day she was returning to the Center from a ride and the stable people were yelling "Put away the horses. Get them into their stalls fast! There's a mountain lion on the prowl!" Ginny explained, "I observed the lion boldly walking along the berm next to the stable. He seemed to settle in the brush, but we could see his face. I was told that earlier he had stalked a youth and that one of the trainers grabbed the boy and locked him in a stall until it was safe to come out. The trails along the Creek and our center were held hostage by that lion for two weeks. Finally, Fish and Game officers were able to apprehend it, but it was considered too dangerous to be relocated and it was destroyed."

Ginny continued, "We had another such scare a few years later." She shared this with me.

"A lion was seen prowling around the river bed just east of the La Novia Bridge. The students at Ambuehl School were kept inside the classrooms for a few days until, finally a small Sheltie dog was able to scare the lion into a tree until Fish and Game officers tranquilized it. That lion was relocated."

By far the most frightening experience Ginny had to share for this book was the time in January 2014, after she had just gotten her five-year-old horse. She and Ward were walking their horses in the creek bed just east of the La Novia bridge, near the abandoned water pump, when suddenly her horse took off running and bucking. She stayed on until, with one of the bucks, she lost a stirrup and flew off the horse. The next thing she knew, the paramedics were loading her onto a stretcher and carrying her up the side of the creek into an ambulance. After two weeks of surgery for her fractured pelvis and sacrum, she was released to go home in a wheel chair. By then her concussion had cleared, but she could not put any weight on her injured leg for two months. She says, "I was never afraid. I just accepted this. I didn't worry at all. It was amazing to me that the good Lord was watching out for me. I do think it was divine intervention. I finally got back on my horse ninety nine days later. I knew if I didn't do it then, I never would."

> Becoming fearless isn't the point. That's impossible. Its learning how to control your fear and how to be free from it.

Apparently, a large bee or wasp nest was inside the old metal pump structure. We think my horse was stung between his back legs and that sure did set him off! "

I was sharing these stories with my friend Diana Schmidt and she said. "Oh I've got one too. "My friend Erin and I had gone out really early. As dawn was breaking, we were heading up the hill when suddenly her horse stopped. She said, 'Diana, she just won't go.' Being English I guess, I said, 'Well make her go!' After being stopped there on the hill for a few minutes, we noticed either the biggest bobcat you've ever seen or a mountain lion skulking by." Diana looked at me and in a knowing way replied, "The horse *knew...*"

These experiences reminded me of a situation that I observed early one morning. I was riding alone on the north berm of the creek. In the distance, I could see two people on horseback down in the creek bed with what I thought was a big hostile dog. I watched for a minute and became worried as a family with small children on horseback was approaching and would soon be upon them. It looked dangerous to me. I could see the dog was not restrained as it seemed to be going after the two riders. As my horse brought me closer, I realized that the big "dog" was actually an oversized coyote and he was aggressing on the riders. I saw them go up the bank on the other side of the creek toward safety, but the family was drawing closer. I sped ahead, and called and gestured for them to go another way. They heard me and turned toward me and came up to me on the berm. We were able to watch the animal for some time, until finally he headed out of the creek and up into the hills. It had surprised me that he was aggressive toward those two riders. It scared me, actually, and I kept out of there for the next few weeks. Those instances serve as a reminder that being out in nature on a 1500 pound animal does present certain risks. With all that said, we need to remember that part of the wonder of a place like San Juan Capistrano is our ability to share the natural environment with God's creatures.

Unforeseen Events Can Also Occur in the Riding Ring
Dan Almquist's Story

One evening in late June, I was chatting with San Juan Capistrano residents and horse enthusiasts, Dan and Lindsay Almquist. Before long the conversation turned to Dan's cane and his recent and most unexpected turn of events in the riding ring at Sycamore Trails. Dan shared this with me:

"On the morning of April 11th, 2018, I was riding our four year-old Quarter Horse, Socks. He was broke in Texas and bought to be a cutting horse. I purchased him with the intent of having an athletic horse that I could ride for the foreseeable future. I now know that a horse which is that young needs to be ridden every day by the same rider. I think he was broke hard and fast by a male rider. Hence, he still has issues with men. It's funny how horses and humans can have similar life experiences and carry those feelings forward as they get older.

I had been riding another one of our horses for the month prior to get her ready for a weekend trail ride. This was the first day I was getting back to training with Socks. He turned his back on me in the stall, but I finally got him haltered and saddled. After warming him up, I asked him to cantor. No spur, just my calf. He took off! It was like nothing I had felt before. When I tried to turn his head he started to crow-hop and then he went into full buck. After three or four bucks, I came flying off, right to left. We were riding counter clockwise in the ring, so my head was going straight for the rail. I landed two inches from the rail.

The rails at Sycamore are two-inch tubular steel. Two more inches to the left and I would now be in heaven with my Heavenly Father. I remember hitting the ground solidly and very hard. My eyes were open. I saw my left leg going in front of my face, like it was unattached to the rest of my body. It landed over my right leg. My body immediately went into shock. I knew my leg was toast. I told our trainer, who was also in the ring, to call the paramedics and then I called my wife. I was taken to Mission Hospital and put into surgery that afternoon. I had multiple doctors tell me it was the worst break they had ever seen. My femur was in nine different pieces at the top and splintered to the point of almost a compound break at the bottom. Five and a half hours of surgery was needed to put me back together. I now have a titanium rod down the middle of my femur. In addition, I have multiple screws, plates, and cables holding the bone in place. I spent 17 days in the hospital.

The hardest part of it all was seeing my kids so frightened, knowing that their dad was so badly hurt, and thinking what if I had been killed, and never saw them or my wife again. I wondered if they would have remembered me and know how much I loved them. It makes me cry even now.

My take-away from the experience is a reaffirmation that God is in total control. At any moment, our life on earth can be taken, so one must have trust in God and believe in something beyond this world. My priority to my family was hardened in my heart. I was humbled and I prayed long and hard about all aspects of my life, including my work in San Juan. I was affirmed and I left with a sense of peace. What does not kill you makes you stronger and more determined and resolute. I will not quit for anything."

True to his word, Dan was not about to quit. By Sunday June 24th, just over two months after the accident, Dan had a new horse, Casey, an 18 year-old mare. In the meantime, Socks, the dangerous one, went off to a new home. Dan shared this with me, "It was a big day today as I decided to get back in the saddle. It was a sobering reality. I need more time to heal." Clearly, Dan is a fighter and will have many years in the future to enjoy riding horses with his beautiful family. Dan's experience is a valuable lesson in not taking anything in life for granted, our families, nor our times in the saddle.

Dan Almquist, Back in the Saddle

Elaine and Liberty

As the research for this work was drawing to a close, I became more ardent in culling anecdotes during our morning rides from fellow riders on the trail. One such morning, my pal, Christine, and I met Elaine Holroyd on her handsome mount, Liberty, and she gave us two horse stories.

The first account was another quicksand story. This has become a dangerous recurring theme. She and Liberty were out riding in the creek and suddenly he was stuck in quick sand all the way up to his belly. She frantically began digging before Liberty became completely mired. She dug and dug. Finally she stood up and with a steady pull she kept telling him to come forward. Somehow, Liberty got a holding and climbed out. After that trauma, Elaine sat down to catch her breath, and Liberty, being the guy he was, ambled over to the brushes and began eating. He seemed quite unfazed by it all!

Another startling tale she shared was the day that she and her gal friend were out riding. Her friend was leading, when suddenly her horse spooked and turned around and collided with Elaine and Liberty. This freaked Liberty out and he took off. Elaine knew that her leg was injured from the collision. When Liberty finally stopped, she did not dare get off him. She was not sure her leg could stand her weight. During all this, her friend was thrown and landed in the dirt and her horse ran into the street, and then ran home to Tar Farms. It was scary for a while. Luckily, a Good Samaritan came by and grabbed Elaine's reins. He walked her and Liberty back to Tar Farms. The next day, realizing that, indeed, she needed to have an x-ray, she convinced her friend to go as well. When Elaine arrived at the ER, she said to the receptionist, "Victim Number One here now. Victim Number Two arriving soon!" Happily both were okay; no concussions, nor broken legs, but it was a horse accident that they would both remember for a long time.

As I said good bye to my new acquaintance, Elaine Holroyd, I knew that I had to follow up on her plans to use her mini horse in a program at Tar Farms for children learning to read. She had already explained that she marches in the Swallows Parade with the mini horses. I recalled seeing her. I thanked her for the story and got her contact information.

As I was riding away, a lady strode over to the horse and stated, "I can't see so well, but I just overhead your conversation about your book." I introduced myself. "Oh, I know you. I read about you in the newspaper. I live next door to Brad and Dee Dee Gates, I'm Brandy. I might not have a horse story, but I sure have a surfing story." She proceeded to tell us about surfing at the Trestles in south San Clemente, near the Western White House, which would have been during Nixon's 1970's days. She explained that armed guards shot at her. As she ran away and climbed over a barbed wire fence, she hurt her leg. With that she pointed to her leg and explained that she still had the scar! Her story wasn't really a horse story but the fact that she wanted to tell it to me reflects an eagerness to connect held by so many in a community like ours. It also reminded me of an experience my husband, Ken, tells about sneaking into Trestles to surf in 1958. This was before the Marines allowed it to become a State Park. He and two friends had hiked in from the highway with their surfboards. They had been in the water for about 30 minutes when a young Marine ordered them out of the water. Knowing their boards would be confiscated, they chose to wait him out, and refused to come ashore.

The Marine, who was probably not a lot older than they were, began shooting at spots near them as a warning. Not really sure how much danger they were in, Ken and his friends stayed in the water, and paddled about a mile north to a place called Cotton's Point (near where the Nixon Western White House would eventually be located). It was outside the Camp Pendleton boundaries. They hung out at the beach until dark when they walked down to the highway to their car. Sometimes I wonder how my husband managed to survive to old age given some of his many "adventures." But that is a topic for another book.

RMV Rodeo - 2017

Chapter Thirteen

Born Free – Horse Memories from the 1970's

"Horse sense is the thing a horse has which keeps it from betting on people!" W. C. Fields

As the population of San Juan began to expand, some of the new arrivals were young families who turned to the undeveloped forty-acre equestrian-zoned valley adjacent to the Lacouague Citrus Ranch. There were about twelve such families and they embraced the horse life-style with great zeal. It was known as Hidden Valley because when people asked where the homes in Hidden Valley were, the general response in the City was that they were in a valley hidden out by the Lacouague Ranch.

John and Sherry Clifton shared more of their favorite memories with me, and added to mine.

More John and Sherry Clifton Memories

As a long-time horse man, John Clifton, reminded me, there were about ten of the men of our little community (including Dan Doyle, Don Shaw, John Clifton, Ken Friess, Stan Griffith, and Bob Youngren) who each purchased a roping steer to keep over at Jimmy Jackson's horse operation. It was probably around 1975. Jimmy, a well known cowboy and farrier, had leased the range land that stretched across where the Hunt Club would eventually be built to what would someday be Stone Ridge. John thought Jimmy probably had about 600 or 700 acres and 90 horses. There was an old barn on the place (the former Belford property, perhaps Father Quetu's old horse barn?) The guys were all in, seeing themselves as ropers. They created a friendly competition, putting

John Clifton. Courtesy John Clifton

money in the pot for the winner of the roping contest.

One day Jimmy Jackson called the newspaper to tell a reporter that a famous trick roper was going to be in town named "Monty Clifton." When the reporter showed up to grab the scoop, John Clifton had to confess that it was a prank, he was neither a famous roper, nor named "Monty." John says to this day, 40 some years later, many of his friends call him "Monty." Many don't know him by any other name! To make matters worse, recently he joined a paddle board club, and even they call him "Monty!" John chuckled while he shared that with me.

I wasn't any too aware of the guys' roping activities until one Sunday afternoon when my mother was visiting from Los Angeles. I decided to drive over and show her what fun the neighborhood dads were having. We crossed Ortega Highway which in those days was a very curvy two lane road, more crowded on the weekends than during the week, and headed up the dirt road to Jimmy's. It turned out to be a day none of us would ever forget.

Calf Roping with Jimmy Jackson

On this day, the fathers challenged their sons, maybe ten boys, to try riding the calves, sort of a junior version of bull riding. When 10 year-old Rick climbed up on the steer and raced crookedly across the competition field, staying on a long half minute or so, my mother looked horrified. She was already skeptical of all the dangerous horse antics she knew our kids were up to, and this was over the top for her. When four year-old Danny, with his long hair blowing, and his hand bandaged from an earlier injury, got up on a calf, and began across the field, my mother had to turn away. It was just too much for her. It was a good thing, because before long, young Danny was thrown to the ground, but not before he had won a nice purse for his age group. Dan commented on his experience saying, "What I remember most was walking up the stairs at home, covered in dirt, wearing a proud smile,

Dan Friess Calf Riding c. 1970's

because those winnings seemed like a fortune. I was dismayed to see that my mom and grandmother were none too happy." We still laugh about it today, (well, my mother isn't laughing, she is more upset about it now than ever!). Of course, my sons, and the others, dusted themselves off and tried a few more times. It would take a lot more than young steers to stop those kids. To add to the drama, someone was filming the kids in their competition, ensuring that the scene would be replayed across the years.

John summed up his memories. "I joined a group of men known as the Las Tortuga Riders and I've ridden with them for forty some years. The group started on Camp Pendleton in the 1950's but eventually disbanded. Under Cab Crowl, the group reassembled in the late 1970's. There are about 100 Tortuga Riders; Jim Verbeerst, John and his sons, and even his grandsons have ridden with them." At this writing, the group is planning their next adventure; riding for four days at Cajon Ranch at the Grapevine, outside of Bakersfield. They will bring tents and their own food. Some of the riders pitch in to cook. They will have lobster and steak one night, ribs, beans and corn another. Full breakfasts, but mostly they will enjoy treasured friendships and camaraderie. John says that for the kids growing up, the horses taught them so much. "For guys and gals too, to work a horse builds confidence. The kids are all successful. For me, horses have brought me a lifetime of friendships."

The Fred and Fran Hill Family

Hidden Valley neighbors Fred and Fran Hill, founders of the world-wide Ronald McDonald's Houses had a story to add. Fred and Fran were not really riders, but their three daughters, Kim, Kyle and Kristen were, and they challenged them to go on a big trail ride to Casper's Park. Fred borrowed Ken

Fred and Fran Hill Family Trail Ride c. 1970's

Friess' horse, Paiute, which Ken delivered, saddled to Fred's door. The girls rode their ponies. Fran rode Kim's horse, Johnnie. The riders gathered in the big field which in today covered over in houses on a street named Paseo Michelle. Fran was shocked to see so many horses and ponies for this ride; maybe 50 or more. It was a day that they could not believe. Once on the trail, following dozens of horses and their dust, as they made their way up San Juan Creek, Fred couldn't breathe. He came to understand why cowboys use bandanas. Having no bandana, he improvised and pulled his tee shirt up around his nose. The ride seemed interminable, though the girls were having the time of their lives. "Fred thought he'd die," said Fran. "People and horses were getting kicked! Poor Fred! Once they finally got to Casper's Park for a big picnic, Fred could hardly stand up." Laughing as she remembered her former NFL player husband's discomfort. Fran concluded, "He found a man who let him pay him to ride Paiute back home. It was a day we will never forget!"

Fran added. "Do you remember when John Clifton held all those little-kid rodeos (gymkhanas) in the field in front of his house? He held pony races for them and then stunts like putting a potty in the field and they had to get off and sit on it and then drink a soda. He was so great about that. The kids never forgot it."

John Clifton Hosts Kids' Games c. 1970's

Julie and Dan Friess

Julie Friess Bert, smiling at her lifetime of memories, reported that some of the most fun times were of just hanging around the back yard, barefoot, and then deciding to vault onto the back of the pony, Connie. Julie enjoyed lying on Connie facing backwards. As she got older, still in bare feet, she liked to jump, bareback onto Windy or Paiute and take off to visit her friends in the Valley. She had a sweet nostalgic expression as she recalled the long summers riding around the creek. Then she remembered that a whole gang of the kids liked to race in the dry creek bed as fast as they could, brushing bare legs against brambles and trees, racing as far as possible. "Mom, that was when I knew I wasn't allergic to poison oak, like you are. We ran through it all the time." Of course in those days, the 70's, there was only the dirt and gravel road leading to the Lacouague Citrus Ranch, with a turn to our few homes, so there was no traffic to worry about.

Dan Friess recalls riding in the creek on pony Connie. He said, "Connie would always sprint up the berm toward the road from the creek, and then she would stop and look both ways, on her

Julie on Connie, Rick on Pony Cart with Cousins c. 1978

own accord, just in case there was a vehicle. Connie seemed to sense that she had a very young rider on her, and that she was the grown up."

Lacouague Girls

One of my favorite memories from those years was of Renee Lacouague (Bondi) at about age 15 racing up our road on Tar Baby, her beautiful black horse. Both Renee and Tar Baby would look like they were flying, full out, hair and mane trailing in the wind. When I asked veterinarian, Dr. Julie Ryan-Johnson for a horse memory, she said, "Renee and Tar Baby were my heroes. I remember looking up and seeing her laughing all the way around those barrels!" Renee was a champion barrel racer.

Denise Lacouague Loyatho shared this memory. Denise was one of the three Lacouague girls (Denise, Michelle, and Renée) one could see riding full out all around the valley. Her family had owned the Lacouague Citrus Ranch at the end of San Juan Creek Road since 1921. When I asked for her memory she said, "As I got older and no longer had a horse, what I remember was riding with our neighbors, Dennis and Barbara Rude, who lived next door to you. They had two horses and typically four of us wanted to ride, so we rode bareback, double. I always rode on the back of

Lacouague Ranch 1970's

Dennis' Palomino, Pal. We would play tag in the dirt fields which are now the homes on Paseo Michelle. The one on the back tagged as the other 'drove'. You had to tag the person, you could not tag the horse. Pal, a big Quarter Horse, had a good sized rump. Dennis would get really close to our opponents, then quickly turn and butt swipe their legs nearly knocking them off the horse!

Another way that we played was in the creek, again riding double, but the one in back stood with a death grip on the driver's shoulders. Yes, standing right up on the person. We would see who could get the farthest, the fastest, by trotting and loping. Circus acrobats we were not! Of course we fell off a lot, dodging rocks as we did. I do remember riding down the side of the San Juan Creek Road once, beside the Golf Club, which we did only a few times. It is a nice stretch. We decided to lope. Well, Pal was a fabulous horse when he wanted to be, but he could also be stubborn, and every bit earned his owner's name of "Butt Head" when Pal did not choose to mind Dennis. That day was one of those times. When the lope extended to a gallop, then, bit in his teeth, Pal stretched out flat and it was Del Mar Racetrack without the crowd. It was definitely not a time to come off. I was grateful for the straight away, but I was worried about what he would do at its end. Would he cross the street and head up the dump road? [Editor's note: The county landfill was on the knoll between San Juan Creek Road and La Novia. The old landfill is currently zoned for a stable.]

Thankfully, he didn't. He slowed at the end, out of steam. As we turned around, Dennis yelled, 'You butt head" a few times. We both had the same idea at the same time, which was to run him back home. Dennis did. When we returned home, Pal was one lathered and slippery horse, our jeans were drenched. I think the horse was the most exhausted, but that could be a toss-up! That's it. It was one of the most memorable days of my growing up on the Citrus Ranch and enjoying my friends and the horses."

Escapees
Lorie Porter

Around this same time across the Creek, Lorie Porter was enjoying her horses and raising her kids. One day while Lorie was away, her young horse, Beaver chewed open the corral. Beaver's mom, Ginger, eager to keep an eye on her young son, followed him out. Beaver led the way down the steep hill to Ortega Highway. As the horses were nosing around the highway, Lori's neighbor, Martha Griver was driving by. Martha recognized the horses and knew instantly that two horses did not belong near the highway with the traffic. Martha pulled her car to the shoulder and in an expert motion, loosened the leather belt holding up her jeans, and grabbed Beaver. Using the belt as a lead in one hand, and holding her pants up with the other, she walked all the way up the steep hill with Ginger following, and secured the two recalcitrant horses in their corral. When Lorie arrived home later in the day, she had no suspicion of the dangerous adventure her two horses had enjoyed. Lorie was thankful to have such a good friend who could keep her cool and think on the spot! Martha's generous action was typical in our community, how neighbors looked out for, and helped each other; all for one and one for all.

Raised on a Horse
Fred Love

Sitting with me in his office, Fred Love explained, "I was raised on a horse. My dad had Love's Pet Store in Orange. Then we had Freddy's Western Wear. I joined the military and when I returned my dad was ready to sell. That's when I turned to training horses and making my living as a farrier. I raised and traded horses my whole life. I had ten brood mares while I worked the Whiting Ranch in El Toro. When Rancho Mission Viejo shut down the *plano* up on Trabuco, I leased it from them. It's where Santa Margarita Ford is today. I had it for one and a half years and ran 10-15 horses and fifty dairy and beef cattle up there.

I was a farrier for 25 years, that's how I met my wife, Leslie Canon. She was training horses at the Orange County Fair Grounds and I came to work on her horses' feet. We got married. Leslie trained and rode Western Cutters in the shows. She competed a lot and was very successful. She and I also trained at the Coto de Caza Equestrian Preserve. Before San Juan Hills High School was built, I had a stable on La Pata right above where the football stadium is now. I trained ropers there and kept ten or so brood mares."

Fred's pride in his career was apparent. Our interview took place at the Ortega Tack and Feed Store in the week before the store closed forever. Fred had opened the business in 2000. Fred explained that he joined the El Viaje de Portola in 1976 and only ever missed one of the rides. "In the early days we rode on the Irvine Ranch until the late 1980's. Now we only ride on the Ranch. One year there was a terrible flash flood. We had to run, grabbing our sleeping bags. The water was coming fast. Our heavy water truck got stuck and we all had to push it out." He smiled at the memory of the wild waters. I was invited to photograph the awards and honors he had hanging on the wall of the office. I could tell how much being a part of the Ride and being friends with so many of the men has meant to him.

On a personal note there were two times over the years when I called upon Fred Love for help. The first time was when we decided that we needed some miniature horses, or small Shetland ponies for our eleven grandchildren. Taking off from the store, Fred had me climb up into the cab of his truck and away we went. During our ride to Santa Ana Canyon, Fred regaled me with stories of his horse and cattle operation on the plane [*plano*, as he called it] of Rancho Santa Margarita. He took me to a big horse operation in Santa Ana Canyon, where we looked over several ponies. I didn't get one that day, but I always knew that Fred was there to help. No questions asked.

Some years later, I was in big trouble with a high strung Pony-of-America, named Pixie which had been evacuated when the San Diego fires erupted in North San Diego County. We were still in the market for a pony, so Ken and our daughter looked her over during her long evacuation at the Del Mar Race Track. They liked what they saw and brought her home. She was a twelve-year old

Pony-of-America Pixie

pedigreed beauty. However, she was also a handful, skittish and jiggy. Her high carriage Arabian tail flouncing about, however, stirred my heart.

Across about six years I got her to settle down. She pranced when she walked. She was a delight to ride, until she wasn't. After a while she became difficult to catch in the mornings. Things devolved from there. By the time I had to call in Fred Love, she had tried to kill me! She stood on her hind legs and battered her front hooves as close to my face as she could get. This was the day after she had tried to kick me, and had, in fact, connected with Christine's leg, knocking her into the mud. I knew then that Pixie was too much for me. I called Fred, and as before, he knew whom to call. Soon after, Pixie left for a new home with someone better equipped to handle her than I was.

Fred closed the business right after our talk, but he remains in our hearts as a true friend, living out the idea of being a good neighbor, and that one's word is one's bond. He has added so much to the equestrian story that is San Juan's.

Fred Love at Round-up. Courtesy Fred Love

Jennifer and John Agostini

Long time San Juan resident and horse lover Jennifer Agostini shared a favorite memory with me. This was long before she met her veterinarian husband, John. They eventually moved to our little Hidden Valley. She was Jennifer Casper then. Her horse story began when she was ten years-old with a 15

161

month-old horse named Raindrop. They taught each other all about riding. As the years passed Raindrop birthed a colt named Eagle.

In addition to Raindrop, Jennifer adopted a very beautiful, 16 hand-high female mule named Herbie. Herbie's first owner had been a little girl who loved the movie, "Herbie the Love Bug," thus the name. Jen was so proud of her beautiful black mule with its white socks, that she paraded her in Bishop, California's Mule Days, and even took a first place with her in English Jumping. Jennifer understood that mules, which cannot reproduce, were not of any interest to stallions, or so she thought!

On this day, teenaged Jennifer was riding Herbie along San Juan Creek Road next to the golf course and reining Eagle behind her. She was trying to wean nine-month old Eagle from nursing Raindrop. Jen was trotting along on Herbie, having a lovely ride, when all of a sudden she felt hooves encircling her waist! Cars were whizzing. *What?* She was soon knocked to the ground. Feeling a bit dazed, she turned her head around to see young Eagle mounting Herbie the mule! Luckily, a passerby in a car, an older man, stopped to assist. As he helped the very frightened Jennifer up, he reassured her that everything was okay. He managed to calm the young girl, and to get the stallion off the mule.

A while later, again in the saddle, Jen realized she had learned an important lesson; she would always rein Eagle right next to her, not behind her, and that thing about horses and mules not mixing, well it might not be all that true!

Jen explained, "Raindrop was the love of my life." She lived a long time. Eagle, too, and he found a good home. Today Jennifer is married. She and husband, John, have a 26 year-old mare named Ginger and John's rescue horse, Joe Dirt, who probably came from Mexico. Their horses are stabled at Mission Trails. Jen summed up her story: "Horses last a long time and can become good friends for a big part of one's life."

> *When a rider looks into a horse's eyes, they find a part of their soul.*

"Cowboying with Uncle Charlie"
Domingo Belardes

When I asked Domingo Belardes, Blas Aguilar Adobe Foundation President and descendent of the Acjachemen people, if there was a horse story passed down in his family, he shared this with me. It seems back in the day, maybe the 1950's, his father's brother; Uncle Charlie had an experience that was the stuff of family legend. Charlie Belardes was many years older than David, Domingo's father. Charlie worked "cowboying," as Domingo said, at Rancho Mission Viejo. One day his foreman asked Charlie to exercise a particularly big stallion. Charlie had an idea. He rode him out to San Clemente Pier and then, staying on the horse, had the horse swim around the entire pier! That was his exercise. When Charlie got back to the Ranch no one thought much about it. After all, he *had* exercised the stallion! What appeals to me, is the idea that the area was so open that one could even get their horse to the beach. These days if your leashed dog even touches a paw on the sand, there will be a Lifeguard Services person giving you a citation!

Vic and Diane Starnes

Vic and Diane Starnes have lived in our valley for 43 years. Vic explained that after he mustered out of the Navy, at the end of the Korean War, he and Diane lived for a time in Yorba Linda. However, they had long been enamored with the idea of living closer to the ocean, and having a place for their teenage daughter, Renee, to keep her horses.

Diane spent many months searching for such a place, and they found it in San Juan Capistrano, where they settled in. Before long their daughter Renee's Palomino foaled a beautiful Palomino colt. The day of his birth was a neighborhood event, and several of the kids stayed home from school to be part of the wonderful happening!

"Joey, the Colt, turned out to be a very special high spirited horse whose legendary deeds included climbing a new pipe corral fence to impregnate a neighbor's mare. Moving to San Juan was one of the best decisions we ever made."

"Oh What A Big Surprise!"

Vic's story about Joey, the colt, scaling the pipe corral, reminds me of something that occurred at our home around 1975. I wrote this up for our grandchildren when they were young. It is a true accounting written for children.

One day, when our daughter, Julie, was around eight years-old, she went out to the barn to put the hay out for her pony, Connie, when she noticed that there was something in the corral. It was wet and lumpy. "*What is this*?" thought Julie.

Julie moved slowly toward the wet lump to get a better look. It wriggled. "*It's alive*!" thought Julie to herself. "*What could it be*?" She stared at the wet thing lying on the ground and noticed that it had mud and dirt stuck to its fur. "*Fur*?" thought Julie. "*Fur*?" For a long time she looked and watched. Then it moved.

That was scary! Julie turned and raced back up to the house to get her dad.

"Daddy! Daddy! Come quickly. It's furry and it's alive! I'm not sure what it is but it moved. It's wet!"

Julie's dad, and then her mom, then both of her brothers, all went out to the corral to have a look. Julie's dad went up to the wet lump.

"Why it's a foal!" he exclaimed excitedly.

"Where did it come from?" asked her older brother Rick.

"Daddy, where did it come from?" asked her younger brother Danny.

Julie and her family looked all around the yard. They looked under the fence and up the road, they walked all around the neighborhood asking if anyone had lost a baby horse.

No one had lost a horse. Everyone was very confused. "*Where did it come from?*" They all wondered. The family even walked down to Rocky's stable to see if anyone there knew anything about a missing foal.

The more people they asked, the more the mystery deepened. Before the family had taken off searching for the baby's family, Julie's dad had set it on a soft blanket to keep it warm. Returning after their fruitless search, the family decided to clean up the baby.

To their great surprise, Connie came over and licked at its fur, and began to clean it up. The family watched in amazement. After a long while the little foal tried to stand up. It was very shaky and awkward, but eventually it stumbled over to Connie and began to nurse milk from her. Finally, everyone realized that it was Connie's baby! They all agreed that the foal would have to be named "Surprise." The children declared the day to be a school holiday and stayed home to help Connie.

For many years after that amazing event, Julie, Rick and Dan, all played with Surprise. The children agreed that Surprise was the perfect size for Danny. Julie trained her enough so that Danny could ride on her back without being bucked off. The children loved Surprise. She grew into a beautiful little pony who looked like her mom. The children's dad even taught Surprise how to give kisses. She had a sweet nature and lived happily ever after, going on nature rides in the creek and watching the swallows flitting and the bunnies playing.

The family never did know who Surprise's father was, or how Connie came to be expecting, as they did not think she had gotten out. But then they did not even know she was pregnant. They just thought she was getting fat, and even cut back on her feed! Poor Connie.

Perhaps, the mystery of where Surprise came from has at last been solved, perhaps it was the Starnes' colt, Joey? He did live next door…

Ken Friess Shows Connie her Foal

Surprise Joins Friess Family c. 1970's

Baby Surprise with Donna and Julie Friess

Julie Friess Trains Young Pony Surprise c. 1970s

166

Chapter Fourteen

Trails Leading to San Juan: The 1980's

"Riding was pure exhilaration! I've never felt so much freedom and independence as I felt on horseback during those joyous times." Michelle Kelly

During the months I spent collecting horse stories for this project, I was interested in discovering the many different routes which have led some of our residents toward horses. Here are two very different such examples: Millie and Gil Jones, who founded the Jones Mini-Farm, now Zoomars, and were Grand Marshalls of the Swallows Day Parade are the first. The other is Steve Nordeck, philanthropist, managing-owner of local businesses, and also a Grand Marshal of the Swallows Day Parade 2017.

Millie and Gil Jones

In 1979, I was just starting to learn how to paint on china with nationally recognized artist, Millie Jones. One afternoon as I took a lesson in her studio in an industrial building in Lake Forest, California, Millie asked me, "Is there anywhere down where you live, that my husband and I might like to live; somewhere for his construction company office and my art studio?"

Coincidentally, the afternoon before, Ken and I had attended an event at the O'Neill Museum on Los Rios Street. As we had walked past the old clapboard Olivares home on the way to the event, an enthusiastic realtor had called to us from the front porch. Perhaps Ken knew him. We stopped and chatted with him. He explained that the property was for sale. Being the good salesperson that he was, he told us all about the possibilities of the historic home, that it had been on the market for some time and the owners were pretty flexible. He said, "with a lot of tender love and care it could be restored." We smiled our good-byes and went on to the Historical Society's reception in the O'Neill Museum.

Back in the studio with Millie Jones' question, I recall stammering out, "Ah…well… yesterday we became aware of a home for sale in the Historic District of San Juan. It's a bit of a wreck, but it is on a large lot. The neighborhood includes a trash truck yard, a wrecked-car storage lot, and a tree trimming company which parks their trucks nearby. This property is full of weeds, Millie, but it might be worth looking into."

That evening, her contractor husband, Gil, called Ken, and after a very long conversation, the Joneses came and looked at the property. They immediately purchased it. Three historic structures sat on the property. Gil restored them. The front home became Millie's china

painting studio where we students took lessons. The house in the back, beautifully restored, served as their private residence. As the years passed, Gil began acquiring animals in the back yard. Before too long, he had developed a children's petting zoo. It was a huge attraction for children and families who came from near and far for birthday parties and good times for the kids.

Zoomars Petting Zoo, Structures Restored by Gil Jones

Early on, Gil and Millie acquired two draft horses, Duke and Dan. Those stunning horses could often be found pulling a hay wagon around town with a load of delighted passengers. Duke and Dan became local celebrities, with frequent newspapers stories written about them and the petting zoo. A host of bunnies, guinea pigs, llamas, and many friendly goats, excited eager children, with pony rides available to complete the day. Across more than ten years, on my way in to paint, I would set my materials down, and reach in and pet the soft fur of their llama, which leaned over, hoping for a treat. Millie and Gil Jones operated the petting zoo for more than 25 years, attracting thousands of visitors each year. It was an interactive experience for the children with the animals and it was a delight for families. One mother described it as "a little piece of heaven for my kids." When our grandchildren were young it was a favorite Saturday morning stop for them. The mini-farm became a noteworthy subject for reporters, and as a person visiting the historic art studio each week across a decade, I, too, felt compelled to write about it. My story was published in the May 1988 issue of *China Decorator Magazine* and as a cover story in the local paper. It is included below.

Zoomars Petting Zoo Offers Pony Rides for Kids

In time Gil became active in the community, serving on the Planning Commission, and then was elected to the City Council for two terms, serving three different terms as Mayor, 1991,1992, 1997. Millie continued as a rising star in the china painting world, publishing articles about her beautiful china pieces, and being an active member in the national and international china painting associations.

When Millie and Gil Jones decided to sell their mini-farm, it became Zoomar's Petting Zoo, and continues to be a great attraction for young families with children. It was honored as the *"2007 Business of the Year"* by the San Juan Capistrano Chamber of Commerce.

August 28, 2007
SAN JUAN CAPISTRANO. "A New San Juan Tradition at Zoomars." Less than two years after opening Zoomars Petting Zoo, Carolyn [Franks] and Omar Gonzalez have become fixtures in the community, creating a new community draw at the site of the former Jones Mini-Farm.

The Gonzalez's efforts were recently recognized by the Chamber of Commerce, who chose Zoomars as the 2007 Business of the Year. Carolyn Gonzalez recently spoke of the award, and her efforts to update the business. "It's an interactive, hands-on petting zoo, geared towards children under 10. We have more than a hundred animals there that the kids can pet and feed. We also do pony rides and train rides. We are now doing a lot of educational animal shows there, too, on animals, birds and reptiles." *(Los Angeles Times,* S. Emery, August 8, 2007)

Story by Donna L. Friess. Featured in the May 1988 edition of *The China Decorator*.

China Painting in a Time Capsule: A Visit to Millie Jones' Studio

This morning as I sat in my china painting class I had the eeriest feeling that somehow I had been strangely transported back through time one hundred years or more. Here I was a sensible 41-year-old mother of three and college teacher, suddenly believing that I was in a time warp. As I sat in my familiar place in the unique studio of my teacher, Millie Jones, I wondered what had triggered this strange feeling today? With a new awareness I mentally retraced my steps of that morning.

Perhaps the feeling began on the way to class. I had driven slowly by the fabulous new basilica across the street from Millie's which is being completed next to the historic Mission San Juan Capistrano. That mission, famous for the mysterious return of the swallows each March 19th, is finally getting back a near replica of the wonderful old stone church lost in the earthquake of 1812. Was it the grandeur of the breathtaking new church or the silent strength of the old mission? Or did it occur as I drove toward class and crossed a time line instead of a railroad track. I felt myself to be back in an era of yesteryear.

As I entered the timeless world known as Los Rios, which is the heart of the historic district of San Juan Capistrano, California. I thought about this ancient street. I remembered that it is said to be the oldest street in all of California where people have continually lived. In fact, the adobe house right next to Millie Jones' property once belonged to Feliciano Rios, one of the first mission soldiers, whose relatives today continue to occupy the same tiny adobe. I reflected on the rich history of the area. Here beneath blue skies of spring where ocean breezes sweep the mind clean, it somehow seems important to reflect on one's heritage.

I recall now that I looked across the tiny lane, past the art studio to an absolutely immaculate Victorian style structure known as the O'Neill home which has been moved to its present site and restored to house the local historical society and museum.

My eye continued down the dusty lane and the clock seemed to turn back to 1794 when the little ramshackle neighborhood began, even then much as it is today. For hundreds of years before that however, it was part of the peaceful village of the Juaneno Indian tribe. In fact, as I thought of the Indians, I had looked the other way down the street to see if I could see the home of Millie's daughter. She is Jennifer Baldridge and she lives in a quaint wood-sided home that once belonged to Juaneno chief, Clarence Lobo. The Lobo family can trace their origins back to the days before the arrival of the Spanish explorers!

I remembered as I retraced that morning, that I had parked my car and walked into the tree- shaded lane. I had noticed the colorful morning glories creeping silently across sagging porches, the rich and muted crow of some distant rooster, and I had inhaled the scent of freshly mowed grass mixed with the familiar barnyard smells. I had smiled as I thought of the huge blonde Clydesdale-type horses named Duke and Dan which Millie and her handsome husband, Gil, so proudly keep in the large corral behind their home.

That reminded me of where I was headed. Art class. My attention quickly focused on the charming old one story early California style house on the corner. The signs in front of it once declared: "Carriage for hire." "Home of Delfina Olivares in the 1890's", and a more modern sign, "Porcelain Art Creations."

Enjoying my journey back in time I recalled how dreadful that property had been eight years ago, before Millie and Gil got the restoration spirit and purchased the three dilapidated old structures which rested on over an acre of property. Gil restored the front house and created such a charming art studio for Millie that it received the prestigious San Juan Beautiful award for excellence that year. It was also declared an historic site by the state of California. The house behind the front house was in such disrepair that it had to be raised. However, Gil was able to salvage much of the original material so that the house he built is really a replica of its former self. Today it is a charming blend of the old and the new and is the personal residence for Millie and Gil. Millie has added such touches as her won hand-painted tiles in the bathroom, which go beautifully with the lovely floral carpeting and her own hand-painted porcelain pieces. The third structure was an interesting old bathhouse, which had been moved onto the property in 1936. It had come from a famous old Hot Springs in the area. Now it is something of a gallery for the Jones' collection of memorabilia as well as an office for Gil's construction company.

I stared as I had realized that my little mental meanderings were about to make me late for class. I moved along more briskly and came to the picket gate in front of Porcelain Art Creation. I opened it. I passed a sleeping German Shepherd, several idle chickens and then I silently slipped by the familiar sight of sleeping little Lacey Baldridge. At nine months of age, the tiny blonde granddaughter of Millie was fast asleep in her porch swing with her bottle still in her mouth.

Upon entering the studio, my eyes noticed the interior as they had never before. I saw gleaming tables filled with pristine white china. I noticed the old gramophone in the corner by the collection of antique dolls and then my eyes rested on the glistening surfaces of the private collection of antique porcelain which Millie has treasured and stored in specially lighted and secured cabinets which line the back walls of the studio. What a sight all of this was! And busy at work were my fellow classmates, many of who have been painting with Millie since she began in the 1960's. Many of the students are teachers themselves by now but they so enjoy the unique atmosphere at the Los Rios studio that they keep coming to class.

I remember taking my place. It was at that point that I had realized that I had been lost in time. I pulled myself to the present and examined the lovely lady gowned in a long-skirted Victorian dress reminiscent of the colorful past of early California. She is Millie Jones and she made all of this happen. I recalled the celebration last year of National Porcelain Art month so beautifully orchestrated. I remembered how all of the members of the Orange County Porcelain Artists climbed up into the huge hay wagon driven by Gil Jones and pulled by those big Belgium horses, Duke and Dan. We here quite a sight as Gil drove us through the historic streets of San Juan Capistrano. The tourists stopped and waved to us as we clopped by. What a memorable time, and all made possible through the quiet efforts of Millie Jones.

But it is more than the historic area, or the lace curtains at the windows or the occasional egg some forgetful chicken has mistakenly laid by the front door. Rather it is a special feeling. It is a feeling of peacefulness, reverence for nature, the past and a real appreciation for the beautiful. In five years I have never heard Millie say or do anything which was unkind. Each day she is filled with the joy of life. Today she was so excited about three new baby goats born in the little pen in the backyard.

Somehow it all seems so right. The past and the present locked together in this special place.

I could clearly see then why my flight into fantasy. It all just fits so well. Here we are enjoying an art form that dates back to early man. The Chinese perfected the production and decoration of hard paste porcelain between the 7th and the 14th centuries. Marco Polo explored China and brought back porcelain in 1295. It was the envy of European royalty. After four hundred years of attempts western man finally discovered the secrets of making porcelain. A German alchemist named Johann Bottger in 1715 was finally the person to master the secrets. After that, serious production and decoration of porcelain proliferated throughout Europe. Finally in the 1870's porcelain painting spread across the Atlantic to be a popular past time of the ladies of the 19th century.

Long before that time, however, those Indian women of the Los Rios area sat along the banks of the Trabuco Creek, which courses toward the Pacific Ocean behind Millie's studio. I could almost see them as they meticulously shaped eating vessels out of adobe clay and water and later, decorating them with paints and beads. Such a rich and colorful heritage from ancient man, to western man, beautifully preserved and protected here on Los Rios Street with Mr. and Mrs. Gil Jones. We hail the artists of Los Rios Street of the past and glory in being the Los Rios Artists of the present.

Donna Friess

Steve Nordeck

Businessman Steve Nordeck came to San Juan Capistrano with yet another perspective, a very different one from that of the Joneses. His path toward the equestrian life is equally fascinating. It is interesting that there are so many different paths that can lead toward horses, and it speaks to the fact that one does not have to "be born in a saddle" to come to appreciate horses.

Sadly, as this book went to press, the town of San Juan Capistrano learned that on June 25, 2018, Mr. Steve Nordeck, philanthropist, horse lover, business man and all-around great guy, passed away from cancer. Mechelle Lawrence-Adams eulogized him stating: "Throughout my near 30 year career in town, Steve was always in my corner and a great example of dynamism and strength to those who loved him. He loved the Mission San Juan Capistrano and was an icon in this town as the face of the Swallows Inn and our beloved El Adobe Restaurant."

The fact that there was standing room only at the great Mission Basilica for his funeral Mass, is a testament to how well respected Steve was. It was a deeply moving service. For me personally, I am grateful for having met Steve, and having had a chance to get to know him as he shared his favorite horse stories with me. During our time together, I was impressed by his down-to-earth humility, and his delightful sense of humor. He will be deeply missed.

Steve Nordeck Entrepreneur was Passionate about His Horses

Steve was a proud member of El Viaje de Portolâ for the past 24 years. He has served as the managing owner of El Adobe Restaurant (14 years), The Swallows Inn (26 years), and the Mission Promenade (24 years.) In the late 1970's, Steve was finishing his political career on the City Council in Manhattan Beach, California, where he also served as Mayor. He was ready for a change. He built one of the first of five homes in Coto de Caza and began watching the horse jumping practices in the large equestrian center nearby. He decided at age 35, that he wanted to jump horses. His friends could not believe what he was doing! Before long, he became proficient enough to compete and did so for some 15 years, sometimes even taking time off from work for the events. He was having a wonderful time with his new horse jumping friends who were also fox hunters. They invited

Stephen Nordeck 2017 Grand Marshall of the Swallows Day Parade

him to be a part of their events. He joined the West Hills Fox Hunt Club in Chatsworth, California, and discovered another way to enjoy his horse. They went on fox hunts all over Southern California. When the fox hunters decided to go to Ireland, to hunt in the home of fox hunting, Steve, explained, during our interview, that he went along, but with great trepidation. "I was scared to death!" He sensed that chasing hounds over fences and bushes would be even more dangerous than the hunts he routinely enjoyed in Southern California. He joined in for two exhilarating hunts in Ireland, and his prediction proved correct, it was even more hazardous than their other hunts!

Back in California, with his relationship with the fox hunters growing, one of them asked, "Steve, don't you know them down at the 'Ranch'? Could there be a fox hunt on the Ranch? Can you arrange it?"

Steve scheduled a meeting with Gilbert Aguirre, an acquaintance from his gym in Coto de Caza, and Executive Vice President of the Ranch. Sitting down with Mr. Aguirre, Steve asked the big question. "Could there be a fox hunt on the Ranch?" Chuckling at the memory, Steve admitted that he was nervous making this request. Mr. Aguirre responded, "I don't like those pants you wear. I don't like those boots." Steve tried to explain that with the English saddle, there wasn't the protection as on a Western saddle. It didn't matter. Gilbert Aguirre said no. The West Hills Fox Hunters did not come onto the Ranch.

Sometime later, Steve learned that the Trabuco Steak House in Trabuco Canyon was up for sale. He very much wanted to purchase it, however, he would need a financial partner. He thought and thought. Whom did he know in the cowboy world that could be his partner? He thought of Gilbert Aguirre. Nervously, one day he scheduled another meeting with Mr. Aguirre and presented, as he said, "my dog and pony show."

No questions asked, Gilbert rolled back in his chair, opened his desk drawer, pulled out his check book, and asked, "So how much do you need? I'm your partner now."

That was the start of a partnership that continued for many years. Eventually, Steve was invited on the Portolá Ride and became a member. He quickly learned to ride Western style. When Steve decided that he wanted to learn how to pen cows, Gilbert offered to teach him to pen, however Steve's horse was awfully big for penning. Steve got a Quarter Horse and learned how to pen.

As mentioned earlier, there was an episode with fox hunters, hounds, and sleeping Portolá Riders. This is the back story to that event. Steve explained that as the years passed, he had an opportunity to grant a favor to Gilbert. One day, Gilbert, took Steve aside, and asked, "You still involved with that fox hunting outfit?"

Steve replied, "Yes."

"Well can you get us some horses and hounds so we can really surprise the guys on Sunday morning of the Ride?"

The prank went off, which was described earlier in this book, and according to Steve, Gilbert found great glee in the chaos which followed the yipping hounds turned loose on the sleeping Riders! Clearly the prank was a lot of fun for those who orchestrated it. Laughing, as he ended his story, he said, "The Ride has a lot of skullduggery. It is wonderful! I enjoy it!"

As our interview wound down, Steve, summed up what we had been saying, "From 1990-1993, I served on the Orange County Planning Commission. That work helped me to appreciate the fact that the Ranch has kept 25,000 acres that will never be touched. That is something." He paused. "I live in San Juan now, but even when I lived in Coto, the town I wanted to hang out in was San Juan. I love the cowboys, the Indians, the Mexicans. I love it here!"

Steve Nordeck and the Jones family have left a lasting imprint on San Juan, Steve did so through his donations to Mission Preservation and other civic organizations, as well as his participation in community life. The Joneses have left their marks through Gil's civic work, Millie's nationally recognized artistic accomplishments, and both for the legacy of the creation of the very popular petting zoo.

Dick Paulsen's Adventure – See Next Page

Chapter Fifteen

Horse Stories Around the 1990'S

"Two feet move your body, four feet move your soul!" (Rancho Chilamate)

Tom Hribar's Story on Dick Paulsen

During my horse story round ups, I chatted with former Councilman, Tom Hribar, who told me this tale. This is a paraphrase of Tom's story: Prior to and during my Council term, there was a San Juan Capistrano Open Space Committee that was created by a previous City Council. This committee had about twelve members who worked on the open space issue including securing grants from the State, improving trails and helping pass a $30 million Open Space Bond in 2008, that eventually led to the purchase of the Rancho Mission Viejo Riding Park at San Juan Capistrano. During the promotion of this bond which was passed by 71% of the San Juan Capistrano voters, we had a community trails ride with close to 100 riders. The ride was held north of town over a 150-acre parcel of land that the committee had persuaded the City Council to purchase for $2 million dollars using funds from the 1990 Open Space Bond. [The Bond was implemented in 1992] There were mostly "rookie" riders on this ride with a few experienced riders like Dick Paulsen. Dick was a Portolá Rider, a horse owner, and an active member of the Open Space Committee. As we crossed Trabuco Creek, behind Saddleback School, Dick's horse decided to roll in the water. It was the funniest thing we had ever seen. The novices on the ride all enjoyed his predicament. He was the only real horse guy, and the only one to fall into the water, while we novices, laughing, all stayed dry. It was a slice of life. You have to know Dick to appreciate this as he is one of the nicest people you hope to meet.

After hearing Tom's story, I responded. "Tom, there's no way I can tell a story on Dick Paulsen like that without his permission."

"No, of course not. Call him."

Tom gave me the number and I called Dick. He answered right away. He explained that he was in Tahiti. I asked him about the incident and he replied. "Oh," then he was laughing. "Our committee photographer, Eddie, was with us that day. He was across the creek taking pictures for the Open Space Committee, just as my horse, Willie, decided that it would be nice to cool off and have a roll in the water. I had been aware that Willie was pawing at the water, but I thought, surely he would never roll over with me on him. I was wrong. Over we rolled, saddle and rider and all! We were in about four feet of water, so we got completely soaked." He paused to chuckle a bit. "It got worse. By the time we got back for the after-ride barbeque, Eddie had the whole event up on a big screen for everyone to see!"

"Donna, it wasn't bad enough that the story made it to the front page of the local newspaper. No, it got worse. On the next Portolá Ride the guys made me wear water wings!"

It's Never Too Late!
Gerry Williamson

It was my pleasure to meet 85 year-old Gerry Williamson at the Ortega Equestrian Center. Gerry, like Millie and Gil Jones, and Steve Nordeck, came to enjoy the equestrian life from yet another point of view. A career educator, Gerry retired at age 65. Her youthful fantasy of being able to swiftly ride like the wind had a chance to come true. One day she was walking her dog over by Ortega Equestrian Center and a young woman rode by on her horse. Gerry shyly, asked, "I would like to ride a horse. Is there anywhere I can do that?" The young woman immediately told her to come on over to the stable.

Before long Gerry was learning not just to ride, but to jump hurdles. Gerry fell in love with riding and bought her own horse named Roy. That was the beginning of a twenty-year infatuation with horses, competing in equestrian jumping events, and discovering a whole new world of friends. As Roy, a beautiful sorrel Quarter Horse, got older she sent him to Colorado to live with a young lady on a vast ranch. She showed me photos of Roy galloping across the pasture to chat with the mares. Roy has a best friend, a goat named "Coconut." Gerry considers her twenty years with the horse some of the best years of her life. "I raised two red-headed humans, and then I adopted a red horse!" she added, smiling, as she returned her phone with Roy and Coconut's photos back into her purse.

These stories illustrate that one can fall in love with horses at any time in life. It's possible to take up new interests later in life and start a whole new way of looking at the world. Roy's retirement to Colorado reminded me of when our big Appaloosa, Paiute went into retirement. Our kids had grown up and left the nest. The other horses had slowly passed away, leaving Paiute alone and lonely.

Paiute was in his mid 20's, getting pretty old. About this time, he was diagnosed with terminal cancer on his privates. The doctor recommended amputation of his penis. Ken asked how long Paiute might live after the surgery. The doctor said perhaps a year and a half. Ken then asked how long might he live without the surgery? The answer was, perhaps one and a half years. We opted for no surgery.

Considering our lonely horse, Ken made an arrangement with our neighbor, Mary Doyle, to stable her horse with Paiute at our barn. For a while, both horses were enjoying life together, when Mary announced that she and her horse were moving to Idaho. Not wanting our big boy to again feel lonely, Mary agreed to take Paiute with her. She made arrangements for Paiute to live near her new home, on a 40 acre horse breeding farm. Paiute had a new job as "uncle," socializing newly weaned foals at that ranch. Each Christmas Mary would send us an update on all the young ones Paiute was guiding. Interestingly, he lived four more years taking care of the young foals, in spite of his cancer diagnosis.

Phillip Schwartze – Lover of Horses

When I asked my long-time friend, former Mayor and Councilman, Phil Schwartze for a horse story he laughed. It turns out that his name, "Phillip" means "lover of horses." Clearly he was a prime candidate for supplying this project with a story. Phil explained that he grew up in Wickenberg, Arizona, which describes itself as the "Dude Ranch Capital of the World." From Arizona, Phil's family moved to Springfield, Missouri. "I have been surrounded by horses for my entire life. Horses have been a common aspect for me. One year I was part of a pack train expedition in the mountains of Colorado with its Governor."

When Phil came to San Juan Capistrano, he was elected three terms to the City Council serving two terms as Mayor. "When we moved to San Juan, I thought it would be fun to get my young sons riding horses. I took them to Kathy Holman over at Ortega Equestrian Center and the boys spent the summer learning to ride. One day Kathy looked at me and asked, 'why don't you get up there?' Once a week for that whole summer of 1986, I took lessons with my sons John and Ryan. It was such a nice way of having fun with them. Across the years, I rode several times in the Swallows Day Parade with the City Council."

Phil continued, "Perhaps all those lessons laid the foundation for me to be ready for my current wife. When I met American Quarter Horse All-Around Champion, Joan Saunders, who rode both English and Western, a real equestrian had come into my life. As a result, so did horses. We were married in 2013, and now we live on a ranch in Fallbrook. Every day, I look out my windows at our horses in their corrals knowing I enjoy their presence. They tell me life is good. I have never been happier!!"

Joan Saunders and Husband Phil Schwartze with Horses Erin, Darla and Jazzy

Wyatt Hart meets Mexican Prancer, "Quapo"

Recently, I was at an evening event inside the Mission where I had a chance to chat with Wyatt and Sue Hart. As long time residents and horse people, I knew that they might have a story. Wyatt is a former Mayor, an involved community-minded person, and an active Portolá Rider. "Well, I've been riding horses my whole life," he began. "I have a friend and he had a horse that had not been ridden much and he asked me to take it on a big ride. Now some good advice is: if you go trail riding, it is best to go on a horse that is as close to a plow horse as you can find."

"Anyway, this friend had two horses, one named "Guapo" which was a gelding up from Mexico. Now Guapo had been trained as a Mexican Prancing Horse. You've seen them in the Swallows Day Parade. They keep their head up high and go into their prance step. They train them with a severe bit. The pressure on their long tongue forces their head up and they prance. Once they are trained, the bit is removed and they continue with that high step which looks magnificent.

On one of the big Portolá Rides, I agreed to ride Quapo. The five or so miles seemed twice that long with all that bouncing and jigging. When I finally got to camp, all I could think about was finding some liniment. When my friend came over for my opinion on Guapo, I said, 'Sell that horse!'"

My First Internet Date
Jim Verbeerst

Ever eager for a horse story, I asked our neighbor and Las Tortugas Rider, Jim Verbeerst, for a horse memory. He offered this up. "A good story about my horse, Chip, is a tale with my friend, Dr. Tom Geisz. One year after a heavy rain we decided to go riding. It had been raining a long time. We were brave enough to take a trail ride in the Creek. The Creek was pretty full of water. As we rode we tried to miss any deep water holes. At a certain juncture, Tom went one way to check out the water issue and I went another. Unfortunately, the route I took had very soggy ground and I had what seemed to be fairly deep water on both sides of the ground I was riding on. Chip started to lose his footing. Before we knew it we were in about five feet of water. I did a complete flip smoothly exiting off Chip. Chip tried his best to imitate me. We both surfaced at the same time and stared at each other over the strange incident. Good old Chip did not act up at all. He allowed me to remount as he valiantly struggled to get us out of our predicament. He got us both to high ground. This is something I will never forget and I certainly felt like a "real" cowboy after that ordeal!"

I very much enjoyed Jim's story and asked him how long he had been riding, and about how he came to our little valley. In Jim's words:

I am a wanna-be cowboy from Detroit. I grew up watching Roy Rogers, Gene Autry, Hopalong Cassidy and the Lone Ranger. I always had my cap pistol ready in case any desperados found their way to our home. I used to go to a stable north of Detroit and ride rental horses. I once even raced a friend of mine who was a much better rider. During the race we came to a dry creek which he jumped nicely. I did too except my horse stopped just as he reached the edge of the dry creek. Fortunately, young bodies can take those kinds of falls!

Fast forward to the early 1980's in California where I met Gretchen, who later became my wife. We both had an interest in horses and began taking English riding lessons at Sycamore Trails Stable. Yes, I did say English. I wore the funny pants and hat, but was told this would make a better rider out of me. When I could not figure out how to attach my saddlebags full of beer to the English saddle, I switched over to Western lessons, which I took for a number of years. I got to meet a lot of nice stable folks and became a pretty good rider in the process.

At the time we were living at the golf course community of Marbella and did not find it to our taste. Fortunately, we went to Kate Wells' Christmas party each year in Hidden Valley. We immediately fell in love with the neighborhood and started to look at every house that went up for sale in Hidden Valley. We didn't find a house that fit our needs, so we started to look at vacant lots. With a stroke of incredible luck, the lot next to Donna and Ken Friess became available. Gretchen had spoken with the owner and she was promised the right of first refusal, should they ever decide to sell. They did decide to sell. We built our dream house and moved in. I soon found a 16 hand horse named Timmie and proceeded to set up a corral and tack shed for him.

Soon after moving in, I met John Clifton who invited me on a one-day ride with the Padre Junipero Serra Riders (The Las Tortugas). It was like a dream come true. He introduced me to a group of the nicest "wanna-be" cowboys, and also some real cowboys that were members of the men's club. That was nearly 20 years ago. Unfortunately, Timmie was a "jigger" and the more I rode, the less I liked him. Ultimately, I put him up for sale and began looking for a new horse around Orange County. I couldn't find anything I liked. John Clifton suggested looking on the Internet at a site located in Texas. Well, Chip was my first "internet date" and the love affair has lasted for over ten years. He is a great horse. He has been used in cattle sorting at our yearly Tortuga Ride and he has helped me and several others win Sorting buckles!

The Founding of Las Tortugas – Padre Junipero Serra Riders
A Men's Riding Club

This ride was originally known as The Camp Pendleton Ride. In 1959, Colonel Allen C. "Ace" Bowen and Victor York of Whittier, along with a few selected men, including Los Angeles County Sheriff Peter Pitchess and Retired Los Angeles Sheriff Gene Biscailuz founded this men's riding club. The purpose of the initial ride was to establish camaraderie, and to raise funds to support the annual Navy

Las Tortugas Riders on a Trail Ride Courtesy John Clifton

Las Tortugas. Courtesy John Clifton

Relief Rodeo at Camp Pendleton. However, there was also another aspect to the origins of the riding group. Camp Pendleton was a litigant in the up-stream water rights for the Santa Margarita River with the Vail Ranch [which became Rancho California] and the Village of Fallbrook. Fallbrook leaders wanted to build a dam on the river. The Marine Corps needed a water expert and pressed Reserve Captain Bowen, a water expert, into active service. He had water expertise stemming from his involvement in the Imperial Valley Water Project. Returned to active duty, Bowen also started up the Camp Pendleton Rodeo and taught young Marines how to ride. Colonel Bowen's contributions to the Western and equestrian traditions at Camp Pendleton resulted in the rodeo grounds at the base being named for him in 1982. The Ride went on a hiatus, but with the energy of "Cap" Crowl and the leadership of Ace Bowen, the Ride began again in 1976 and has been going ever since. Their symbol is the turtle, and their official name is Padre Junipero Serra Riders. One of the longest running traditions of the group is the belief that they have never had a bad ride. John Clifton shared some of the photos from the various rides. They showed long caravans of horse trailers heading up into the mountains. I saw photos of the Riders erecting a huge tent, preparing delicious meals, chilling around the campfire and participating in many horse-type competitions. The adventures looked epic to me. I laughed at the photo of one of the men stashing the fish he had caught in his underwear!

Las Tortugas Riders Prepare for a Big Trail Ride. Courtesy John Clifton

Las Vaqueras Women's Riding Club

In 1993 Judy Foster began a women's riding group, Las Vaqueras, which is going strong today. The club, which has a sponsored membership, sets a limit at 150 members. The goal is equestrian recreation and increasing the members' horsemanship skills. Their website explains: "We are daughters, sisters, mothers, and grandmothers coming together to value and maintain the traditional Western cowgirl way. Our Vaqueras' values bring together the past and the present for the future. Horses, hearts and friends." Across the many months of interviews, I enjoyed learning about some of the members' love of the group. In the weeks to follow, I would learn of Jana Adams' fun times inviting some of the Las Vaqueras Riders to her ranch up north and the adventures they had discovering the wineries in the area. You will read about that soon.

Las Tortugas Riders Enjoying a Trail Ride Courtesy John Clifton

Sam Allevato with Las Tortugas Riders

Chapter Sixteen

Around Town: More Horse Stories

"Preserving homes and buildings just goes hand in hand with horses and preserving our lifestyle." Ilse Byrnes, 2017

The Story of the Bucking Stallion and the Young Nurse:
Greg Sykes

Recently we attended a "Leaders for Philanthropy Night" at the Shea Center which included an equestrian demonstration, speaker, and a time for networking. At the event, we were chatting with several long time San Juan residents. They were eager to join in telling horse memories. Rotarian, Greg Sykes, was chatting with us and before long, I asked, "Do you have a horse story for me?" Well indeed he did!

"It seems back around 1944 my mom and dad were set up on a date by a fellow young Army officer. My dad, Larry, had a friend who knew some graduating Army nurses. He invited a few of the nurses to watch them ride horses at Central Park in New York City. While making the riding arrangements, my dad's friend learned that there was a stallion which had not been saddle broken. He did know my dad was from Wyoming, but for some reason he thought it would be pretty entertaining for the group to watch my dad get bucked off. To make it more exciting for the group, my dad was not told that this horse was quite wild. My dad sensed something was up just before mounting the unruly horse. He had actually trained a lot horses while growing up, and had a sense about them. When he got on the horse, it took off wildly across the corral. Dad spun the horse in a tight circle as it bucked and bucked, until finally, it tired. Then, he rode it back to the rail. Of course the nurses were very interested in the demonstration. One of them, a beauty named Anne, turned out to be my future mother. All the horse heroics caused Anne to take an interest in Larry, my dad. Soon thereafter they began dating, and then were married. I am the happy result of the stunt my dad's buddy tried to play on him.

Greg Sykes' Parents Wed in Wake of Bucking Stallion Episode. Courtesy Greg Sykes

The moral of the story is you better know more about the person on whom you are trying to play a trick, as they may just outsmart you and it could backfire! Although, this time it went well for all.

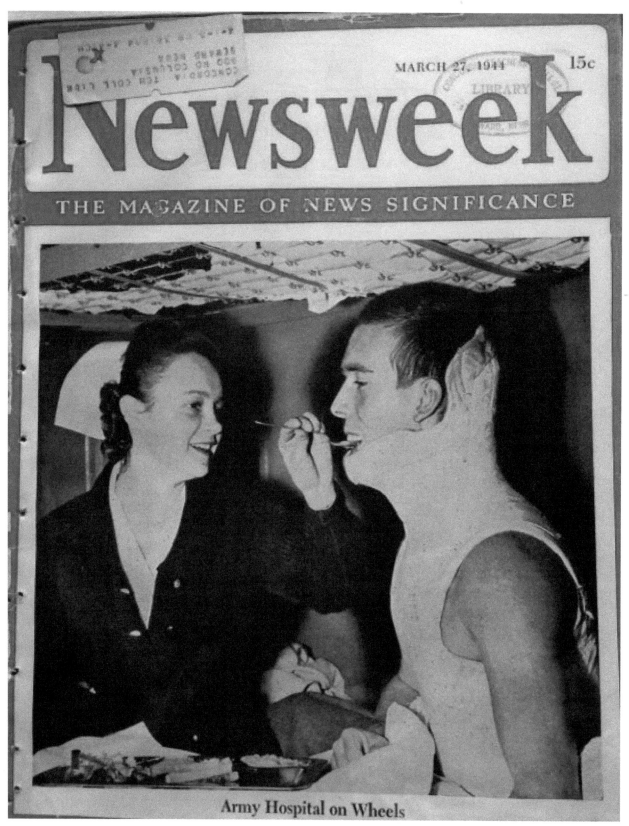

Greg Sykes' Mother, Nurse Anne. Courtesy Greg Sykes

A Barn Sour Horse and an Ornery Horse

As a former Mayor, Larry Kramer, and his wife, Christine, joined in our discussion, Chris, too, had a horse memory to share. Smiling, she told me about her "barn sour" horse.

"When I was about seven or eight years-old I would spend the summer at my grandma's house in Michigan. My father got me a big black stallion named Chico so that I would not be lonely during the summer. Well, when I got on him, he would just take off through fields and gardens and clothes lines, soon bringing me back to the barn. He was too much for me, so my parents gave him to my cousin and they got me Toby. Toby was blind in one eye, smaller than Chico and ornery. Those two horses were not the best to teach me a love of horses. I learned to stick with my beloved horse books by Walter Farley such as *The Black Stallion Adventures* and his many other books about horses and other animals. Marguerite Henry's *King of the Wind,* was my favorite. I enjoyed horses vicariously."

Chris earned a Master's Degree in Library Science and devoted her life to helping children enjoy reading, the past ten years she has volunteered at Concordia Elementary School where she uses innovative ideas to get the children excited about reading. I did ask about the cowboys on television when she was a child, she confided in me that she had an affection for Roy Rogers and Dale Evans. Chris' husband, Larry, joined in, explaining that his favorite cowboy was Hopalong Cassidy. Smiles erupted on our faces as our little conversational group remembered those old time TV cowboys.

Don't Be Afraid to Get Your Feet Wet

When I asked my riding partner, Christine Baumgartner, for her favorite horse story, she shared this: "When I ride with Donna, I often ride Donna's 6 year-old mare, Dancer, while Donna rides her 26 year-old Quarter Horse mare, Blaze. Dancer recently had to learn how to approach and survive new experiences. It makes me smile.

Donna and I had ridden in the river bed countless times when it was dry. Dancer was fine with that. But then came our ride after winter rains had turned the dry river-bed into a shallow, fast moving stream. It was the first time Dancer had been asked to walk through water! Since Blaze is 26, she's "been there and done that." She sniffed the water, put her front feet in, took a drink, and then walked to the other side. Dancer, on the other hand, was a wreck!

She wouldn't go near the water. She huffed and blew, and paced along the side,

Christine Baumgartner and Dancer 2017

making it very clear that she was not going to go near that unknown stuff. I understood that it was new and that the babbling water was scary. The water felt weird on her feet.

Donna and Blaze circled back to find us. Dancer was excited to see them and happy to whinny about this scary stuff (water), and how she was not going to set one hoof in it.

I guess Dancer finally realized that crossing the water was the only way to reach Blaze. So, she gathered herself together and dashed through it, maybe she thought if she ran fast, she wouldn't have to touch it.

We crossed a couple of other streams that day, but always after much hesitation and huffing. I kept encouraging Dancer and telling her each time how brave she was. The next week we again went riding, and we were able to go further through the water. As long as Dancer was close to Blaze, she was less terrified. In the weeks to come the crossings became easier because Dancer learned that she can survive walking through water."

Christine is a Dating and Relationship coach, and she used the story about Dancer to encourage her clients to "get their feet wet" in the scary world of dating. "Taking it from Dancer; once you get used to something it's not that bad!"

Donna Friess and Blaze 2017

Combining My Passions: Photography and Horse Racing
Tom Baker

When I asked Tom Baker, the former Director of the San Juan Capistrano Department of Parks and Recreation, about his subsequent career in race horse photography he had some great stories. His portrait of 2015 Triple Crown Winner, American Pharaoh, has been my computer screen saver since that Triple Crown. Tom answered me simply, "I found a way to combine my passion for photography with my love of horse racing. Here is Tom's response in his own words:

A Man with Two Passions

I was 29 years old in June of 1975 and I felt like I had just won the Lotto. I was working in the Parks and Recreation field as a Recreation Superintendent for the City of Placentia. At that time, the great City of San Juan Capistrano was looking to hire a person to oversee a parks and recreation needs assessment to determine community priorities and develop such a program. The City gave me a six month contract to complete the study and after the study was completed, they hired me to put that plan into action.

Soon after that, our son was born, I began to take photographs, and developed quite an interest in photography. It seemed I was always the one with the camera. Not only on a personal level, but with my position with various cities, I was always photographing the various activities to promote our programs to the local community. At that time the Assistant City Manager, John O'Sullivan, asked me to go to a local San Juan stable and take a photograph of his horse, "Long Last Love." This was not a problem since I enjoyed taking photographs.

Tom Baker Photo Big Stakes Race 2008 Del Mar Racetrack

He invited me the following week to go to the races at Hollywood Park. It was a wonderful day. I bet on a few races and won; that was the beginning for me. I fell in love with those beautiful animals and began to study their breeding in order to make me a better handicapper.

When I attended the races, I would bring my camera and began to photograph the horses in the paddock areas as well as during the races. My wife's parents lived in Arcadia, California, which is the home of Santa Anita Race Track. We would go to Arcadia for the weekend, and the family could visit while I went to the racetrack. Since we were so close, I could attend morning workouts as well as the races during the day. I was lucky enough to sell some of my photographs to the owners and trainers, thus covering my expenses and allowing me to purchase a more professional camera.

I was contacted by the *California Horsemen's News* to see if I was interested in writing articles and taking photographs of the important horse races. They paid me $5.00 per image and $1.00 per inch of writing. Not a lot of money, but the more important part was that it enabled me to get a press credential which gave me access to the entire track at any time. I was able to go in the backstretch area to photograph horses and talk to the various trainers and jockeys as well as covering the races.

At this time, horse racing was very big. There are three major race tracks in Southern California and I was fortunate to cover those tracks. The next 30 years, I worked for three other publications, including the *Racing Form*. Besides these tracks, I was able to photograph the

Professional Horse Photographer Tom Baker Photo. "Super Saver" - Kentucky Derby Winner 2010

"Triple Crown" which includes the "Kentucky Derby," the "Preakness" and the "Belmont." I was fortunate to also be able to photograph the Championship Breeder's Cup Races held yearly throughout the United States.

I have included two of my favorite photographs, a shot at a big stakes Del Mar Race Track race in 2008, and one of Kentucky Derby Winner "Super Saver" in 2010.

I not only enjoy color photography, but I have also developed an interest in infrared photography. About 15 years ago, I had one of my cameras converted to shoot only infrared photos. With the help of some Photoshop adjustments, I am able to turn a simple photograph into a piece of fine art. The images can range from black and white to a surreal image with the use of color.

I have been able to take two of my favorite pastimes and combine them into one lifetime "daily double".

Professional Horse Photographer Tom Baker Photo. American Pharaoh Triple Crown Winner 2015

"President Lincoln" Comes to San Juan – A Reenactment
Richard Hill-Adams

As my quest continued, and I searched wherever I could to bring the experience of living in an historic equestrian community to life, I came across a very interesting article in the *Capistrano.net* business newsletter for 2003. I must have blanked out back then because I did not recall "President Abraham Lincoln" coming to town! I remembered the Freedom Train for the Bicentennial in 1976, however, Lincoln's arrival at the Depot escaped me. I read the article below written by Richard Hill-Adams, which is compelling in its own right, but I needed the back story, as clearly, once again, the community of San Juan was embracing its history. I called Richard on May 19, 2018 and he filled me in. This is how San Juan Capistrano happened to be the site of an historic reenactment.

Back in 2002 Richard Hill-Adams was supervising the construction of fifty-five homes he was building in Wilmington, California. Many weekends he had his eleven year-old son, Christopher, with him, while his wife, Jana, was riding with Las Vaqueras. The construction site was very near the Drum Barracks left over from the Civil War. Christopher saw that a Civil War reenactment was taking place at the Drum Barracks. Richard looked into it and the actors were very excited about young Christopher's enthusiasm. They invited him to participate (even though he was two years shy of the age limit). Christopher was accompanied by a tutor, Claire Adams, who was quite willing to be present while

Lincoln Reenactment in San Juan Capistrano Brought by Richard Hill-Adams

Christopher marched about with the other "soldiers."

As time passed, Richard became acquainted with the organizers of the activity, Larry and Connie Flowers. When the Flowers learned that Richard was from San Juan Capistrano they commented that they always wanted to do a reenactment down there, and enjoy High Tea at the Tea House, but the City regulations and the Sheriff's Department would not permit holding the event due to the guns. Richard told

Lincoln Meets Richard Hill-Adams 2003. Courtesy Richard Hill-Adams

them he could probably make it happen. Connie Flowers, according to Richard, gave him a very dubious look that said, "I'll believe that when I see it!"

Richard was not one to be turned away. He reached out to the City staff and to the Chief of Police. Richard explained, "I got a lot of push back, because the terror attacks of 9/11 were still fresh in everyone's mind, and the reenactment, included a 21 Gun Salute with muskets. City staff was concerned about the guns. I got a petition up and the business owners, Stephen Rios, and everyone along the route of the reenactment, signed the petition that they wanted the event."

The result was that Richard brought the reenactment to San Juan and as the article explains, "President Lincoln got off the train at the Depot." However, there was more to the story than is in the newsletter. After visiting along Los Rios Street, including the O'Neill Museum, The Tea House, and enjoying lunch for 50 "soldiers" on Sarducci's patio, the entourage entered the Mission for the big confrontation between "President Lincoln" and "Don Juan Forster." You will recall that Don Juan Forster lived in and owned the Mission from 1845-1865 until President Lincoln signed the Declaration that kicked Forster out.

According to Richard there were some 300-400 spectators inside the Mission when Lincoln, portrayed by actor William Peck, declared that Forster return the Mission to the Catholic Church. San Juan's native son, Tony Forster, the biological great great-grandson of Juan Forster, was dressed up as Don Juan.

The confrontation began. Lincoln finally commanded to his soldiers, "Dispatch this man!" At this point the soldiers stormed the stage to drag Don Juan (Tony) away. Don Juan's own vaqueros mounted a defense, coming to his aid, but the soldiers prevailed. As Don Juan (Tony) was dragged from the stage, he called out in typical Tony Forster style, "Mr. President, does this mean we aren't having dinner tonight?"

Richard was chuckling as he shared those parting lines. As our conversation came to a close, he said, "I was Colonel Adams, Special Assistant to the President. We had a lot of fun and staged several more such reenactments in town."

HISTORICAL REENACTMENT

San Juan Capistrano, California

(Capistrano.net Business Newsletter, 2003)

On February 15, 2003 President Abraham Lincoln accompanied by the 116th Pennsylvania Volunteer Infantry Company of the Union Army, will arrive in San Juan Capistrano; they will inspect the Historic Los Rios District and the Mission at San Juan Capistrano.

The Spanish Crown had lost the Missions and their Lands when Mexico confiscated the property after passing the Secularization Act in 1833. California was declared to be an Independent Republic when Captain John C. Fremont raised the Bear Flag in 1846. Mexico ceded California to the United States in 1848, after the Treaty of Guadeloupe Hidalgo, which ended the War between the United States and Mexico. When California became a state in 1850 the Federal Government agreed to uphold the claims of the legal landowners and provide Patents for their lands. At the request of the Catholic Church, President Lincoln returned the all of the Mission's to the Catholic Church in March of 1865.

President Lincoln who will be accompanied by several Union Officers, their ladies and an escort detail of soldiers will arrive by train on February 15th, 2003 in San Juan Capistrano. The Presidents entourage will be met at the San Juan Capistrano Train Station by the 116th, Pennsylvania Volunteer Infantry Company, a local Union Army Civil War re-enactment group. The President will deliver a speech, visit the Historic Los Rios District, which has the oldest adobe homes in Orange County, and then the Mission at San Juan Capistrano. The Mission was the seventh to be built of the twenty-one Missions in California; Father Junipero Serra founded this Mission in 1776.

During President Lincoln's visit to the Mission at San Juan Capistrano, he will settle the differences between the former landowner Don Juan Forster who had purchased the Mission, in 1845 from his brother-in-law, California Governor Pio Pico. Don Juan Forster lived at the Mission as his home for twenty years until President Lincoln returned the Missions to the Catholic Church in 1865.

The local cowboys represented by the members Cross Creek Cowboys and the Border Renegades will protect the Mission and the Priests until President Lincoln arrives with the Federal Troops. After resolving the former landowners' issues and inspecting the Mission; the President along with his entourage of Union Officers and their ladies will be escorted by the 116th Volunteer Infantry Company back to the Historic Los Rios District, for a High Tea, at the Tea House on Los Rios Street in the afternoon. Later in the day President Lincoln will tour some of the local merchants and then depart by train with his entourage.

Come and enjoy a day of Living History in the oldest town in Orange County, a town famous for its rich historical background. The events begin in the early morning with the President's arrival at 8:30 AM and continue into, the late afternoon. The public is invited to all aspects of the program and they can follow the President's entourage from the Train Station up Los Rios Street and over to the Mission. All of the re-enactors will dress in authentic period clothing with weapons of the era. Children may have their parents take photographs with the President, Federal Troops and the Cowboys in the afternoon. Richard Hill Adams.

FYI: This program is being sponsored by:

The 116th Pennsylvania Volunteer Infantry Company
Richard Hill Adams
The City of San Juan Capistrano
The San Juan Capistrano Historical Society
Sarducci's Restaurant
Staples The Office Superstore Store
The Old Town Merchants Association
San Juan Depot & Grill
The San Juan Capistrano Chamber of Commerce

Kinkos Copy Center
The Mission at San Juan Capistrano
The Capistrano Dispatch
The Capistrano Valley News/Freedom News
Friess Company Builders
Pekarek-Carnadell Architects

Lincoln Reenactment San Juan Capistrano 2003. Courtesy Richard Hill-Adams

Golden Boy and the Girl with the Mega-Watt Smile
Richard Hill-Adams

One day I was visiting our dentist, and, of course, I was looking for stories. Dr. Carol Daderian has been our family dentist for a long time. Among other community service involvements, she is a past President of the Rotary. Carol suggested that the tale of Golden Boy and his owner, Jana Adams would be nice in the book. The story involved reenactment leader, Richard Hill-Adams. On a warm Sunday afternoon, I called Richard, who was Jana's husband. "Can you tell me the story of Jana and Golden Boy?" I asked.

"Oh, Golden Boy loved his mom. When Jana would come into the gate at Tar Farms, he recognized the sound of her truck and he would begin to whinny," explained Richard.

Of course I was intrigued and asked more about his wife and his life with her. In his words: "It was 1982, and as always, I was driving my El Dorado in the fast lane hitting high speeds when I passed a car and saw this young woman behind the wheel. I tapped the brakes (much to the alarm of the car behind me) and slowed next to her. I caught her attention. She tapped her watch as if to say she needed to get to work. It didn't matter. I followed her. I was not going to let her get away. I followed her all the way up the freeway to MacArthur near the airport when she finally pulled over. It was 7:30 in the morning. I looked good as I was ready for work in a suit and tie and the whole works. 'Good morning," I said, 'I know this is not a proper introduction. I'm Richard Hill-Adams and I work up there.' I explained pointing to the top floor of a nearby building. 'Here is my card. I'd like to know your name and have your phone number. I'd like to see you again, maybe buy you lunch, or you and a girlfriend some lunch.' I asked, hopefully."

'Um…err.. okay. My name is Jana… Um…okay… here's my card.'

As soon as I got to the office, I called my florist and asked her to send the biggest bouquet of big, bright, beautiful flowers she could, big enough that she could not see any other guys coming by.

From that day on we were together. She had one request, that was 'that you take care of my family, (I was thinking she meant a lot of brothers and sisters), my horse, Tadjur, and my dog, Yukon.' I answered her, 'Of course, and I will take care of you all the days of your life.' Seven months later, on March 26, 1983 we were married. We traveled the world and welcomed a son, Christopher.

Jana was a horse woman, a 20 year member of Las Vaqueras where she was the Trail Boss and served on the Board of Directors for years. The women rode from Casper's Park to Rancho Santa Margarita and beyond, over hill and dale. They called her the girl with the "mega-watt smile." She rode her horse

Jana Adams and Richard Hill-Adams

196

Golden Boy who was a big 16 hands high, Palomino Quarter Horse.

Jana's dream always was to own a ranch near where she once lived near Paso Robles. We searched for some time and eventually found a perfect 33 acre place which she named Blue Oaks. It had a big house, a barn, a six mare motel, arenas, and two pastures. It was situated in the middle of 275 wineries. She and her girlfriends, like Renee Ritchie, would trailer up their horses in her big ¾ ton GMC truck. I went up a few times, the place would be crawling with women. They enjoyed riding out to the wineries to sample wines. Jana would like to say, 'the horses know their way back to the ranch...'

Jana enjoyed the ranch from 2006 until 2016. She was diagnosed with an aggressive form of Parkinson's disease, but even with that, as she became more fragile, for three of the five years she was ill, she and Golden Boy would go riding. As her equilibrium began to falter, I would walk next to her, to ensure that she stayed in the saddle. When she rode with her gals, like Renee, they would ride next to her, to right her or warn her to straighten up. Golden Boy understood all of this. He walked more slowly, and more carefully.

Jana and I had a great life. We traveled the world. She loved her family, her friends, and her horses. At the end, the hospice nurse complimented me. I was the night care. Each day when the hospice nurse noticed how clean and well-groomed Jana was, she mentioned, 'you don't see that too often.' Jana had a good quality of life. Our son, Christopher, quit school and work to take care of his mom. She passed away at home on December 27, 2017. I kept my promise. I cared for her all the days of her life."

Jana Adams on Golden Boy. Courtesy Richard Hill-Adams

Unexpected Sightings
Sarah Moore

When I asked Sarah Moore, the Office Manager at Dr. Carol Daderian's dental office, for a horse story, she smiled and shared this with me. "One day, I was beaching in the sun in my bikini with my water bottle close by in south San Clemente just above Camp Pendleton. I had been lying on the sand, enjoying the beautiful Southern California day, listening to the waves as they gently lulled me. Thirsty, I sat up to take a drink of water, and met with the most unexpected sight. Just down the beach from me were mounted military security officers patrolling along the water's edge. I did a double take as I was not expecting to see horses riding along the shore!"

That memory led to another unexpected sighting by Sarah. This time she and her friends were having a late afternoon beer at the Swallows Inn when she looked up and a big horse suddenly poked his nose in the front door! Again, Sarah had to do a double take. Reflecting, she added, "Sometimes, I think I am in a regular city, but then something like that happens and I once again am reminded of what a truly unique character our town really has."

From the Child's Point of View

Hopefully, across these chapters, you have seen a beauty in the tradition of oral history; how it allows the contributor a place to share his or her lived experience. For many of us, some of our most profound moments are from childhood, which in looking back, might seem trivial. Nevertheless, when they are powerful enough to share, even years later, it says something about the impact of that experience on the person. The following are, perhaps, small stories, but for the children who lived them, they were so memorable that years later they chose to share them...

Annika's Scary Moment

I occasionally see our family friend, Adri Vander Broek, on the trail. When I asked her for a horse story, she immediately knew what she wanted to share. It was a very scary experience for her 14 year-old daughter, Annika, who was on her beloved horse, Roca. Roca is stabled at the Ortega Equestrian Center.

As Adri told the story: "Annika and her friend were enjoying an afternoon trail ride on their horses when they came to the water in San Juan Creek. Suddenly, out of nowhere, Roca, dropped to her knees and started to Roll! Annika was horrified! She kept her wits about her and quickly hopped off. Standing in the water, she knew to pull up on the reins. Finally, after what felt like a long time, Roca

Annika Vander Broek and Her Mother Adri with Roca 2017

198

reluctantly got up. They both walked out of the water. Roca was soaked and sandy, and the saddle was trenched and scratched. Luckily, neither Annika nor the horse were hurt, but it was a scary moment and it taught Annika to never let her guard down when riding."

As a reader you may have noticed that horses rolling in rivers and streams with their riders aboard has been a recurring theme!

One afternoon, as my grandchildren dropped in after school, they found me at the computer, and of course, they wondered what was going on. "Girls, I'm finishing the horse book I was telling you about. Do you have a story for it?" [Of course I would be in grandma trouble if I did not share their thoughts with you!]

Two Miniature Shetland Ponies Arrive

Laughing Ella shared this. "I was only about eight years-old that time you and Poppa decided to buy us kids a Shetland pony. Pixie, your Pony-of-America, was a bit too jumpy for us. The day that the horse seller rolled up in front of your house and drove into the back yard pulling a horse trailer with two of the most adorable mini Shetlands, we'd ever seen, well that was the

Git Up! Enjoying the Mini Shetlands

beginning. Mimi, we kids knew you only had planned to purchase one mini pony, but when my mom looked at how adorable they were, and you looked at her, the deal was sealed. That horse trader knew what he was doing by bringing both of them! I remember you told the man that *both* ponies could stay.

The mini Shetlands had long hair and one of them was a paint with white in his mane and some white spots, the other was all black, and looked like a miniature black stallion. We kids were just delighted. On the way to walking them to the barn, of course,

Ella, Ashley and Elizabeth Friess Mini Sheltlands

with no saddle, Poppa put me on the little black horse. He was a very short pony, maybe three feet tall, but I was also pretty small. I was heading for the barn, when all of a sudden, he lurched and reared. Oh my goodness! My heart stood still, then it pounded like crazy, while I hung on to the mane. The whole thing only took a few seconds, and I stayed on, but forever after we kids named him Bucca for bucking, though, he actually just reared! After that I always rode Freddie, the paint. He was much nicer."

Friess Girls and their Mini Shetland Ponies, Bucca and Freddie

"Oh, I have another one. This happened one day when Elizabeth, and Emily, and I went riding. We were up in the hills. Elizabeth was on Dancer and I was riding Blaze, Emily was behind us on Mr. T. We had a nice ride in the hills, and on the way home Elizabeth and I let our horses lope for a while. Emily held Mr. T back because he was so old, however, he got excited seeing his stable mates loping along, and whoa! He took off loping. In the meanwhile, Elizabeth and I slowed our horses down, and we were waiting at the crest of the little hill, when, oh goodness, the trouble started. Mr. T hadn't planned on how he was going to slow down, and we pretty much were blocking the trail. All of a sudden, the excited old Thoroughbred banged right into Dancer. Surprisingly, she was not that upset. She turned her head around as to say, "What the heck, Dude, you are rude!" After that we all just walked the horses back home. It could have been bad. I'm just thankful Dancer didn't spook and we didn't fall off"

Girl Dangling
Megan Friess

Granddaughter Megan wanted to share one of her most memorable moments on the horses. "This was about twelve years ago when Lucky (a gift from Ron Hanson at Sycamore Trails) came to live with you. I was about nine years-old and Poppa was letting us take turns riding on her bare back around the corral. The big pepper tree was hanging over the corral and had a low, thick-hanging branch which stuck out into the corral. It was covered by the drooping leaves. I didn't have any reins. I was just riding around the arena holding on to her mane, so I had no control over where she decided to go. She walked

Friess Girls - Ella, Jillian, Katie and Megan

through the leaves and that big branch caught me right in the stomach. I was stuck. I was in shock for a minute, and then somehow hoisted myself sideways as Lucky just kept on walking. I knew to hold on to the branch. There I was, dangling from the branch. Girl dangling! Poppa walked over and saw me just chilling there, hanging. He got me down, but I never forgot it. It seems funny now, but it wasn't that funny back then!"

The Case of the Run-Away Ponies

Elizabeth and Ashley Friess wanted to get their unforgettable experience into this accounting. Ashley wrote: "Elizabeth and I were riding the mini Shetlands one day with our dad. We were heading back from a trail ride in the hills. I was about five years-old and Elizabeth was seven. We were in front of our dad on the trail behind the Neighborhood Park, when suddenly Freddie takes off with Elizabeth. She knew to jump off. My dad was screaming 'get off the horse! Get off!' He was yelling in pure panic and had evident terror in his voice. He

Elizabeth and Ashley Friess Braid Dancer's Mane

did not stop yelling as he was afraid the pony would run away with me across busy San Juan Creek Road and we would be hit by the fast cars. I finally did manage to jump off! Whew! The moral of the story: Be careful where you ride!"

Why I Love Horses: Emily Friess

When I asked our granddaughter, San Juan Hills High School senior and Camp Rawhide Ranch graduate, Emily Friess, about horses and why she loves them, she answered. "I love horses because they are very intelligent and understanding animals. They each have their own personality; some are lazy, while others are overly energetic. One of my favorite things that horses do is when they come up to a person and try to use them as a scratching post. These many hundred pound animals are gentle giants."

Donna and Pixie, Jillian and Mr. T

Caroline Enjoys Feeding Carrots 2017

Caroline Friess

Eight year-old Caroline walked into the room as she had just completed her china painting project. "Caroline, do you want to add a horse moment to the book?" I asked. She responded in a shy little voice, "I like to feed the horses because it's fun feeding them. I like to touch their soft pink noses because they are pretty. I like riding horses."

Life With a Dare-Devil Brother

Our granddaughter, Jaycelin Bert, has just one very vivid memory of her childhood horseback riding adventures with our horses. One day when she was about seven years-old, she went riding with her novice-rider, ten year-old brother, Jake, and her mother. They had enjoyed a leisurely trail ride and were some distance in front of their mother, heading for home when Jake rode up alongside Jaycelin and challenged her, grinning, "You wanna race?" Jaycelin had chosen to ride Mr. T, the calm former race horse, because she could trust him. She said, no, and was not concerned because Mr. T was old. Jake was on the big Quarter Horse, Lucky, who was more high strung. As Jaycelin described the incident;

Jaycelin Bert with Blaze

"About a second after Jake made the challenge, he and Lucky bolted off. I thought, Mr. T would hold back, but, being the former race horse he was, he was up for the challenge and took off running behind Lucky. I wasn't sure what to do. At this point, our mother could see what was going on, and yelled to Jake to stop! I knew I could not stop Mr. T so I threw myself off. By now, our mom was running on her horse to stop Mr. T before he crossed the busy street. Once she had him

Jake Bert on Lucky

in tow, and Jake had finally slowed down, she circled back to me. She climbed off her horse and brushed the dust from me. I was crying and scared, but I had gotten myself safely off, and I wasn't hurt. I never did really want to go riding with Jake after that. He was so new to horses that he had no idea that telling the horse, "Git" would have such a big reaction! I suppose if there are any lessons here, one might be, do not trust your older brother on the horses, while the other might be, don't be discounting a former race horse, just because he's old!!"

Julina Bert with Jaycelin on Mr. T c. 2004

Elizabeth, Ella and Emily on a Ride

Saddle Up! Ashley and Elizabeth Friess with Mr. T and Lucky c. 2008

Friess Family on the Trail c. 2009

Jaycelin Bert With Her Grandmother Mimi
(Donna)

Julie and Jaycelin Bert Going Riding

Elizabeth Practices for Barrel Racing on Dancer 2017

Elizabeth with Dancer

Trail Riders Jenny and Emily Friess c. 2008

Chapter Seventeen

"Hi-Ho, Silver, Away!"

"That all things change but truth, and that truth alone, lives on forever."
(The Lone Ranger Creed)

Gone Missing
Kay Richardson

My neighbor Kay Richardson has lived near me for a quarter of a century. I have enjoyed her friendship very much, and we have discussed our fond memories of being inspired by the old-time TV cowboys. I saved this story until now because I thought you would get a kick out of it. It took place back in the days when the Lacouague Citrus Ranch was behind our homes and Rocky's Stable was located where Tar Farms is today.

Kay shared this. "One afternoon I went out to feed my Arabian horse, Tiger, and he was missing from our barn. My heart started racing as I panicked. *Where was Tiger?* I set out on foot with a halter and searched everywhere I could. I returned home wondering what to do next. I was getting really worried, when out of the corner of my eye, way up on the hill, I spotted him on the ridge behind our houses on the Lacouague Ranch. I knew the Lacouague family rented out a small pasture. He was just standing there, my white horse, minding his own business. I grabbed the halter again and quickly hiked the half mile up the hill to get him. Breathlessly, I haltered him up and rode bareback all the way home. I was so relieved that he had not gotten into trouble with a car or worse. Later that afternoon my husband, Don, came home and stopped to say hi to the horse before he came inside. I was upstairs in the kitchen when he called to me.

"Kay, where is Tiger?
"What? …He's out in his stall."
"No, that's not him?"
"Yes it is!"
"No Kay, it is not!"

At this point Kay went out to Don and "Tiger" in the corral. She studied her horse and realized instantly that Don was correct. This was NOT Tiger! She was puzzled and worried. *Where was her horse?* She went out searching the neighborhood once again, this time more thoroughly. When she went back to Rocky's stable, down the street from her home, she examined each stall. It was a big stable. Finally, there he was, merrily munching on some fresh hay in an open stall. He had gone visiting and took advantage of the opportunity for a snack!

With the real Tiger safely in his stall, Kay once again haltered up the look-alike horse and hiked up the hill. When she crested it, she saw a young girl clearly looking for her horse. I never knew exactly how she explained the whole incident to the girl, but the story ended happily. Kay now realizes that she could have been killed, jumping on a strange horse, bareback, like that! She shook her head as she concluded, "That's typical me!"

San Juan Feels Right to Us
JoAnn and Richard Cramer

Hopalong Cassidy was especially interested in teaching us youngsters about right and wrong. At the end of the show he would always talk about the importance of good behavior.
Michelle Kelley

JoAnn Cramer is the President of the Mission San Juan Capistrano Docent Society, where she has volunteered for six years. Her husband, Richard (Dick) has volunteered as a Gardening Angel at the Mission for the past eight years. They are San Juan residents with an appreciation for the equestrian culture we share.

Dick explained, "I didn't grow up in San Juan Capistrano but visited occasionally with my family. I grew up in the Pomona Valley and our family had a horse (Cherokee, known as Cherry) that we boarded in West Covina. As such, I was constantly around horses from an early age. In fact, we didn't live far from the old Kellogg's Arabian Horse Ranch which is now Cal Poly Pomona [California State University at Pomona]. I often rode my bicycle over to the Ranch and watched the beautiful Arabian Horses.

Our horse was a brown and white Morgan gelding that had previously been a show horse. We went to many horse shows, parades and rodeos on the weekends which I enjoyed very much. My father, an architect and artist, made rawhide hackamores that he sold to Western and Saddle Shops. I used to like going to these shops and looking at all the cowboy boots and clothing, especially the leather fringe jackets.

I was influenced by the likes of Gene Autry, Roy Rogers and Dale Evans, Hopalong Cassidy, the Lone Ranger, Tom Mix and others; as well as the great old Western music with the Sons of the Pioneers. "Ghost Riders in the Sky" is still one of my favorite songs along with many of Marty Robbin's ballads. Every Saturday growing up in Pomona we would go to the Fox Theater to see the latest Western movies; more innocent times than we have today. San Juan feels comfortable to me.

JoAnn shared that she rode as a youth and invariably got the horse that took off running away with her. "I was scared to death, holding on for dear life! I was the one the guide had to circle back and bring back into the group." She admits that she recently had a lovely ride in the hills above Rosarito Beach with her family. She is the first to say that Dick is the horseman. They both enjoy living in San Juan Capistrano and seeing the horses out and about.

The Influence of Television on America's First Generation of Youth with TV's

Dick Cramer's memory of the powerful effect of the movie and television cowboys on him as a youth was another recurring theme which evolved from the interviews. I enjoyed the many happy recollections people had about them. In Chapter Fifteen you read Tortuga Rider Jim Verbeerst's story. I admired his honest way of admitting that he was a "wanna-be" cowboy, that he had admired the cowboys on TV as he grew up. I, too, as I revealed earlier, had a childhood admiration for Roy Rogers and Hopalong Cassidy. Across the months of talking to people about horses, I discovered the powerful impact that television cowboys and cowgirls had on so many of us growing up as the first generation watching television. I never asked about it, the topic just came up. Sam Allevato told me that as a child, he was so taken with Hoppy that his young friends actually called him "Hoppy." He still owns a nice collection of Hoppy memorabilia. When I talked with Kathy Holman of the Ortega Equestrian Center, she, too, mentioned Hoppy early in our conversation. One of her most cherished mementos is a signed Hoppy poster given to her by a friend.

I went back and asked John and Sherry Clifton about the TV heroes of their youth. Sherry answered me. "I lived right across from Hoppy Land on Clune Avenue in Venice. My dad was a Venice police officer and he would take me to see Hoppy. Once I got to sit on a horse with him. John said, "I used to ride horses at Grant's Stables in Playa Del Rey, right near Hoppyland."

Christine Baumgartner shared, "I remember seeking out happy couples on TV since my parents weren't happy people and not happy with each other. Luckily in the 1950's there were plenty of happy couples. I liked how happy Roy Rogers always was and how he and Dale Evans seemed together, their singing together, and that Roy Rogers was so nice to his horse Trigger. I watched all of his shows.

Without meaning to, I have discovered that Jim, Sam, Kathy, Donna, Sherry, Christine, Dick, now Michelle might be members, if there were such a thing, of a fan club for grown-ups who loved the old TV cowboy legends.

It only took a little digging on the U.S. History.org website to find an article, "Land of Television." The case is made that perhaps no phenomenon shaped American life in the 1950's more than the invention of television. At the close of World War II, a television set was a toy for a few thousand American families who could afford them. Ten years later nearly two-thirds of American households had televisions, and the invention of TV dinners in 1954 allowed families to dine while watching their favorite shows.

"Television brought Western heroes into American homes and turned that fascination into a love affair. Cowboys and lawmen such as Hopalong Cassidy, Wyatt Earp and the Cisco Kid galloped across televisions every night." One Western, *Gunsmoke*, ran for 20 years, longer than any other prime time drama in television history. The report went on to describe the Saturday morning shows with Roy Rogers, Rin Tin Tin, Howdy Doody and Davy Crockett. At the close of the 1950's decade, 30 Westerns aired on prime time each week, and Westerns occupied 7 spots on the Nielsen Top-10."

The themes of the Westerns drew a sharp line between "good" and "bad" and "reinforced the notion that everything was okay in America as good triumphed over evil." The report concluded that as the Civil Rights Movement gathered momentum in the 1960's, the simplistic version of right and wrong began to blur as society tackled issues which had long been left in the shadows.

That United States History report proved to me that, truly, my generation, the first to have televisions, could hardly have NOT been heavily influenced by Western shows playing in our living rooms.

"Hi-Ho, Silver, Away"
Michelle Kelly

When I asked San Juan resident and Mission San Juan Capistrano docent, Michelle Kelly for a horse memory, she said, "When I was in my teens, I had an aunt and uncle who had a small horse ranch in Beaumont, California. Whenever I stayed with them on vacations, my cousin and I would ride like crazy into the nearby hills as fast as the Lone Ranger rode ""Silver." It was pure exhilaration! I've never felt so much freedom and independence as I felt on horseback during those joyous times." I went back and asked Michelle about the TV cowboys. She reminded me, "Hopalong Cassidy was especially interested in teaching us youngsters the difference between right and wrong. I remember him riding up on the camera at the end of the show and talking about the importance of good behavior. Roy Rogers, The Lone Ranger, and all those other Cowboys and Cowgirls would also do the same within the contexts of their weekly shows. The stories were like secular morality plays, and the "Romance" of the Old West served as their back ground. How could we kids not fall for those shows? I did Hook, Line and Spur!"

The Evolution of El Viaje de Portolá Man
Borre Winckel

San Juan Capistrano resident and Portolá Rider, Borre Winckel, wrote a series of articles describing his introduction into being a part of the Ride. This is excerpted from his first article, *The Evolution of EVP-Man. [El Viaje de Portolá Man], 2003,* and shows the influence of TV cowboys on young children.

"There was neither a horse nor much horsing around in my pre-Portolá days. Life revolved around work, raising a family, a couple of obscure hobbies and joining the wife in church, and perhaps in that order. I could have been *anybody* and I might even have been *you.*

For many years, I had a vague notion that outside of town something was going on involving large four footers and men taking to the hill in Western gear. The closest I had come to these fellows was seeing them saddled up on the wall in the Swallows Inn.

For most of my early life, anything that had to do with the West and Western living came from watching *Bonanza, Gunsmoke, The Virginian,* and my favorite program, *Rawhide.* As a kid, cowboys were the good guys and Indians had to be played by others, usually a younger brother whose preference was ignored. No wonder we always won, even, or especially, when pretending.

In those days, we attached PVC pipe to scrap wood mouthing gunfire sound effects with amazing accuracy and results. John Wayne had nothing on us. Horses were missing though, so our bikes substituted.

A few friends rode along with swords, wearing capes-made from old curtains-while engaging in a parallel action form another bygone age. We were young and our battles always ended at dark, at dinnertime, whenever mom called us in or when our enemies got tired of being the enemy. But, admittedly our bikes made for poor substitutes of the horse.

I had only truly ridden a horse for as many times as my hands have fingers. I confess, I somewhat feared the beast, especially the kick from its mighty hind quarters. I was under no illusion; the horse was riding me. Then one, day a dear friend asked if I had ever heard of a Ride called El Viaje de Portolá and would I like to join in for just one day? My life would never be the same again."

Borre's story goes on to include more newbie adventures from his first Ride in 1998, when he was paired with a rental horse that was supposed to be for "greenhorns," but took off galloping with him well ahead of his host, Gilbert Aguirre. Borre says, "that wasn't even on my list of "no-no's!" His conclusions provide insight as to why the Portolás have persevered.

"One thing was for sure, friendships for life were already being made and I hadn't even yet entered the hallowed grounds of Campo Portolá. This rider-in-training owes it all to his host and to the kind fellows who tolerated a greenhorn's first hours on the trail of Gaspar de Portolá."

The Lone Ranger and Silver. Famous Television Icons

A Moral Compass

Another long-time San Juan equestrian confided in me that he grew up in a chaotic family and that the Boy Scout Oath and the Lone Ranger Creed provided him with a moral compass which has served him throughout his life. Perhaps, it is safe to say that the life lessons taught by the television cowboys and cowgirls of the 1950's, have had a lasting impact, at least on some of us, who were the first generation to grow up with a television.

The Lone Ranger Creed:

I believe: That to have a friend,
a man must be one.
That all men are created equal
and that everyone has within himself
the power to make this a better world.

That God put the firewood there
but that every man
must gather it and light it himself.

In being prepared physically, mentally, and morally
To fight when necessary
For that which is right.
That a man should make the most
Of what equipment he has.

That 'this government,
Of the people, by the people
And for the people'
Shall live always.

That men should live by the
The rule of what is best
For the greatest number.

That sooner or later...
Somewhere...somehow...
We must settle with the world
And make payment for what we have taken.

That all things change but truth,
And that truth alone, lives on forever.

In my Creator, my country, my fellow man."
The Lone Ranger

Western Heroes as Cultural Icons

Southern Californian artist, Katie West, specializes in Western art which she combines with her love of country. A good deal of her past work can be found in San Juan Capistrano on wall displays and historic depiction monuments. In her art book, *Legends of the American West*, she points out that the theme of patriotism was modeled by many of the celebrities portraying legends of the Old West. Katie's art book includes memorable cowboys in the section entitled: "Cowboy Up America," where such favorites as: Roy Rogers, Dale Evans and Trigger, John Wayne, The Lone Ranger and Tonto, Marshall Dillon, Zorro, John Wayne, Hoppy, Gene Autry, Tex Ritter, James Arness, and others appear. Clearly, many heroes of the Old West became cultural icons, sharing values of patriotism and courage, as good won out over evil. It is no wonder so many of those whom I interviewed held such precious memories of those legendary giants from their youth. Here, once again, are those values as described in *Cowboy Ethics* by James Owen.

The Code of the West:

1. **Live Each Day with Courage**
2. **Take Pride in Your Work**
3. **Always Finish What You Start**
4. **Do What Has to Be Done**
5. **Be Tough, But Fair**
6. **When you Make a Promise, Keep It**
7. **Ride for the Brand**
8. **Talk Less and Say More**
9. **Remember That Some Things Aren't For Sale**
10. **Know Where to Draw the Line**

Entering Cowboy Country
Dan Almquist

Every time I come into town via Del Obispo Street from the harbor in Dana Point, my eyes search out the statues welcoming those passing by. A trickle of joy runs through me. Intrigued to know their origins, I contacted the owners, Dan and Lindsay Almquist, who shared this explanation.

"Our family attends the final weekend of the National Finals Rodeo (NFR) in Las Vegas, Nevada, every year. During the rodeo, the convention hall is filled with vendors describing their wares as "Cowboy Christmas." One year, artist, Bradford Williams, had a booth displaying his art. The piece we purchased was entitled "Binding Contract" and is one and a half times life size. It consists of three separate pieces and weighs over 3000 pounds. Bradford is a true Cowboy artist. Our property runs right up to Del Obispo Street and we live on the border between Dana Point and San Juan. I thought the piece would be a perfect welcoming for those coming into our beloved and special City of San Juan Capistrano; a way to announce that this is "Cowboy Country," a place where people deal with integrity, and a reminder that one's word and handshake means something. We, the Almquist family, are new to San Juan, having only lived here for five years. That being said, I think there are even greater days ahead for San Juan if we can come together and get past some of the divisiveness that has hindered our town in recent years. Hence, the image of one Cowboy reaching over the split rail fence to shake another Cowboy's hand. The title is "Binding Contract." Bradford obviously envisioned the Cowboys making a deal and solidifying it with their handshake. Perhaps, they were settling a dispute? Maybe they were just saying hello to one another. Whatever story one wants to picture, it is a powerful image. I have four young children, who like all children, are impressionable. The statue is a daily reminder for each of them, and for my wife and myself, to live with integrity and to honor our word."

"Binding Contract" Statue. Courtesy Dan Almquist

A Public Art Project
Mustangs Symbolizing San Juan

"Wild Horses Return to San Juan Capistrano" was the headline of an *Orange County Register* article in October, 2015, describing the public art project of painted wild mustang sculptures which San Juan artists took on to paint for charity. Dana Yarger of Dana Point and Tom Scott, President of the El Camino Real Playhouse, spearheaded the project to promote local businesses. Other cities have been successful with such projects; Avalon, California, for example, proudly displayed buffalos, Fullerton enjoyed painted sheep statues, London, England boasted cow statues, and Zurich chose lions. According to the *Register* article, "Dana Yarger chose wild mustangs, because the City is the self-proclaimed 'equestrian capital of the West Coast.' The history of horses in the region extends back centuries, and the sprawling ranches and equestrian centers that exist today represent that history."

San Juan Capistrano artist, Art Guevara, is known for his vibrant, sometimes magical art work. He has been creating public art in the form of murals, sculptures, and paintings in San Juan Capistrano for over 30 years. For the particular public art project mentioned above, he painted three sculptures; one celebrated the story of "Zorro: The Curse of Capistrano," taken from the early 20th Century novel and silent film that brought fame to San Juan Capistrano, while "Saving the Wild Mustangs," was the theme of another, painted in patriotic colors with an American flag. At another time, he painted a longhorn bull sculpture to honor Native Americans, entitled "The Story of Native Americans."

Art Guevara is a highly celebrated and prolific artist. He uses his work not only to raise money for charity, but to expose social injustice. His paintings bring attention to issues such as: domestic violence, child sexual abuse, drug addiction, and prostitution. His work has received international recognition. Recently the City of Guanajuata, Mexico sent a

Wild Mustang Public Art Project - El Camino Real Playhouse

television network crew to San Juan Capistrano to interview him. A psychologist in Columbia commissioned Art to create a work that could illustrate the problem of human trafficking to help victims in their country. Art created a big four-part mural depicting wild horses adorning the temporary construction fence for the new Marriott Hotel being built on Ortega Highway at El Camino Real.

Art Guevara Painted Mural on Construction Fence at new Marriott Hotel Site.
Courtesy Art Guevara 2017

Wild Mustang Public Art Project. Courtesy
The Capistrano Dispatch

Art Guevara's Beautiful Work. Courtesy *The Capistrano Dispatch*

At The End of the Trail

As my eighteen months of research came to a close, it seemed prophetic to discover that San Juan Capistrano's public art competition would involve the horse. They go hand-in-hand, San Juan Capistrano, and the horse. In the same way, when San Juan again built its own high school, the students chose a stallion as their mascot. They persuaded the City to rename the entrance street to "Stallion Ridge," and selected, "Ride for the Brand," as the school's motto. It is no surprise to enter the football and track stadium at the High School and read the billboard announcing that you have arrived in "The Badlands." Symbolically, the Old West is all around us.

Sitting in the bleachers at the Bren Events Center, at the University of California at Irvine, for the graduation of the San Juan Hills High School Class of 2018, on Thursday night, June 7th, we enjoyed the massive letters RFTB which repeatedly flashed across the big screens at the front of the stadium. Certainly the 630 graduates understood that RFTB means RIDE FOR THE BRAND. The Mistress of Ceremonies, the Principal, Jennifer Smalley, in her prepared remarks to the class, made some astute observations about this particular Class. Above all else, she described their passion. She pointed out that the students showed their passion to change the world as they protested gun violence by joining the national high-school walk-out to stop bloodshed, and by registering to vote in record numbers. In her observation they also demonstrated a passion toward each other. It seems to me that she was pointing out that the students of San Juan Hills High School, indeed, symbolize what it is to "Ride for the Brand," that they adopted a culture of: "all for one and one for all." That is a very telling statement coming from the school Principal, and not one I have heard at other such graduations. Later, in private, I asked my granddaughter, Emily, the recent graduate, about this. Her immediate response was, "we believe in inclusiveness above all else."

217

It is not just the High School students who get it about "Ride for the Brand." Across the nearly half century in which I have lived in town, I have seen the same theme played out countless times in our community: when Gilbert Aquirre rode his horse across the raging flood waters of San Juan Creek, clutching the desperately ill child to him, determined to get medical help; when Ron Hanson asked Ken Friess, "How much do you need for the youth wrestling mats?"; when Kathy Holman helped a 65 year-old retired school teacher learn how to jump her horse; when thousands of volunteer hours are put in each year to help children to increase their mobility and confidence at The Shea Center; or when a passerby stops and dusts off a teenager who has been knocked off her mule by a randy young colt!

This theme was demonstrated decades ago when the City residents blazed a new trail and elected a Council committed to reducing the City's proposed build-out from 85,000 people to 40,000; when

determined voters were inspired to approve millions of dollars in Open Space Bonds for our children and grandchildren to enjoy; when community members valued the beauty of our ridgelines and stood up to protect them; and when powerful efforts are put forth to ensure the continuation of our Swallows Day traditions through the Fiesta Association; when residents donate hundreds of thousands of dollars to ensure after-school safety for our youth though the Boys and Girls Clubs of Capistrano Valley; when the Historical Society galvanizes the townsfolk toward important preservation projects; or when parents and volunteers dedicate countless numbers of hours to the American Youth Soccer Association programs. I see it in every corner of San Juan Capistrano, in daily acts of goodwill and kindness by the residents.

My take-away from gathering the material for this book is that living in a town such as ours offers a uniqueness that has evolved from the cherished traditions of old; that we get our strength from knowing what is right and what is wrong, being true to our beliefs, being willing to discuss our differences with each other, while continuing to look out for our neighbors, which is essentially the "Code of the Old West" (*Cowboy Ethics*, 2004).

As our journey through the equestrian story that is San Juan's comes to a close, I hope you have come to have, perhaps, a new respect for the countless ways in which the lives of our residents are enriched not only by the presence of horses, but through our devotion to the larger cultural celebration of our Western heritage. This book has been a way to memorialize the lived experience of some in a place such as ours.

As the personal stories have shown; we have ridden horses in competitions, raced on them for sport, bet on them for fun, cantered with them on the trails, depended upon them as therapy assistants, have needed their help in transporting us, in cultivating the soil, in harvesting the crops, in carrying those crops to market, and in some cases even carried ammunition across enemy lines. Many of us have relied upon them for our livelihood as stable owners, trainers, veterinarians, breeders, grooms, competition judges, and/or feed and tack store owners. We have enjoyed photographing them, painting their images, reading about them, writing about them, and making movies about them. We even take pleasure in grooming them, and sometimes, in simply looking at them, while also keeping alive our rich Western traditions.

The concept of horses as a philosophical, therapeutic, and recreational entity is being threatened across Southern California. San Juan Capistrano is among the last of the cities in our area to have preserved their presence. If, we, the people, do not continue to fight to protect them, and to treasure this rich legacy, San Juan will succumb to, yet, more concrete, steel, and glass.

My hope is that this trip backward in time has allowed you moments of reflection, and, perhaps a renewed interest in cherishing our four-legged equine friends. We, with our children and grandchildren, and future generations, have the opportunity to help preserve this unique aspect of Western culture in our little corner of the planet, at the edge of the continent.

My best, Donna
www.drdonnafriess.com
donna@yourtimenow.org

References and Appendices

"Whether you are riding a horse or not, it's good
for people to be around horses."
(San Juan Capistrano Veterinarian, Mark Secor, 2014)

References
Primary Sources

Oral Histories

Adams, Mechelle Lawrence March, 20, 2017, April 21, 2018, May 4, 2018.

Adams, Richard Hill, May, 7, 10, 20, 2018.

Aguirre, Gilbert. Interview, March 22, 2017.

Agostini, Jennifer Casper. May 6,7, 2018.

Allevato, Sam. June 14, 2017.

Almquist, Dan and Lindsay, June 23, 2018.

Baker, Tom. May 8, 2018.

Baumgartner, Christine

Belardes, Domingo. Blas Aguilar Adobe foundation President and descendent
of the Acjachmen people, April, 2018.

Berney, John. Emails. May 2018.

Bert, Jaycelin. June 4, 2018.

Bondi, Renee Lacouague, April 13, 2017.

Butler-Moburg, Dana. April 24, 2018.

Brandes, Melissa. April 26, 2018.

Burgess, Shane. Dean of the College of Agriculture and Life Sciences. Video. 2013. University of
Arizona.

Byrnes, Ilse. March 27, 2017.

Caldwell, Eileen, May 7, 2018.

California State University at Fullerton's Oral Documentation. Testimony of Albert Launer taken
December 11, 1964).

Clifton, John and Sherry. April 26, 2018.

Cramer, JoAnn and Richard, May 10, 2018.

Dupont, Allison Powell, May 16, 2018.

Friess, Ashley, May 15, 2018.

Friess, Caroline, May 20, 2018.

Friess, Ella, May 10, 2018.

Friess, Emily, May 15, 2018.

Friess, Jillian. April 20, 2018.

Friess, Megan. May 29, 2018.

Greenbush, Barbara. Lecture. "Courage under Fire: The Story of Staff Sergeant Reckless." August
9, 2017.

Hart, Wyatt and Sue, June 9, 2018.

Holman, Kathy, April 18, 2018.

Holroyd, Elaine. April13, 2018.

Hribar, Tom, May 7, 2017.

Johnson, Julie Ryan. Email. May 19,2018.

Kelly, Michelle, May 13, 2018.

Kerr, Ginny. Interview January 13, 2018.

Kramer, Christine. May 4, 2018.

Lacouague, Marie. April 13, 2018.

Love, Fred. March 17, 2017.

Loyatho, Denise Lacouague, April 10, 2018.

Miller, Jacqueline. April 21, 2018.

Moiso, Tony. May 31, 2017.

Moore, Sarah. April, 2018.

Nordeck , Steve. July 10, 2017.

Oehlett, Molly. May, 2018.

Paulsen, Dick, May 15, 2018.

Porter, Lorie. April, 2018.

Powell, Hilary. March, 2018.

Richardson, Kay. February, 2018.

Ritchie, Renee. March through May, 2018.

Saint Margaret's Episcopal High School Newsletter , April 4, 2018.

Schmidt, Diana. February 10, 2018.

Scott, Eric. Lecture June 3, 2017.

Schwartze, Phillip. Conversation May 4, 2018.

Smith, Michelle Lacouague. April, 2018.

Smith, Morton. April 16, 2018.

Stewart, Kerilyn. April 10, 2018, May 12, 2018.

Sykes, Greg. May 7, 2018.

Thompson, Gretchen Stroscher, July 19, 2017.

Vander Broek, Adri. May, 15, 2018.

Verbeerst, James. April 13, 2018.

Von Aldenbruck, Cherylin. September, 2017.

Williams, Colonel James. October 2017.

Williamson, Gerry, May 7, 2018.

Whitney, Kevin. Videotaped testimony. https://vimeo.com/195773694. Shea Center.

Field Trips

Blas Aguilar Adobe, Grand Opening. August 21, 2017.

Irvine Museum, March 2017.

La Brea Tar Pits and Page Museum. July 17, 2017

Laguna Art Museum, January 3, 2017.

Mission San Diego, October 5, 2017.

Montenz Adobe. June, 2017.

Owens Valley, California Historical Landmark 349,where the military installation of Camp Independence once stood during the California-Indian Wars. January, 2018.

Presidio and Father Serra Museum, San Diego, October 5, 2017.

References: Secondary Sources

Adams, Richard Hill. 2003. *Historical Reenactment.* Capistrano.net. Business Newsletter.

Amor, Samuel. 1921. History *of Orange County, California with Biographical Sketches Part I.* Los Angeles Historic Record Company. Google Books. Com. accessed Aug. 27,2017.

Anton, Mike. May 12, 2009."Hidden in O.C.'s Foothills, a gnarled reminder of California's Past. *Los Angeles Times.*

Armstrong, Scott Elias, "Bering Land bridge." *Scientific American: The Conversation,* March 4, 2014).

Baumgartner, Jerome, W. 1989. *Rancho Santa Margarita Remembered: An Oral History.* Santa Barbara, CA. Fithian Press.

Blumer, Herbert. 1962. Society as Symbolic Interaction," *Human Behavior and Social Process: An Interactionist Approach.*Boston. Rose, Arnold, editor.

City Historical Roster: Roster of City Council , Members, Staff and Committees, San ;Juan Capistrano Housing Authority and Board of Directors, Staff and Committees of the Former Community Redevelopment Agency. City of San Juan Capistrano. Accessed, May 18, 2018.

Cleland, Robert Glass. 1922. *A History of California: The American Period.* New York. The Macmillan Company.

Cleland, Robert Glass. 1941. Reprinted 1975. *The Cattle on a Thousand Hills: Southern California 1850-1880.* San Morino, Ca. The Huntington Library.

Collings, Adam. 2003.*California: West of the West.* Orange County, CA. Adam Collings Enterprises.

Dana, Richard Henry, Jr. *Two Years before the Mast.* 1968 Original Copyright. 2005. New York. Literary Class of the United States, Inc.

DeFord, Frank. "The Horse who Picked up a Paintbrush." Aired on NPR's Morning Edition. Nov. 27. 2013. Accessed April 7, 2018

Design Group.1992. *City of San Juan Capistrano Open Space Master Plan.* San Clemente, CA.

Engelhardt, Zephryrin, Fr. 1922. *San Juan Capistrano: The Jewel of the Missions.* Los Angeles, Ca. Printed by Engelhardt, Zephryrin.

Engelhardt, Zephryrin, Fr. 1920. *San Diego Mission: The Mother of the Missions.* Los Angeles, CA. Printed by the author.

Engelhardt, Zephryrin. Fr. 1921. *San Luis Rey Mission: The King of the Missions.* San Francisco CA., James H. Barry Company,

Engelhardt, Zephryrin, Fr. 1927. San Fernando Rey: The Mission of the Valley. Chicago, Ill. Franciscan Herald Press.

Equestrian Subcommittee: City of San Juan Capistrano. 2008. Members: Sam Allevato, Council Member, Dr. Lon Uso, Council Member, Ginny Kerr, Planning Commissioner, Ken Friess, Former Mayor, Joyce Hoffman, Tar Farms Stables, Patricia Harris, Rancho Sierra Vista Stables, Ron Hanson, Sycamore Trails Stables, Kathy Holman, Ortega Equestrian Center.

Friess, Donna. 1998, reprinted 2016. *Whispering Waters: Historic Weesha and the Settling of Southern California.* California. H.I.H. Publishing.

Friess, Donna. 2000. *Historic Weesha and the Upper Santa Ana River Valley.* California. H.I.H. Publishing.

Friess, Donna. 2010. *One Hundred Years of Weesha.* California. H.I.H. Publishing.

Gonzales-Day, Ken. 2006. "Lynchings in the West," and chronicled 350 such cases in California between 1850-1935. North Carolina. Duke University.

Gonzalez- Day, Ken. Lynchings in the Wrestles Angeles Downtown Walking Tour. Accessed www.Kengonzalesday.com. website. August 29, 2017.

Gray, Paul Bryan. *Forster vs. Pico: the Struggle for Rancho Santa Margarita*. Spokane, WA. 1998. Walking Around Books. Hath Trust Digital Library.

Greshko, Michael. 2017. "Ice Age Predators Found Alongside Oldest Human in Americas.". Published Aug 25, 2017. *National Geographic*."

Hallan-Gibson, Pamela. 1986. *Two Hundred Years in San Juan Capistrano*. Virginia. The Donning Company.

Hallan-Gibson, Pamela. 1990. *The Golden Promise: Illustrated History of Orange County*. California. Windsor Publications.

Hoffman, Abraham. 2003 (*Los Angeles Westerners Corral*, The Branding Bar. Los Angeles Corral 234.) Western Theme in American film and television

Hoffman, Nancy. 1992."Sgt Reckless: Combat Veteran. Hoffman, Nancy. Nov. 1992. Republished in Marine Corps Official website. www.mca-marines.org

Johnson, Julie Ryan. March 17, 2017. "The Riding Park: 60 Acres of Fun." *The San Juan Scoop*.

Kirkham, Chris. ."How One Developer Learned Not to Put the House Before the Horse." *Wall Street Journal*. August 9, 2016

Krist, Gary.2018. *The Mirage Factory: Illusion, imagination, and the Invention of Los Angeles*. New York. Crown, a division of Penguin Random House.

Las Tortugas: 35 Years. 2010.Padre Junipero Serra Riders. Pamphlet.

Lindsay, Brendan C. 2012. *Murder State: California's Native American Genocide 1846-1873*. Lincoln, Nebraska. University of Nebraska Press.

Los Angeles City and County Directory. 1926.

Los Angeles City and County Directory. 1926.

Magalousis, Nicholas M. Editor 1987. *Early California Reflections*. National Endowment of the Humanities.

Marines official website. https://en.wikipedia.org./sergeatn Reckless. Accessed April 5, 2018.

Meadows, Don. 1967. *Southern California Quarterly,* Vol. 49. No. 3 (September 1967) pp. 337-343. Published by University of California Press on behalf of the Historical Society of Southern California. (Accessed February 2, 2017).

Metro Meteor. www.paintdbymetrol.com. Accessed March, 20, 2018.

"Operation Reckless." "Building monuments to America's Greatest War Horse." www.ssergeantreckless.com. accessed 4/8/2018

O'Sullivan, Saint John. 1920. Saunders Charles Francis. *Capistrano Nights: Tales of a California Mission Town*. New York. Robert McBride and Company.

Owen, James P. and Stoecklein, David R. 2004. *Cowboy Ethics: What Wall Street Can Learn from the Code of the West*. Ketchum, Idaho. Stoecklein Publishing & Photography.

Preserving Agriculture in San Juan Capistrano. City Document Summarizing the Agricultural Preservation Program. Preface by Mayor Gary Hausdorfer. 1981.

Pleiades, Fullerton High School Yearbook, 1909.

Rancho Mission Viejo and David R. Stoecklein.2013. El Viaje de Portolā. San Juan Capistrano, CA. Rancho Mission Viejo.

Rancho Mission Viejo. El Viaje de Portolā 25th Silver Edition. April 1988. San Juan Capistrano, CA. Rancho Mission Viejo.

Reichman, Louis and Cardinale, Gary. 1988. *The Orange County Experience*. Temple City, CA. Pacific Shoreville Press.

Richards, Susan. 2006. *Chosen by a Horse*. San Diego, CA. Harvest Books.

Ritchie, Erika. "Old War Horse to get Deserved Recognition*,*" *Orange County Register*, Tuesday May 8, 2018.

Ryan, Julie Johnson. May 17, 2017. "The Riding Park: 60 Acres of Fun!" *The San Juan Scoop.*

St. Margaret's Episcopal High School Newsletter. April 20, 2018.

San Juan Hills High School. Accessed 3/8/2018 https://en.wikipedia.or/wiki,/san-juan-Hills-High-School

San Juan Capistrano General Plan. City of San Juan Capistrano.

San Juan Capistrano Historical Society, Website. Accessed, February 2018.

Science Daily. November 18, 2004. "New Evidence Puts Man in North America 50,000 Year Ago." University of South Carolina. From Research Organizations.

Scott, Eric. Lecture. He served as Curator of Paleontology at the San Bernardino County Museum for 24 years and Ancient horses years (Prehistoric Horses of North America, Statelinetack.com accessed 7/25/2017)

Sergeant Reckless. https://wikipedia.org. Accessed 4/7/2018

Slayton, Robert A. and Estes, Leland. 1988. *Proceedings of the Conference of Orange County History.* Orange, Ca. Chapman College Department of History.;

Smith, Joan Irvine and Stern, Jean. 2001. *California: This Golden Land of Promise.* Chapman University Press, Orange, CA.

Smith, Joan Irvine. 2006. *A California Woman's Story.* Irvine, CA. Irvine Museum.

Stant, James E. Jr. *Don Juan Forster: Southern California Pioneer and Rancher: A pugnacious Brit ruled Southern California.* A Master's Thesis. University of San Diego, 1977. Article in *The San Diego Reader, Jeff Smith, July 5, 1977. Accessed on line June 9, 2018.*

Taylor, Alan. 2001.*American Colonies: The Settling of North America.* Penguin Books, New York, New York. [Pulitzer Prize Winner].

The Capistrano Dispatch. May 24, 2013. Isle Byrnes subject of story.

The Capistrano Dispatch. July 24, 2014. *Sparing the Horse* [Kathy Homan Horse Rehabilitation]. Written by Brian Park. San Juan Capistrano, California.

The O'Neills: The County's Pioneer Ranch Family. Article reprinted from book *Orange County Scene.* Sponsored by Joe MacPherson in *The Orange County Register.* November, 1997.

Teyes, Daniel. August 19, 2006. *Video Taped Interview with Tony Forster: History of Mission Hill in San Juan Capistrano* for a California State University at Fullerton, History Class and class paper. The Teyes paper includes testimony provided by Karen T. Wilson, great-granddaughter of Nathaniel Pryor, from an Interview taken August 28, 1975 by Gladys Landell as a part of California State University, Fullerton's Oral History Project, *General History of San Juan Capistrano, California.*

Townhall Association. 1978. *San Juan Capistrano. 1974-1978.* "A Citizens group dedicated to controlled growth and the preservation of a rural, self-contained, village-like community."

Tyron, Don. February 7, 2007. *Ama Daisy Saved the Mission Viejo Ranch.* Looking Back.

Tyron, Don. May, 2007. *A Tribute to Tony, 1935-2007.* The Journal. Offices of O'Neill Museum, San Juan Capistrano, California.

Tyron, Mary Ellen.1999. *A Guide to Historic San Juan Capistrano.* The Paragon Agency. Produced by the San Juan Capistrano Historical Society. San Juan Capistrano, CA.

U.S. History.org. "The 1950's: Happy Days." *53.c. The Land of Television.* Accessed, June 4, 2018.

University of Arizona News. May 3, 2018. *"UA to Award Honorary Degrees to Two Alumni."* University Communications.

University of Arizona Alumni Association Newsletter. 2013. "Gilbert Aguirre, Alumnus of the Year 2013." University of Arizona Video.

West, Katie. 2007. *The Art of Katie West Presents Legends of the American West.* California. Free Style Graphics and Publishing.

Winckel, Borre. 1998. *The Evolution of EVP-Man.* Portolá Newsletter. Rancho Mission Viejo.

APPENDIX A
Eric Scott Abstract on *Equus Occidentalis*

EQUUS OCCIDENTALIS CONFERRENCE PAPER ABSTRACT

Conference Paper: FIRST RECORD OF EQUUS OCCIDENTALIS FROM ORANGE COUNTY, CALIFORNIA, WITH IMPLICATIONS FOR THE LATE PLEISTOCENE DISTRIBUTION OF EQUUS IN THE AMERICAN SOUTHWEST

Maree Michelle Kutcher and Eric Scott

Abstract: Horses (genus Equus) are common in Pleistocene faunas throughout North America. Despite this abundance, the number of species occurring remains unresolved. Molecular data from fossils has been employed to suggest no more than two species, one stout-limbed and the other stilt-legged, while morphology-based paleontological investigations propose multiple species. In the late Pleistocene, two morphospecies of large stout-limbed horses have been documented from the American southwest: Equus Occidentalis and/or E. Scotti are known from only five localities in the region.

Conference Paper · Jan 2016

Abstract

Assessing whether the hypothesized distribution of these two large horse morphs is real, or instead is an artifact of the dearth of diagnostic material, therefore requires additional fossils. To test this hypothesis, we examined a previously undescribed late Pleistocene horse from San Juan Capistrano, Orange County, California. Remains include a skull, mandible, articulated right hind leg, and other postcrania recovered from nonmarine terrace deposits that also yielded remains of Bison, an index taxon for the late Pleistocene. Metric data confirm that this is a large species of horse; the metapodials are stout rather than slender, whole the lower incisors lace infundibula. These characters demonstrate clear affinity with Equus occidentalis. Based upon size and morphology, this is the first confirmed record of Equus occidental from Orange County. The presence of Equus occidentalis in this region accords well with the hypothesized distribution of late Pleistocene large stout-limbed Equus in the American southwest. Our result indicates that multiple horse species inhabited North America during the late Pleistocene.

APPENDIX B
Don Meadows. September 1967. *Southern California Quarterly*. Abstract

"The Original Site of Mission San Juan Capistrano."

**SUMMARY OF HISTORIAN DON MEADOWS'
1967 ARTICLE "THE ORIGINAL SITE OF
MISSION SAN JUAN CAPISTRANO"**
Excerpted from *Southern California Quarterly, September, 1967.*

Don Meadows cites the 1783 report from Father Mugârtegui which stated: "On the first of November 1776—this mission [Mission San Juan Capistrano] was founded in the glen popularly known as El Arroyo de la Quema *at a site three-fourths of a league distant from what is called the Old Road, and about a league and a half from the seashore.* [Italics are Don Meadows']. Father Mugârtegui continues: "There the mission remained for two years under many difficulties especially because the water which was insufficient not only for irrigating the planting but for drinking purposes so we were obliged to conduct it for our needs almost a quarter of a league. For this reason the mission was transferred to the site where it stands today [1783] about three quarters of a league distant from the original glen."

The article continues with some aspects of the original report that were omitted. The omitted portion reads: "in the following spring, which was April 1777, eight almudes [4 bushels] of corn were planted *at a distance of a quarter of a league, more or less, from the mission,* [italics are Meadows'] but all the sowing was lost from the drought."

Meadows concluded, based upon measuring distances from definite reference points, that the original site of Mission San Juan Capistrano can be located with reasonable margin of error. The site was in San Juan Canyon (Arroyo de la Quema) two miles (three-fourths of a league) above the present mission. According to the data the site was four miles (one and one-half leagues) from the seashore. Land that could be irrigated from San Juan Creek was within a radius of .7 of a mile (one-fourth of a league)of the mission, and at times drinking water had to be carried an equal distance. According to Meadows, "these conditions and distances check out perfectly on the U.S. Geological Survey maps of the region. There, the site of the original mission was somewhere in the Northeast Quarter of Section 5, township 8 South, Range 7 West."

Meadows offers an intensive explanation of the area and why others locales are ruled out as the site of the first mission. He explains, "the knoll covered by a large citrus grove is owned by the Lacouague family of San Juan Capistrano. Through the kindness of Mr. Jean Lacouague I was taken into the orchard and on the ridge or knoll was shown an area perhaps fifty yards in diameter where, when the orange trees were planted some thirty years ago; an extremely large number of morteros, mutates, manos, cog stones, etc. were uncovered. Many of the artifacts were given to friends, but some are still in the hands of the Lacouague family…Without doubt here was the original Indian village of Quanis-savit mentioned by Father Serra. Due west of the village site, at a distance of 125 yards, is the tile-roofed home of Pierre Lacouague who purchased the acreage in 1920."

Meadows further explains that the ocean cannot be seen from that location. He states that when Father Palôu wrote that, "from the houses one can see the ocean and the ships as they pass, for the beach is only half a league away," Meadows believes Palôu was describing the mission at the second location, where it is today. Meadows further states that Father Palôu was writing from hearsay, and that Father Maynard Geiger points out, that there is no evidence that Father Palôu ever visited either one of the mission sites, so "he could be confused in his viewpoint and distances."

[Father Maynard Geiger,(O.E. M. letter of May 29, 1967) discovered and published in the *Quarterly* the reports made by Fray Pablo Mugârtegui, the priest in charge of the mission in 1782-83.]

In Don Meadows' well published and respected report, he summarizes:

"In conclusion, available data indicated that Mission San Juan Capistrano was originally located in San Juan Canyon on the Lacouague ranch, two miles east-northeast of its present location, on a knoll on the south side of the stream, and was moved it its present site on October 4, 1778. Historians will always be indebted to Father Maynard Geiger for discovering and making known the Mugârtegui reports of 1782 and 1783. From them a legend has been confirmed and new light has been cast on the "Jewel of the Missions."

Don Meadows. *Southern California Quarterly,* Vol. 49. No. 3 (September 1967) pp. 337-343. Published by University of California Press on behalf of the Historical Society of Southern California. (Accessed February 2, 2017).

Don Meadows. *Orange County under Spain, Mexico and the United States* (3 vols. Whittier, CA. 1963.

[Note: Meadows defines "a league" as 2.7 miles. Friess research shows 3.4 miles to a league.]

APPENDIX C
City of San Juan Capistrano City Time Line. 2009. Tom Tomlinson
City Planning Director.

Taken from www.sanjuancapistrano.org

Dated: 3/30/2009

City Timeline

1700's

1776:   Father Junipero Serra establishes Mission San Juan Capistrano.
Originally founded by Father Fermin Lausen on October 30, 1775, San Juan Capistrano has the unique distinction of being twice founded. Eight days after the first occasion news of an impending Indian attack forced Fr. Lausen and his party to bury the bells of the mission and returned to San Diego. One year later Father Junipero Serra was the head of the founding party as he and his men arrived at the former site to find the cross still standing. Soon the bells of the Mission were recovered and the date of the second founding is November 1, 1776.

The first chapel was built, completed, and is still in use today. It is believed to be the oldest church in California, and since it is one of only two still standing where Father Serra is known to have said Mass it is called "Father Serra's Church."

1794:   Construction of what were probably the first structures within the vicinity of present day El Camino Real occurred.

Forty adobe dwellings were built south of the quadrangle as permanent housing for the Mission Indians. The fact that neophytes later occupied most of the structures on El Camino Real at the time the lands were granted (in 1841) suggests that these buildings were constructed as part of the 74 neophyte dwellings building in 1794 and within the vicinity of present day El Camino Real and Camino Capistrano.

Work begins on a large stone church, it was to be the most magnificent of all the California mission churches. The Great Stone Church was built in the shape of a cross, 180 feet long and 40 feet wide with a bell tower of 120 feet tall that could be seen for miles.

1800's

1806:   **Dedication of The Great Stone Church**
        According to Mission history, September 7, 1806 is the official dedication date of The
        Great Stone Church, which for the next six years becomes the splendid edifice and pride of
        the Mission.

        Deemed the most prosperous year for the Capistrano Mission, it produced 500,000 pounds
        of wheat, 190,000 pounds of barley, 202,000 pounds of corn, 20,600 pounds of beans,
        14,000 cattle, 16,000 sheep, and 740 horses.

1812:   **Earthquake destroys The Great Stone Church**
        December 8, 1812, a devastating earthquake strikes during a Mass and destroys The Great
        Stone Church, as well as the lives of 40 people. The magnificent church would lay in ruin
        until attempts at restorations were made some forty years later. Until then, Liturgical
        services were once again held in the little Serra Chapel with the bells of the fallen tower
        hung in the wall. In fact, this sight can still be seen today.

        In an attempt to provide Indians with an opportunity for independence, Governor Figueroa
        chose Capistrano as the site for a pueblo of "free" Indians. During this period of
        secularization, the land soon gravitated into the hands of settlers and the last of San Juan
        Capistrano's property was sold by Pio Pico to his brother-in-law (Juan Forster) and a
        partner (James McKinley) in 1845 in exchange for hide and tallow equal to the amount of
        $710 dollars.

        The Forster Family resides on Mission grounds and occupies the rooms that make up the
        present day museum and gift shop, while allowing Church authorities to keep the Serra
        Chapel and a small room for the priest. In 1864 the Forster's move out of the Mission and
        onto their Santa Margarita Ranch.

1865:   **Mission lands returned to Catholic Church**
        A portion of the Mission lands are returned to the Catholic Church by the United States
        Government on March 18, 1865 after the signing of the Patient by President Abraham
        Lincoln which gave the Bishop of Monterey and his successors rights to this land for the
        practices of religious purpose and use.

1877:   San Juan Capistrano consisted of a school telegraph office, post office, two stores, hotel,
        four saloons, and forty to fifty homes, mostly of Adobe.

1880:   A total of 31 non-Spanish speaking residents and 345 native born Californios of Mexican
        descent reside in San Juan Capistrano.

1881: **Arrival of the railroad**
Arrival of the railroad brings significant changes and establishes a link with the outside world. This marks the beginning of San Juan Capistrano as "visitor destination" during a time when there is intense public interest in the Spanish and Mexican periods of California, which had been popularized as a "golden age" by such writers, as Helen Hunt Jackson, Charles Lummis and Hubert Howe Bancroft.

1889: Orange County incorporates, breaking off from Los Angeles County. San Juan Capistrano is already 113 years old as a community.

San Juan Capistrano resident Modesta Avila is ordered to stand trial for attempted obstruction of the railroad by hanging laundry across the track. She is convicted and later dies in prison, the first female prisoner in newly incorporated Orange County.

1900's

1936: Beginning of Fiesta de las Golondrinas
A popular radio host broadcasts from the Mission, announcing to the world the return of the swallows. Hence began the Fiesta de las Golondrinas, a celebration marking the return of the swallows that still takes place today.

1958: San Diego freeway built
The San Diego freeway is built, changing the face of the small town forever by splitting the community in half with a ribbon of concrete.

July 21, five residents take out incorporation papers to initiate the City's incorporation process. These residents were: Carl Buchheim, Larry Buchheim, Reginald Erikson, C. Fulton Shaw, and Henry Stewart.

1961: San Juan Capistrano becomes an official City
In April, San Juan Capistrano becomes an official City with its incorporation. Population is: 1130. The first five Council Members are Bill Bathgate, Carl Buchheim, Ed Chermak, Don Durnford, and Tony Olivares.

1965: City adopts first General Plan that establishes a goal to become a large urban community with a projected population of 84,000.

1974: City adopts a new General Plan which significantly changes the direction of the community by emphasizing its small village-like character, preservation of major ridgelines to define the limits of the community by these natural features, setting aside a minimum of 30% of the City as open space (including areas for preserving active agricultural operations), maintaining a rural equestrian lifestyle and establishment of goals and policies for the future management of growth in the community.

City establishes the Cultural Heritage Commission and adopts a resolution designating historically and culturally significant structures throughout the community.

1976:   City adopts first ever Home Warranty Program for new residential construction in California. All residential developments to have a minimum three-year warranty on all aspects of a new residence.

City adopts Agriculture Preservation Program that is designed to preserve approximately 220 acres of active agricultural operations. City establishes funding mechanism that is applied to new development to assist in financing this program. Eventually, approximately 120 acres would be purchased through an Open Space Bond measure approved in 1990 by approximately 74% of the voters.

City hosts Freedom Train to celebrate the bi-centennial of the Country. The train is a moving museum of major historic documents of the Country's history. San Juan Capistrano is one of only four stops in Southern California to host the train.

1978:   Los Rios Precise Plan adopted to preserve and guide development in the oldest residential neighborhood in California. Portions of the neighborhood along Los Rios Street is recognized as an Historic District and placed on the National Inventory.

City adopts first growth management program in Orange County, and one of the first in California. Program restricted residential development to a maximum of 400 building permits in any given year. Was designed to extend buildout of the community from 1985 to 1990 (population projected at 42,000 by General Plan). Program is still in effect with the population at 33,826 (2000 Census).

1980:   City and Glendale Savings and Loan execute an agreement for development of 1,220 acres of land that includes dedication of approximately 700 acres of open space to the City, including the major ridgelines that form the natural separation between the community and the City of San Clemente to the southeast.

1983:   City creates a Community Redevelopment Agency to assist in the financing of major infrastructure improvements and create an economic development package for improving the viability of the downtown commercial sector.

1984:   Library designed by renowned architect Michael Graves opens and immediately becomes a tourist attraction for architects from all over the world, Librarian has to limit tour groups to certain days in order to keep the facility open and maintain availability for residents

The new Catholic Church (which is a recreation of the original Stone Church destroyed by an earthquake in 1812) is completed. It represents the tallest building in the community with its bell tower at 104 feet and the main rotunda at 85 feet in height.

1986:	City assembles vacant land parcels in the downtown core for future commercial development and selects a developer to create a commercial plaza and hotel in the area known as the Historic Town Center.

1986: City assembles vacant land parcels in the downtown core for future commercial development and selects a developer to create a commercial plaza and hotel in the area known as the Historic Town Center.

City celebrates its 25th anniversary in a tent during a major rainstorm. Although water was running through the tent, the celebrants took off their shoes and danced the night away.

1987: City-retained archaeologist team conducting survey testing of the Historic Town Center discover major building foundations and Native American artifacts. Due to the presence of these artifacts, City puts Historic Town Center project on hold.

City approves the Franciscan Plaza project that represents the first large-scale redevelopment project in the downtown. It is to include retail shops, a five screen Edwards Theater and parking structure. During construction, a number of artifacts are revealed and recovered prior to construction of the buildings. Project was completed in 1989.

City prohibits sale and discharge of fireworks and establishes program to conduct a free fireworks program for celebration of Fourth of July.

1989: Citizens Committee formed to investigate and support a possible $21 million Open Space Bond measure to acquire approximately 120 acres of land for open space/recreation use. In April 1990, this bond measure passes with 74% support of the voters. In subsequent years, the approved funds are used to acquire 120 acres, including the area known as "Kinoshita Farms". The 56 acres have been developed with the San Juan Community Center and Sports Park, along with the preservation of a 28 acre active farming operation. Most recently the original farm house has been restored (Condgon House, first wood frame building in the Capistrano Valley).

1990: City embarks on the preparation and approval of an Open Space Master Plan for the City. Its adoption in 1991 establishes the priorities for the development of open space properties throughout the City. It is recognized for its comprehensive planning by the Orange County Chapter of the American Planning Association excellence in Comprehensive Planning.

1992: City conducts a public participation planning program to consider development options for the Historic Town Center Project. In 1993, the City adopts the Historic Town Center Master Plan which established a central park area that includes the location of significant historic artifacts that are located below the ground. Also included in the park is the Blas Aguilar Adobe that is now being used as a Native American History Museum.

The Associated Senior Action Program (ASAP) is established as a volunteer group to assist San Juan Capistrano Police Services with everything from clerical support and bike patrol to vacation-home checks and help with special events.

1993:   The period 1993/1994 saw a major adjustment in the City's organization due to the recession. The staffing levels were reduced by approximately 30%. In order to meet the needs of the community, computers and other technology were employed to maintain the same service levels that the residents had expected. Today, although workloads have increased, the use of technology efficiencies have not resulted in increased staffing levels to those of the pre-recession years. In many instances department levels have not changed from that of post 1994.

First woman Mayor selected by City Council colleagues, Collene Campbell.

Capistrano Depot celebrates its 100th Birthday.

1995:   City approves, and provides, financial assistance for first 100% affordable housing senior apartment project within the City.

1996:   City approves a major historic renovation of the Mission Promenade property (Ferris-Kelly Buildings) across from Mission San Juan Capistrano.
San Juan Capistrano becomes the first city in the nation to adopt a Rodeo Ordinance to ensure humane treatment of rodeo animals. The ordinance is set to the safety standards of the Professional Rodeo Cowboy Association.

Over 20 historic buildings receive plaques through a generous donation of The Decorative Arts Study Center.

City Motto is adopted "Preserving the Past to Enhance the Future."

1997:   Grand opening of the new sports field complex made possible by Open Space Bond proceeds. Complex included lighted baseball fields, three regulation soccer fields, community gardens, refreshment building and parking.

City celebrates the first Holiday Tree Lighting at Historic Town Center Park, despite the El Nino storms.

City develops its first official Web site **www.sanjuancapistrano.org**.

City initiates Rental Subsidy Program for residents, which is designed to help low-income residents improve their financial situation and become more self-sufficient within two years.

City enters into lease with South Coast Farms to operate the Kinoshita Farm, agricultural land at Camino Del Avion and Alipaz Street. Ultimately farmer George Kibby receives certification to farm the land as the first active organic farm site in Orange County.

1998:   City Council initiates a comprehensive update to the City's General Plan that had sewed as the vision for the community since its adoption in 1974. This intense update program that included a significant number of public meetings and community workshops concludes in December 1999 with the adoption of a new General Plan. The adoption of the new plan comes almost exactly 25 years from the date of the previous plan approval and will continue to provide major visionary direction of the previous plan approval.

City successfully initiates Summer Concert Series and Shop and Dine Expo in the Historic Town Center area.

December grand opening of phase I of the new community center at the Sports Park. This initial phase includes administrative offices, meeting rooms and main hall, senior center and kitchen facilities.

First time in the City's history, all three incumbent City Council members are elected without need for an election due to no challengers.

1999:   Downtown lighting project, phase 1, is installed bringing lights to the historic downtown. Phase II construction of the gymnasium is completed for the community center complex. Revised General Plan adopted for community, designed to address the needs of the City as it enters the 21st century.

2000's

2000:   Camino Real Bell is replaced at Arguello Way through efforts by the California Federation of Women's Clubs.

Phase III construction of the youth center is completed and opened as part of a joint project with the Capistrano Valley Boys and Girls Club. Construction of this phase was made possible with a grant of $500,000 from the federal government under the sponsorship of Congressman Ron Packard.

Diane Bathgate, daughter of original Council Member Bill Bathgate, is elected to City Council.

City officially names park in downtown "Historic Town Center Park."

San Juan Capistrano proudly hosts the West Coast debut of Olympic Trials Equestrian Competition. Three rounds of show jumping competition grace the field at the Rancho Oaks Blenheim Mission Viejo Riding Park.

2001:   City celebrates 40th Anniversary of Incorporation population is 33,826.
City Council Members include Wyatt Hart, Mayor; David Swerdlin, Mayor Pro-Tem; Diane Bathgate; John Gelff; John Greiner.

2002:   First Leadership Academy started by Mayor Diane Bathgate, informing citizens about city government.

Veteran's monument placed in mini-park, renamed Veteran's Park.

Regional Transportation Strategy developed.

Stone Field renovated with assistance of Mission Hospital; field is one of only a handful of WPA projects left in Orange County.

Joel Congdon House, dating back to 1877, renovated and placed on National Register of Historic Places.

2003:   Construction begins on groundwater recovery plant, which is expected to cut reliance on outside water sources by 50 percent.

Stage completed for Historic Town Center Park through generous donation by Collene and Gary Campbell.

Double-tracking solution found, which removes the threat of double-tracking from the downtown.

Blue Ribbon Committee completes plan to revitalize the downtown business community. City adopts financial strategy designed to protect programs from state cutbacks.

Historic Preservation Manager hired to protect city's historic resources.

2005:   City Guides Program initiated in joint effort between the City, Friends of the Library Walking Tour, and Historical Society Walking Tour to train a pool of docents to lead history and historic architecture walking tours of the historic downtown.

Northwest Area Strategies Ad Hoc Committee established to identify obtainable open space area and funding tactics for acquiring land, and to develop strategies for future land use and infrastructure planning and associated funding. 12 members appointed and meetings begin in early

2006:   Second phase of structural renovation to architecturally renowned SJC Library begins. Previous work included drainage and landscape improvements.

2006:   Two projects completed by the city to renovate and restore original historic paint colors to two landmark farmhouses: the Swanner House complex in the Northwest Open Space Area and the Harrison House on Ortega Highway.

Missing interior ceiling is replaced, period lighting is installed, and front deck is repaired on Harrison House.

Swanner House complex, dating to 1923, is nominated to the National Register of Historic Places by the city, under the name of the original owner, Roger Y. Williams. If accepted by the Keeper of the Register in Washington DC, the site will be the 12th site listed in the National Register within city boundaries.

City Council approves license agreement with San Juan Family Farm Museum to pursue the conversion of the Joel Congdon House to a museum on the ground floor.

Special Thanks
Thank you to everyone who played a part in helping to bring together the celebration of this momentous occasion.
Special Thanks to Mr. Tom Tomlinson for his valuable contributions to this timeline.

APPENDIX D
Don Tyron Article: "Ama Daisy Saves the Rancho Mission Viejo." 2007.

Taken from corp.ranchomissionviejo.com   Dated: February 4, 2007

LOOKING BACK   *February 2, 2007*   19

'Ama Daisy' Saved the Rancho Mission Viejo

Looking Back

By Don Tryon

At one time we had many ranches surrounding our community. All are gone but one, and even that has been reduced over time. Many of the local ranches have been turned into homes, business centers, conservation areas, green belts and parks. Still, much land is used for cattle grazing and agriculture. The last ranch, Rancho Mission Viejo, came very close to being totally subdivided in 1944, thus our whole area would have been a duplicate of Anaheim or the San Fernando Valley. But thanks to a grand old lady, the large ranch was saved for her family and heirs - and quite possibly saved San Juan Capistrano, as we know it.

Marguerite Petra de la Conception Moore was born in Los Angeles in 1879. A fifth generation Californian, she would have added that some of her ancestors were here to greet Father Junipero ⬛Serra and Commander Gaspar de Portolā when they first came to California in 1769. Marguerite was baptized in the old Plaza Church in L.A. and was in the first graduating class at Los Angeles High School in 1898. Her father, Walter S. Moore, came from Philadelphia- settled in L.A. and married Amenaida Rafaela Lanfranco.

At a social event in the old Oceanside Hotel in 1900, Marguerite first met Richard O'Neill Jr. Shortly thereafter she left to visit a sister in South Africa and stayed for six years. She often would reminisce about the Zulu warriors and the snakes she had seen there. When Marguerite came home, she met O'Neill Jr. again and this time romance blossomed. They married in 1916 and sailed to Honolulu for their honeymoon. Then they established a home in Los Angeles. In the meantime, Richard's brother, Jerome, managed the Rancho Santa Margarita y Las Flores, which encompassed an area from El Toro to Oceanside, and was 35 miles long. The ranch had been owned by James Flood and managed by Richard O'Neill Sr. When Flood passed away in 1888, his son, James Flood Jr., gained ownership. He fulfilled his father's long- time promise, based on a handshake, and gave Richard Sr. half interest in the ranch.

Richard Sr. passed away in 1910 and gave his half interest in the ranch to his crippled son, Jerome, who always had an active interest in the ranch. Jerome and Flood Jr. formed their joint partnership into a corporation. The two passed away two days apart, in 1926. Jerome had established a trust dividing his half share of stock benefiting his sister, Mary Baumgartner, and his brother Richard O'Neill Jr.

In 1940 the ranch was divided up between the Flood's, Baumgartner's, and Richard O'Neill Jr. Fortunately O'Neill Jr. took the Rancho Mission Viejo portion, which was 52,000 acres in Orange County. In 1942 the Navy purchased the San Diego portion from the Flood's and Baumgartner's to create Camp Pendleton for the Marines.

O'Neill Jr. managed the ranch for a while, but later the Jerome O'Neill Trust hired other managers. Upon his death in 1943, the ownership of Rancho Mission Viejo remained in the trust. The beneficiaries were Marguerite, affectionately known as Daisy or "Ama Daisy", and their two children, Alice O'Neill Moiso Avery and Richard Jerome O'Neill. In 1944 the Bank Trust officers tried to sell the ranch without the beneficiary's approval. The Bank Trust had an offer of $1.2 million; they had very little interest in ranch operations and they just wanted to get out of the situation. But Daisy refused to sell, held firm and continued operations. Her interests were in the land and what it could do for her family. Thereafter, the bank was uncooperative and indecisive. Ranch improvements were stifled. which limited the income. But Daisy persevered. Her decisions prevailed and the ranch eventually provided a generous income.

Marguerite "Ama Daisy" O'Neill

Daisy always had a deep distrust with banks and individuals who tried to manipulate her. Her grandson, Tony Moiso, now CEO for Rancho Mission Viejo, likes to tell the story of when he was twenty-three. he was urged to talk to her about the family idea of developing a portion of the ranch. Other interests were encouraging her to accept another plan - one the family felt was unacceptable. Tony was successful, but Daisy said, "Okay. If that's what you and (uncle) Richard want to do. Take care of the Ranch, watch out for connivers. and be sure that I get paid." As a result, a partnership was formed with Donald Bren, and it was called the Mission Viejo Company. This company was formed to develop what is known today as the City of Mission Viejo. Tony Moiso has a great affection for his "Ama Daisy" as she would often take him on many visits to the Ranch, to the horse races. visiting old timers in Oceanside and San Juan Capistrano, and to eat at the former Las Rosas Café, where the Birtcher Plaza is now, and later to the El Adobe Restaurant. She always admonished him to "eat beef." Interestingly, years later, the land and building that the El Adobe is located were acquired by Rancho

Richard O'Neill Jr. & Marguerite

Mission Viejo. The Portolá Riders have dedicated a plaque at the Campo de los Amantes on the Ranch to Daisy. It quotes her as saying, "Always take care of the Ranch; It has always taken care of the family." The O'Neill heirs have done just that and they feel she would have approved their stewardship. As a result of having just a few in control, the developments have been well planned, with huge tracts donated for parks and conservation areas, and still much land set aside for grazing and crops. Marguerite "Daisy" O'Neill passed away at the age of 102 in 1981 and she has left us all with a great legacy. (Don Tryon is the Director and Archivist for the San Juan Capistrano Historical Society.)

Index

CPSIA information can be obtained
at www.ICGtesting.com
Printed in the USA
BVHW052151300120
571049BV00001B/7

9 780981 576756